A LIFE WORTH LIVING

PUBLICATIONS BY JOHN HOLT

How Children Fail, 1964; revised edition, 1982

How Children Learn, 1967; revised edition, 1983

The Underachieving School, 1969

What Do I Do Monday?, 1970

Freedom and Beyond, 1972

Escape from Childhood: The Needs and Rights of Children, 1974

Instead of Education: Ways to Help People Do Things Better, 1976

Never Too Late: My Musical Life Story, 1978

Teach Your Own: A Hopeful Path for Education, 1981

Learning All the Time, 1989

SELECTED LETTERS OF JOHN HOLT

Edited and with an Introduction by Susannah Sheffer

Ohio State University Press/Columbus

Library of Congress Cataloging-in-Publication Data
Holt, John Caldwell, 1923–1985
    A life worth living: selected letters of John Holt / edited
and with an introduction by Susannah Sheffer.
        p. cm.
    ISBN 0–8142–0523–2 (alk. paper)
    ISBN 0–8142–0544–5 (pbk.: alk. paper)
    1. Holt, John Caldwell, 1923–1985—Correspondence.
2. Teachers—United States—Correspondence. 3. Education—
United States—Philosophy. I. Sheffer, Susannah, 1964– . II.
Title.
  LB885.H64L54 1990
  371.1′0092—dc20   90–33342
                                                          CIP

Printed in the U.S.A.

9 8 7 6 5 4 3 2 1

A life worth living and work worth doing—that is what I want for children (and all people), not just, or not even, something called "a better education."

—JOHN HOLT, 1983

CONTENTS

Preface   ix

Acknowledgments   xiii

Introduction   1

1   1945–1963   13

2   1964–1976   30

3   1977–1985   199

Epilogue   274

Appendix: Books Mentioned in the Text   277

Index   281

Illustrations follow page 146

PREFACE

With a couple of exceptions, the letters from which the material in this book is drawn are the carbon copies or photocopies found in John Holt's correspondence files after his death. Holt did not begin the practice of keeping regular copies of correspondence until the early 1960s, but some old friends have generously sent original letters that predate this period. Holt had reclaimed his original letters to his grandmother, Katharine Crocker, after her death in 1956, so these were among his papers and thus available for this collection.

Each of the correspondence files contains the correspondent's original letters, copies of Holt's replies, and, often, material to which the correspondence refers (articles, newspaper clippings, and so on). I have consequently had access, in many cases, to both sides of the correspondence.

During the late 1960s and early 1970s—the period covered by chapter 2 of this volume—Holt was away from his Boston office so much of the time that perhaps three-quarters of his correspondence was dictated onto cassette tapes, which he then sent back to Boston. Associates would type up the dictated letter and mail it from Boston. It should therefore be assumed that all the letters are mailed from Boston unless otherwise indicated. Often Holt mentions his actual location within the text of the letter.

Because much of this book's material was dictated and transcribed in this manner, we cannot assume that every typographical decision within a given letter was Holt's own. The typists sometimes held the transcribed letters before mailing them so that Holt could make any desired corrections, but just as often he was away from the office for too long to make it practical to do so. Holt was quite a skillful speaker, so the reader should not imagine that the transcribers had to clarify or edit his language, but they did often determine the punctuation, paragraphing, and, on occasion, spelling within a letter. For this reason, my adherence to such details has not been as rigid as an editor's in a different situation might have been. I have been conservative about changing punctuation and paragraphing, but more liberal in altering spelling and typographical errors, as such errors seem to tell more about the transcriber than about Holt.

Where an entire word or phrase is missing in my source copies, however, I have been unable to determine whether Holt or his typist was responsible for the omission. To make it easiest on the reader, I have added the word or phrase in brackets when it is obvious what Holt intended, and have added it in brackets with a question mark when I have been unable to do more than guess his intent. I have also added the occasional explanatory word or phrase to Holt's many abbreviations.

Because I worked from copies, not every letter contained a signature. If a letter had no signature at all, I have left it off entirely here. If the signature was handwritten but not typed, I have indicated this by putting brackets around the name as it was signed. Finally, if the letter also included the typed name, I have indicated this by giving the name as it was typed, without brackets.

There are approximately two hundred individual names in the correspondence files, but perhaps only a third of these are people with whom Holt engaged in regular correspondence. In choosing letters for this volume, I have looked for those that show Holt finding and making his "life worth living and work worth doing," and those that in some way look at the relation between struggling for an individual life worth living and a collective one, at what it means to see one's own life's work in terms of the larger world. Specifically, I have looked for letters that show Holt developing an interest in schools, coming to understand what was wrong with schools, struggling to fix those wrongs, and finally realizing that some of the wrongs could not be fixed and that something entirely different was necessary. I have also favored letters that show Holt's thinking about his own books—particularly the process and thought behind them—and about books of others in the school reform movement.

Having these priorities, I have had to leave out a great deal of other material—most of the extensive material about music, for example, and the letters that deal with the daily specifics and legalities of home education. I feel comfortable with these omissions because the former may one day become part of another volume and the latter have to a great extent been published in *Growing Without Schooling* magazine.

Most of Holt's letters are long, and many span several topics, so in some instances I have had to indicate with ellipsis points a deletion of material that does not belong in this particular volume. I have also deleted, and have so indicated, material (such as detailed travel plans) that will be of little interest to the reader, and, though very rarely, passages that might betray the privacy of those mentioned.

A list at the back of the book gives bibliographical information about books mentioned in the text and in the footnotes.

Susannah Sheffer

ACKNOWLEDGMENTS

Many people have contributed to the making of this book. In particular, I owe thanks to:

my colleagues at Holt Associates—Pat and Day Farenga, Donna Richoux, Mary and Tom Maher, Ann Barr—for generously giving me time, space, and encouragement;

Alex Holzman at Ohio State University Press, who showed me how nice it can be for an editor to *have* an editor;

those of John Holt's friends and colleagues with whom I have been able to speak, and whose insights and reflections have added significantly to my understanding: Pamela Dant Christie, Mabel Dennison, Jerry Friedman, Gary Hicks, Merloyd Lawrence, Hope Metcalf, Jennifer Priest, Margot Priest, Dennis Sullivan, and Nelson Talbott;

Ellen Balzé, who lived with it;

Ethel and Isaiah Sheffer, for historical research and technical support, and for showing me, by example, how to care about quality work;

Peter Bergson, for his faith from the beginning, and the Bergson-Shilcock family, whose lives are an example and an inspiration;

Aaron Falbel, fellow traveler, with love and admiration;

Nancy Wallace, true colleague and friend, who is in every way part of this book;

and John Holt, whose letters to me over the years helped me find my own Life Worth Living.

INTRODUCTION

John Holt (1923–1985) was a writer, teacher, and amateur musician, who came to public attention when his first book, *How Children Fail*, was published in 1964. The book was a collection of memos and letters about life in the fifth grade classroom in which Holt taught, and its critique of conventional schooling helped set the school reform movement of the 1960s in motion. After graduating from college in 1943 (an institution that he later would not name, believing that "a person's schooling is as much a part of his private business as his politics or religion"), Holt served for three years on a submarine during World War II, worked in the World Government movement, and finally took a teaching job at a small, experimental boarding school in Colorado. He had no idea that education would become his life's work until he began to ask himself why his students weren't learning what they were supposed to be learning, and found that he had something to say about why that might be, and what we might do about it. The public response to *How Children Fail* showed that people were interested in the opinions of this previously unknown elementary school teacher.

By the mid-1970s, when *How Children Fail* was ten years old and Holt's name had become widely known, he appeared to have given up on schools. The teacher who had cared so passionately about making schools into better places for children seemed to have lost interest. He no longer spoke at meetings if school reform was the topic. He wrote about a society without schools, rather than a society with better schools. To many of his audiences and readers, and likewise to his colleagues in the reform movement, it seemed as if John Holt had left the fight.

But he did not so much leave the fight as reconceive it, redefine what needed to be done. To the extent that he did, in fact, give up

1

the idea that reforming schools was possible or desirable, the giving up was not easy. It was, as he later wrote, one of the hardest things he ever had to do.

To understand John Holt we need to understand why he believed he had to turn his attention away from school reform and classroom education to education in society as a whole. We need to understand the anatomy of that decision, look at what he himself said about it, and place it in the context of the educational activity of the time in which he made it.

Holt was not trained in education. He went into teaching only because it seemed like the most interesting thing to do at the time, and he later argued that this lack of training was his biggest asset:

> My first teaching job was to tutor an otherwise interesting and bright teenager whose school skills were at about second or third grade level. Top specialists had pronounced him "brain-damaged." In spite of the label, he wanted to read, write, and figure like everyone else, and wanted me to help him.
>
> Not having studied "education," I had never heard of "brain-damage," didn't know enough to know that it was just a fancy way of saying, "We don't know what the trouble is." But it was clear to me that brain-damage or no, it was my task and my responsibility to find out what was keeping him from learning and to figure out something to do about it. . . . In short, I was what I call a serious teacher—I would not accept fancy excuses or alibis as a substitute for doing the work I had chosen and had been hired to do—help children learn things. If they were not learning, as many were not, I couldn't blame it on them, but had to keep trying until I found something that worked. As *How Children Fail* makes clear, this often took a long time, and I failed as much as I succeeded.[1]

Holt often failed at getting his students to learn what, according to the curriculum, they were supposed to learn, but he was determined to figure out why. He soon became as interested in the reasons for the failure as he had been in the original task of following the curriculum. Team teaching[2] allowed him long periods of simply observing the children, trying to experience the classroom as they experienced it rather than as he imagined they were experiencing it. He was surprised and puzzled to find that most of the children in his classroom were bored and frightened, intent only on figuring out

1. *Growing Without Schooling*, no. 2, Fall 1977, p. 1.
2. The team teaching, practiced with Bill Hull, is discussed in greater detail in *How Children Fail*.

2

what the teachers wanted and whether or not they should try to give it to them. The classroom was not the place of active learning and exploration that Holt had imagined it to be.

To the thousands and millions of readers of *How Children Fail* who found in the book confirmation of their own school experience, Holt was one of the first to see through educational jargon and theory and to write about what life in school was really like for children and teachers. People reading it and remembering their own childhoods found, often for the first time, someone who said that disliking school made sense. Students and teachers who had suspected that something was wrong but had not been able to say what it was found someone who could articulate it for them. James Herndon, another of the "romantic critics" of the era, wrote many years later, "Reading Holt as beginning teachers, people with questions about the system as we saw it, we were able to feel that possibly we weren't just *crazy,* because here was this guy who was able to articulate for us what we were thinking, and certainly *he* didn't seem crazy."[3]

While teaching in school and writing the notes and memos that would become *How Children Fail,* Holt was also spending time with, and keeping notes about, the young children of relatives and friends. He saw in these young children energy, fearlessness, tolerance for ambiguity and for what adults call failure, and actual skill at learning—all of which were almost wholly absent in his fifth grade students at school. What was it, he wondered, that turned such active and curious young human beings into the fearful, timid, evasive strategists he met at school?

He began to suspect that the fault lay in the way children were treated in school, in the way they were made to feel about themselves. Soon he argued that school's mistake was thinking that we had to *make* children do what they naturally wanted to do, and knew how to do—learn about the world around them.

In arguing that children were innately curious and good at learning, Holt placed himself in the tradition of Rousseau, Tolstoy, Dewey, and A. S. Neill, but on the basis of their similar views, rather than because he had read these educational philosophers or consciously chosen to ally himself with them (though he later became friends

3. Private correspondence with Susannah Sheffer. Herndon is the author of *The Way It Spozed to Be* (New York: Simon & Schuster, 1968) and *How to Survive in Your Native Land* (New York: Simon & Schuster, 1970).

with Neill, he read his work only after coming to similar conclusions himself).[4] The question, for Holt and others arguing similarly about the nature of children, was how to preserve and nourish what was already present in children, how to make schools into places that nurtured and supported children rather than threatened and defeated them.

If bad schools were the problem, it seemed as if better schools ought to be the solution. By the late 1960s several other teachers and ex-teachers—George Dennison, James Herndon, Jonathan Kozol, Herbert Kohl, for example—had published books about their experiences in schools and offered proposals for change. The media began referring to them collectively as the "school reformers" or "romantic critics." Finding himself so categorized, Holt began corresponding with these allies. Though in many ways working toward a common end, these reformers would ultimately prove to be more individual, more distinct in their outlook and in their recommendations, than the collective title suggested. Even when Holt was excited and moved by the work of these allies (and as the letters in this collection will show, this was often) it would be incorrect to say that he was influenced by them, any more than he was influenced by Dewey or Neill. Holt was always more influenced by his own experience, his own observations of children, than by anything else. The work of others sometimes illuminated these observations, to be sure, sometimes helped Holt interpret them in a new way. But, as George Dennison wrote of Holt after his death, he "never derive[d] theory from theory, but stay[ed] as close as possible to experience itself. His entire career was really based on this, this *making sense of experience.*"[5]

During the 1960s, the idea that there ought to be more freedom in education expressed itself both in the school reformers' efforts to make traditional classrooms more open and in the effort to create what came to be known as free schools. Holt involved himself in both efforts. He addressed himself to teachers in conventional classrooms, suggesting changes they could make there (the book *What Do I Do Monday?* was a collection of such suggestions). He visited free schools around the country, took great interest in those that seemed

4. See letter to Jonathan Croall, Oct. 22, 1981.
5. *Growing Without Schooling*, no. 48, Dec. 1985, p. 8.

to be successful, and contributed to discussions in the free school movement's publications.[6]

Discussions among those in the free school movement (and in the school reform movement as a whole) often centered on the meaning of freedom—did it mean letting children do whatever they wanted, for example, and what would happen if they appeared to abuse it once they had it? What was the proper relationship between adults and children? Between schools and society? Would school reform lead to societal reform, or were free schools and open classrooms merely sanctuaries in a troubled world?

For a while it seemed—at least to those right at the center of it— that the movement was making progress. Looking back, years later, on the height of the reform effort, Holt wrote, "Many people . . . seemed to be very interested in and even enthusiastic about the idea of making schools into places in which children would be independent and self-directing learners. . . . For a while it seemed to me and my allies that within a few years such changes might take place in many schools, and in time, even a majority."[7]

But by the mid-1970s the picture was no longer as bright. Many free schools closed for lack of money; changes that had seemed so promising were short-lived; teachers who had tried new methods, succeeded, and written about their successes were fired from their positions; audiences seemed less receptive. Samuel Bowles and Herbert Gintis wrote in *Schooling in Capitalist America* in 1976, "In less than a decade, liberal preeminence in the field of educational theory and policy has been shattered. . . . Today, much of the free school rhetoric has been absorbed into the mainstream of educational thinking as a new wrinkle on how to get kids to work harder."[8]

This was precisely how Holt saw it. He wrote later that he came to realize, "slowly and reluctantly," that

Very few people, inside the schools or out, were willing to support or even tolerate giving more freedom, choice, and self-direction to children. Of the very few who were, most were doing so not because they believed that

6. Primarily *The New Schools Exchange*. For further discussion of the free school movement, see Allen Graubard, *Free the Children: Radical Reform and the Free School Movement* (New York: Pantheon Books, 1972); and Jonathan Kozol, *Free Schools* (Boston: Houghton Mifflin Co., 1972).

7. John Holt, *Teach Your Own* (New York: Delacorte Press, 1981), p. 2.

8. Samuel Bowles and Herbert Gintis, *Schooling in Capitalist America* (New York: Basic Books, 1976), p. 6.

children really wanted and could be trusted to find out about the world, but because they thought that giving children some of the appearances of freedom . . . was a clever way of getting them to do what the school had wanted all along—to learn those school subjects, get into a good college, etc. Freedom was not a serious way of living and working, but only a trick, a "motivational device." When it did not quickly bring the wanted results, the educators gave it up without a thought and without regret.[9]

Holt was not the only one who thought the school reform movement failed, and failed not from lack of effort but because most people did not, despite talk to the contrary, really want the changes in education and society that continued growth of the movement would have created.[10] What is interesting is Holt's particular response to that failure.

Some reformers responded to the alleged failure of the movement by continuing to do what they had been doing—working to make particular classrooms and schools better. They didn't see lack of widespread interest in or acceptance of their ideas as failure, but rather as evidence that more persistence and determination were necessary. Others—usually those who had never supported the reform movement in the first place—used the occasion of its failure to herald the back-to-basics movement of the 1980s.

A third group began—as early as 1970—to talk and write about *deschooling*. Both the word and the idea of deschooling came primarily from Ivan Illich, who perhaps more than anyone else did in fact influence Holt's thinking in obvious ways. Illich and his colleagues at the Center for Intercultural Documentation (CIDOC) in Mexico[11] argued that "How do we make schools better"—the central question of the reform movement—was the wrong question to ask. It was wrong not just because it was ineffectual but because *schooling* did not make educational or political sense, and was indeed educationally and politically harmful. It was not that the school reform movement

9. Holt, *Teach Your Own*, p. 4.
10. Some people—Bowles and Gintis, for example—argued that schooling prepared people for life in a stratified, capitalist society, and that the free school movement challenged this. See also Joel Spring, *Education and the Rise of the Corporate State* (Boston: Beacon Press, 1972). Holt thought the free school movement also challenged the idea that learning must be painful, boring, and separate from the rest of life.
11. The Center for Intercultural Documentation (CIDOC) in Cuernavaca, Mexico, was a kind of low-cost think tank at which Illich and his colleagues discussed various modern institutions, especially the school. North American students paid to attend lectures and seminars, and visitors from the reform movement included Paul Goodman and Jonathan Kozol. CIDOC closed in 1976.

had failed, but that schooling itself had failed—as Holt would later write, the whole design was wrong.

After the book *Deschooling Society* was published in 1970, Illich said that he regretted the title because it implied that doing away with schools would be enough. One of the biggest challenges to Illich's vision was the charge that abolishing schools while leaving unchanged society's class structure and school's influence on the way we think about teaching and learning would accomplish nothing, and would perhaps even make more prevalent the class distinctions that Illich himself claimed to oppose. It is important to understand that by *schooling* Illich did not simply mean school buildings, but rather our view of education as a commodity—something to be gotten, distributed (usually inequitably), and used to measure people—and the link between school credentials and access to jobs, knowledge, skill. He argued that it is *in school* that we learn to expect class distinctions, and to distrust our ability to do things for ourselves. "We can disestablish schools or we can deschool culture," [12] Illich wrote, meaning that if we do not deschool our way of thinking and of structuring society, closing down school buildings would be meaningless (or, again, potentially harmful). Illich may have disagreed with his Marxist and neo-Marxist critics on matters of strategy (what aspects of society to change first), but he was not indifferent to the issues of class inequality about which those critics wrote.

Holt was fascinated by what Illich was saying about making knowledge and skill more accessible; it confirmed and built upon what he had by this time come to believe quite strongly about education. The second big challenge to Illich's vision—that it lacked any concrete proposals for change—was in a sense a challenge to Holt's thinking as well, because Holt saw himself more as a tactician than as a prophet, and could not—temperamentally as well as philosophically and practically—let such a challenge go unmet. He could not stop at the question, "What kind of society do we want?" but had to ask, "How do we get there?" as well. Some of the interplay between Illich the prophet and Holt the tactician comes through in their letters, and it probably shaped Holt's later choices to a large degree.

For a tactical approach to be acceptable to Holt, it had to make sense in both a daily and a long-term way. For him, the answer to the

12. Ivan Illich et al., *After Deschooling, What?* (New York: Harper & Row, 1973), p. 20. See also Ian Lister, *Deschooling: A Reader* (London: Cambridge University Press, 1974).

question, "How do we get there?" soon became home education, or people allowing their children to learn at home and in the surrounding community. Holt founded *Growing Without Schooling* magazine in 1977 as a tactical response to what he had learned at CIDOC. If he could help people find alternatives to school in their own lives, which was *GWS*'s stated goal, then he could feel that he was making a contribution to lasting change.

This belief that change must happen within people's own lives is perhaps more characteristic of Holt's thinking than anything else. It gave him, on the one hand, evidence that what he was talking about was possible. To the claim that without school people could not learn to read, or find work, or make friends, or whatever the particular charge might be, Holt was able to offer (and to publish) stories of actual people who proved this false. On the other hand, the "nickel and dime theory of social change" in which Holt believed so strongly[13] could at times seem *too* nickel and dime for anyone to take notice. Holt's insistence on an individualist ideology meant that not everyone realized that he saw homeschooling not only as an individual solution but also as a vehicle for societal change. The approach also had its risks; not every family who took its children out of school did so with Holt's agenda in mind, and while this did not much trouble him it did mean that the connection between an individual family's decision and the possible greater change was, again, sometimes difficult to see.

Home education as practical deschooling was slow, but, to Holt, ultimately more satisfying than anything else he could think of to do. Again, it was satisfying to him both because of his temperament and because of his philosophy. Being an evolutionary rather than a revolutionary (and it was on just these grounds that the revolutionaries criticized him), he had to see change in small happenings rather than in the whole of the social structure, and it was among other things a certain impatience that made him favor this approach. Holt wanted to see change in his lifetime, to feel it happening. His question, no matter what other larger questions he was also considering, was always, "What do I do Monday?" If schools are bad, now, for these particular children, is there something we can do right away? Home education appealed to him because it was something families could

13. See *Growing Without Schooling*, no. 1, Summer 1977, p. 1.

do without having to wait for anyone else to agree with them, and *at the same time* it demonstrated how people could teach, learn, and find work without school. If Illich thought that our imaginations were even more imprisoned by school than our bodies, Holt wanted to broaden our imaginations by helping us to see—as always, through actual examples—what life without school could be like. And in fact, as home education became not only an individual family decision but also a collective movement, it began, simply in the nature of its own growth, to address some of the charges of individualism that had been leveled against it. As home educators began—and this is something that is in process right now, at this writing—to demand that communities become more welcoming to children and that knowledge and skill become more accessible, they began making the small but significant changes in the broader community that were in keeping with Illich's vision of a deschooled society.

In deciding, as he wrote to Nat Hentoff in 1973, that schooling was a sinking ship, and in turning his attention to something that he could think of as viable, Holt also left himself open to the charge of callousness. Some school reformers (and others writing about the movement) accused Holt of dropping out, of abandoning the people with whom, and for whom, he had struggled for years. Those who continued to work for change within schools thought that he lacked precisely the persistence and determination that would lead to real change. It seemed as if as soon as the climate began to change in the mid-1970s and working for school reform became less fashionable, Holt deserted that ship for one with fewer holes. Those who had criticized the reform movement, on the other hand, thought that in writing about deschooling and home education Holt was being as romantic—in other words, as idealistic and impractical—as ever.

Making schools into better places for children had been the central task of Holt's life for several years. Through it he had earned himself a public name and found many friends and colleagues. It cannot have been easy for him to decide that it was a sinking ship. But, as we have seen, and as the letters in this collection make clear, it was inherent in both his temperament and his philosophy to redefine his work when he felt a redefinition was necessary. He had, after all, once believed wholeheartedly in running a submarine, and in World Federalism, and in classroom teaching. In *How Children Fail* he wrote, "It is a curious and unsettling process, the business of changing your mind on a subject about which you had very positive convictions,"[14] and yet it can be argued that whatever Holt did do or see or achieve in his life was due precisely to his ability to let go of what had once been important, to imagine another ship and jump onto it when the time looked right.

Yet, this said, it is important to understand once again that such decisions to change course were never easy, that if Holt did desert the school reform movement (and, as we will see, it is not even fully clear that he did), he did not do it without thought or feeling. For Holt, life worth living and work worth doing were never separate. He could never quite live by the motto of the sea, "Keep one hand for yourself; one for the ship"; much of his life was characterized by an inability to distinguish between the two hands. The effort to find an individual life worth living was always conducted in the context of trying to find a collective one; he was, in other words, trying simultaneously to find his life's work and to find ways to make the world work. This complete identification with his work was what made redefining it so difficult. In 1978 Holt wrote to Mabel Dennison, the founder of the school that George Dennison wrote about in *The Lives of Children:*

> I reread *The Lives of Children,* for the I don't know how many-th time . . . When I reached the end of the book, I did something I haven't done since my uncle died, and that was the only time in my life that I did it. . . . What I did was burst into sobs. . . . Must be partly this, that I manage to live and actually stay very happy and busy in this society only by agreeing to forget or ignore a large part of what I really know about it, and beyond that, agreeing to accept as more or less natural and unchangeable a lot of things that I once could never have accepted. . . . But there was more to my grief than that. There was something awful about the fact that, having been shown the way, and a way we could so easily have taken without a great deal of trouble, we took another way.[15]

"Having been shown the way . . ." Holt refers here to George Dennison's book, which he believed showed us a great deal of what was possible in education and how we might attain it. But he also refers to the collective wisdom of the school reform movement, his own included. Holt, after all, was not only shown the way; he also showed it to others, and he could not stop trying to show it. During the last years of his life he was collecting material and making notes for a file

14. John Holt, *How Children Fail,* rev. ed. (New York: Delta/Seymour Lawrence, 1982).

15. This letter is included in the present collection.

marked "School Reform Book." Clearly he still believed he had something to say on the subject. Even though he had ostensibly given up the idea of reforming schools years before, even though he had made conscious resolutions to stop trying to change what he could not change, he apparently never quite lost the hope that if shown the way more clearly we would do what needed to be done.

CHAPTER 1

1945-1963

Holt joined the Navy in 1943, anxious to fight the war against Germany and Japan. He didn't expect the Navy to teach him anything about himself or help him begin the search for his life's work, but his submarine experience ended up being pivotal on both counts. Years later, in unpublished notes about the war years, he wrote:

> [In September 1943] I had left submarine school in Key West, Florida, and had come to New London for three months' further training at the sub base there. . . . It was very late in the afternoon of a perfect New England fall day. . . . For no reason at all I had an overpowering feeling that from here on things were going to be completely different. I had not been particularly happy at school, had felt myself, and had been, something of an outsider. This had continued through college. . . . Something about the sight, and sound, and smell, and feel of that evening suddenly gave me an overpowering feeling that this unsatisfactory part of my life was behind me, that from now on I was going to do better. It was something like the feeling of a convalescent, rising out of bed after a long illness. . . . To this day I can feel myself walking up that hill into the cool evening sunlight, like a man released from disease or prison into the full possibilities of life.

Though Holt later wrote about peace and counseled draft resistance, he described the submarine as "the best learning community I have ever seen or been part of." In *Instead of Education* he wrote, "We were not on [the submarine] to 'learn,' but to help fight the war. Like millions of other people at the time, we did not talk or think about 'learning'; we learned from the demanding work we did together,

13

and we shared our experience and skill as widely as we could." The submarine experience exemplified two of his central beliefs about education: that one should not do things in order *to learn,* but because they seem important and worth doing, and that knowledge and skill should be shared rather than hoarded.

By the time the correspondence in this chapter begins—in late 1945—Holt had become frustrated with the limitations of life in the Navy, and was ready to think about what to do next. He ended up working in the World Government movement, for the New York State branch of the United World Federalists. Of this he later wrote:

> The dropping of the atom bomb had convinced me that civilization was in very serious danger and that ways had to be found—ways very different from any yet attempted—to establish some kind of permanent peace— some kind of rule, law, and government over the entire earth. . . . There was a great deal written in those early postwar days about world government. One very striking piece, which appeared in the *Atlantic,* was written by a young ex-marine named Cord Meyer, Jr. As it ended with a call and a plea for world government, I wrote him a letter, saying in effect that I was as convinced as he was of the need for world government, and wanted to give my full time to working for it, and did not know how to go about it, did not know what sort of working opportunities there were. He wrote me back very promptly, saying . . . that the idea did indeed need people who were willing to work for it, and adding the names of a couple of organizations already in existence. I went to see both of them, and talked to their people about what they were doing and what I might be able to do, and eventually found myself working for one of them at a salary which would have scandalized my college associates if they had known of it.

Holt's six years with the World Federalists (1946–52) were filled with writing and lecturing, as the later years of his life would also be. In 1952, Holt left the UWF for a year of travel in Europe. When he returned, his sister, Jane Pitcher, suggested that he visit the Colorado Rocky Mountain School in Carbondale, Colorado. Jane, having seen how much her brother enjoyed her children (and they him), had long urged him to go into teaching. Perhaps she hoped that a visit to this new, experimental boarding school would spark his interest. It did; he wrote about that first visit many years later in *Teach Your Own:*

> I liked it. My insides sent me the same message they had sent years before, when for the first time I went down into a submarine: "Right now, this is the place for you." I said to [director of the school] John Holden, "You know, I like it here, and I'd like to stay and work here." He made what some might have taken as a rather negative reply: "Well, we'd be glad to have you, but the trouble is, we haven't any place to put you, and we

haven't any money to pay you, and we haven't anything for you to do." In return I said, "Well, if you can get some sort of roof over my head, I don't much care where you put me, and if you're feeding me I can probably live without money, for a while at least, and I'm pretty sure I can find something to do." It was an offer he couldn't refuse.

He later used both this and the story of his getting the UWF job as examples of how young people can find work they believe in without going through the usual job-and-career channels. He stayed at the Colorado Rocky Mountain School for four years, teaching English, math, and French. In 1957, having decided that he would like to try living in a bigger city, he moved to Boston's Beacon Hill, to the apartment in which he would live for the rest of his life. He continued to teach, first at Shady Hill School, then at Lesley Ellis School, and finally at Commonwealth School. *How Children Fail*, the book about these teaching experiences, had just been accepted for publication as this chapter closes.

Holt wrote regularly to his maternal grandmother, Katharine Crocker, until her death in 1956. At the time of the following letter the war had ended and his submarine was stationed off the coast of California, preparing for decommissioning.

[TO KATHARINE CROCKER]

[U.S.S. *Barbero*, Mare Island, California]
[postmarked 9/10/45]

Dear Granny,

Well, I am back again in the best of all countries to be in. I am however far away indeed from the cool breezes and dark pines of Seal Harbor where I suppose you still are. I would love to be there with you instead of this relatively dismal place where I am. I refer to Mare Island, California. What I have seen of this so-called sunny state has not inspired in me any desire to stay here any longer than I have to, which will, I am afraid, be a matter of some six months. From where we are tied up I can see the town of Vallejo, a miserable little town that lives off the Navy like one of those sucker parasite fish. No trees are in view. Nevertheless I think I may contrive to enjoy myself here. I have a couple of friends from Yale and other places who will probably be pulling in here on other boats and I feel sure that we can inject ourselves by fair means or foul into the social life of this community. [. . .]

I am also going to get in touch with the job placement people at New Haven and think about getting a job. I have not been able to decide the thing I want to do and I don't yet know what the possibilities are. I think I would like to work in the Manufacturing business, a medium-sized or small one where there would be some opportunity to advance and take a place of some value in the organization. I sense a suspicion on your part that that is a career unworthy of any real talent such as you believe and I hope I have. I hope not, because it is my sincere conviction that insofar as the manufacturers of this country are able to provide for the material welfare of the people of this and other countries during the next few decades there is still hope for the democratic life in the world. I do not expect or intend to spend my life working at it. But although I would like to go some day into politics I have no intention of going into it until I can do so as an independent.

[. . .]

Write again and give my very best to those of my friends who are up there in that lovely place, and have a good time there yourself.

Loads of love,

[John]

[TO KATHARINE CROCKER]

[U.S.S. *Barbero*, San Francisco]
[ca. October 1945]

Dear Granny,

[. . .] I am engaged with the rest of the ship's company in the tedious and difficult job of getting the ship ready for decommissioning. It is a job which I think is unnecessary in the first place, inasmuch as the ship is obsolescent to the point of being worthless in any future combat. In the second place we are plagued by the darndest collection of orders, directives, instructions, and general interference that you ever knew. I no sooner get started doing a job one way than someone comes down and says to do it the opposite way.

[. . .] There isn't much to do during my free time except to reflect gloomily on the world we live in. It is not any different than I thought it would be—but it is still a little discouraging to find after all that suffering and fighting that men are no smarter, no more humane, no more cooperative than they ever were. We have been threatened a long time that the day would come when man would have to change his ways or be eliminated from this planet. The day is here and he has not started to change yet.

[. . .]

Meanwhile the old guard in the Army and Navy, taking advantage of the tremendous wave of esteem and gratitude which they are receiving from the public, are starting to do what they have always wanted to do and have fortunately never been able to do—to maintain a tremendous military machine in peacetime and to exercise a certain amount of control over the lives of a large part of the people. You have to serve in the Armed Forces as I have to realize how burning is the desire of the military man to have his say, how unbearably annoying it is to know that there are men who do not have to obey his orders or believe his opinions. [. . .]

I am needless to say a little downcast and discouraged to see the way things are going. Don't think however that I am moping around in the dumps here because that is far from the truth. I am having a fairly good time and if there was only a little more reason to believe that I might be home sometime in the fairly near future I would feel much better. . . . Enjoy yourself in New York Granny. . . . Hoping I will be there soon on the red couch

loads of love,

[John]

[TO KATHARINE CROCKER]

[U.S.S. *Barbero*, San Francisco]
[postmarked 1/7/46]

Dear Granny,

I'm double spacing these as you see to disguise the fact that they are very skimpy. There is getting to be less and less news out here as time goes by and I just can't think of a thing to write unless I get into some long discussion about the fate of the world, which generally takes me too long. [. . .] I feel a little now like a man in the front seat of a speeding car who presses his feet against the boards and tries to slow the car down. He feels that he is accomplishing something but is not. I have written to our Representative and to several magazine editors about this atomic bomb and its effect on the world, and what we can do to get out of the mess we are in, but I am all the time very conscious that one voice is so weak as to be practically inaudible. The only way I see it is that everyone who thinks about this crisis has got to do all he or she can to bring about the one solution that will save us. We may be too late but at least there will be some salve for our conscience, as there was for those who opposed Hitler in the thirties, that we did what we could.

I am in the process of trying to write an article or exposition of the problem of atomic power and what it means to us, but it goes slowly. It is so long since I have done any creative writing that I [have] lost the power of words to a great extent. The sentences come out rough cast and have to be machined and polished to shape and size, where in college I could put them out as fast as my fingers would hit the keys to the typewriter. I do not know what I will do with it if and when I get it finished. I like to think that someone might publish it, but the only magazines that would interest me, magazines read by more or less intelligent people who would give some attention to such an article, can draw from the output of writers so much more skilled than I am that they would probably not be interested in it. Still I am going to keep sawing away on it. [. . .]

I think I will stop and get this off. Write when you are not too busy and tell me all about yourself, Christmas, the baby[1] and everything. Loads of love,

[John]

1. His sister Jane's.

Holt had been working for the United World
Federalists for two years when he wrote the following letter while on vacation in Connecticut.

[TO KATHARINE CROCKER]

[Southport, Connecticut]
August 2, 1948

Dear Granny,

[. . .]

I am amused at Dick Smith, whom you may know. Every time he
sees me he tries desperately hard to persuade me that I am foolish
and improvident to be working for world government. He does not
try to say that we ought not to have world government. He only tries
to tell me that I should not be working for it. To me it seems that he
is trying to justify his own refusal to work at it, that my work is something of a reproach to him. I begin to see (please don't imagine that
I am making a personal comparison) why the citizen voted to exile
Aristides because he was tired of hearing him called "the just," why
the Athenians poisoned Socrates, why the Romans crucified Christ.
If you know that you ought to do something, and are not doing it,
the sight of someone who is doing it is more than you can bear. [. . .]

The world government business is coming along famously. I expected that the summer would cause a big slackening of effort; but it
has not. A lot of new chapters have been started all over the state. I
feel exactly as I do when I ride a big wave into the beach—the sen-
sation of being carried along by an irresistible force. This thing is
irresistible. It will not be held back. The only thing that might cause
us to fail is our own pessimism and defeatism—and I don't think
they will. If the people who profess to believe in this would give it
their fullest support, we would have world government in a few
years. As it is, I think we may have it in ten or fifteen years.

[. . .]

[Love, John]

[TO KATHARINE CROCKER]

[166 E. 96 St., New York, New York]
6/17/52

Dear Granny,
  [...]
This is most confidential, but I have decided to resign from this job sometime during the summer. There are many reasons. I believe as strongly as ever in world government, and in the importance of doing whatever one can to bring it about. But I have strong reservations about the ways in which the United World Federalists are working toward that goal—so strong that I don't think I can do the job justice. Also, I'm bored with the kind of work I have to do, masses of small details that in most businesses would be handled by clerks and secretaries. My capacities, such as they are, are not being fully used, which is always discouraging. And I feel I need a change.

I have no idea what I will do. I feel a certain interest in teaching, though I have no enthusiasm for going to college for three years to get a Ph.D. The only kind of teaching I think I'd really be interested in and qualified for would be teaching in a preparatory school, like Exeter. I don't know enough about what that would be like to be sure whether I would like it or not.

I am also interested in writing and editing. Here again, I am completely ignorant of the problems and opportunities in this field. I plan to take plenty of time to look around before making a decision.
  [...]
[Much love, John]

After leaving the United World Federalists, Holt
traveled in Europe for a year. Soon after he
returned in the summer of 1953, he visited his
sister's family in New Mexico, and learned about
the Colorado Rocky Mountain School.

[TO KATHARINE CROCKER]

[Arroyo Seco, New Mexico]
9/27/53

Dear Granny,
 [. . .]
Jane heard that a school was starting not far from Aspen, where
she spends the winter, and she thought I might be interested in it. It
turns out that the people who are starting it are planning to put into
practice some of the ideas I have had about schools. I feel that it is
very important that a school raise as much as it can of its own food,
and do as much as it can of its own work. That is what they are doing.
The students, boys and girls, do all the housework, help build the
buildings, raise and put up the food, and so on. It seems to me important, not only because any other way of running a school is pro-
hibitively expensive, but also because that is a very valuable part of a
child's education. I can't tell you how I regret the fact that when I
was growing up I never learned, hardly ever had a chance to learn,
to make or fix anything.
Well, to make a long story short, I am going up there next week to
see what the school is like and, if it looks interesting, whether they
would be interested in having me as a teacher.
 [. . .]
[Much love, John]

[excerpts from letters written to Katharine
Crocker from the Rocky Mountain School,
Carbondale, Colorado]
[12/12/53 and 4/15/54]

This is an extraordinarily interesting and absorbing life. The time
flies by so quickly that I hardly know one week from the next. I am

living in the main boys' dormitory, surrounded, literally, by eight to ten teen-aged boys, living in closer contact with them than their own fathers. As was the case when I stood watches on the boat last summer with Spike Innes, I have to make these boys do a lot of things they would rather not do—get up in the morning, clean their rooms, get to classes, get to bed at night, behave reasonably well in the dorm. In a way, it's too much of a disciplinary load for one person. Still, I don't mind it much; and I manage to get them to do a good deal of what they ought to do without too much yelling at them, and without their getting to feel that I am a policeman. My predecessor, a very nice guy, was completely flummoxed by the job. He kept pretty good order, as good as I do, but he did not enjoy the boys' company and they certainly did not enjoy his.

[. . .]

I am enjoying life so much here. I love these children, a various and often difficult lot, and I think that most of them are fond of me. I seem to be good at teaching; at any rate, my pupils are all learning a good deal. I take a very grave view of the state of the world and our unfortunate country, but the bad news which I see in every day's newspaper does not bother me, as it used to do.

After moving to Boston in 1957, Holt still kept in touch with some friends from the United World Federalists, including Elliot (Mike) and Hope Metcalf. Mike had been on the Executive Council of the New York State branch.

[TO MIKE AND HOPE METCALF]

109 Chestnut St., Boston
Dec. 22 [1957]

Dear Mike and Hope,

It's a quiet Sunday evening. The cars are crashing and banging around on the Storrow Drive a good deal less than usual. I've taken a walk in the park, had dinner, and changed the ribbon on the typewriter. What better time to say hello and Merry Christmas.

There's not much news of me. The book[1] goes slower than I ex-

---

1. The *How Children Fail* manuscript.

pected. For one thing, it is turning out to be longer. I have about 85,000 words written and several chapters to go. I thought it would be about this length when finished. Also, the revising often takes time. I seem very hard to please, and things that I like when I first write them I like less after a second look.

On the whole, though, I think there is good stuff in it. With any luck, and if I get a publisher, it is a book people might very easily buy.

The flute is coming along fairly well. I am a hundred times better than I was when I saw you; but there is a long way to go.

Outside of this, and an occasional outing with one of my friends in Boston, I live a quiet and happy life. The days go by so fast I hardly notice them go. [. . .]

Merry Christmas, Happy New Year

[John]

[TO MIKE AND HOPE METCALF]

109 Chestnut Street
March 11, 1961

Dear Mike and Hope,

What a time has gone by since I wrote. As usual about this time of year, I have a feeling of the waters closing over my head. In January I bought a cello, figuring that I could get about an hour a day to practice on it; but I have not touched it in over a week.

[. . .]

I hope and expect to be doing free-lance research work at our school next year, working with younger kids, all the way down to three years old. It is at this level that I think I can find out most about ways to improve teaching.

Kennedy seems to have made a good start; but the major problems of our society are going to require a good deal more positive action than he has been in a position to give so far. I personally view the problem of unemployment with a good deal of seriousness. In a country where there are 8,000,000 out of work (the quoted figures are seasonally adjusted), men who are still working are going to fight for their jobs with a good deal of bitterness, resisting anything which might displace them, as in the railroads. I find it hard to blame a man who has only his job between disaster and himself and his family for doing everything he has to [to] cling to that job, even if in so doing he goes against the better interests of the community. Also, we cut a very poor figure in the eyes of the world when, with all our wealth, we cannot keep people at work who need work and want to work. And I think the problem of technological unemployment, which most economists tend to wave away as nonexistent, may be more real and permanent than we like to think.

I am more often than not gloomy about the state of our country. There is something dinosaurish about a society that cannot adapt, or that can only adapt slowly and ponderously, to new conditions. Take any one of a host of major social and economic problems—integration, education, urban decay, traffic congestion, unemployment, the decline of public transportation, TV, crime and corruption, juvenile delinquency. In most of these fields there is substantial agreement among thoughtful people and so-called experts about what ought to be done. But it isn't being done. For various reasons, the kind of action needed winds up being called impossible.

[. . .]

I don't know how I got off on this. Maybe reading the Sunday paper does it. We do move; but we move so slowly, and time presses on us. There is so much energy, skill, and good will available in this land; but the gears don't mesh, and we wind up doing less than we could or would like to do. We have a dream of a better America and a better world, but we think that, alas, it must remain a dream. Why must it?

[. . .] Much love to all,
[John]
Another blizzard here!
No school today!

In 1961 Lore Rasmussen, a teacher whom Holt
had come to know,[1] wrote a friend about the book
Holt was working on, and this friend in turn
wrote Frank Jennings, a professor of education at
Columbia. Jennings ultimately passed the letter
on to Jerome Ozer, an editor at Sir Isaac Pitman,
who wrote to Holt saying that he was eager to
publish the book. Holt stayed with Pitman for his
first three books, *How Children Fail*, *How Children
Learn*, and *The Underachieving School*.

[TO FRANK JENNINGS]

109 Chestnut St.
March 31, 1963

———————————————

Dear Frank,

You can imagine how welcome your letter was. I'm not only glad
that Pitman wants to do the book, but even more glad that they are
enthusiastic about it.

I went to a local bookstore, whose proprietor is British by birth,
and asked him what he knew about Pitman. He seemed surprised
that I didn't know of them, said they were a fine British house with
connections and outlets in a great many parts of the world. I am very
pleased to know this, because in some respects I feel that there may
be as good a market for my ideas on education in Britain as here—
perhaps better.

I finished Chapter 8 two or three weeks ago, but then decided that
it wasn't right and had to be done again. When I had re-done it I felt
the need of a chapter which looked ahead, both to the future and to
other books that I have in mind, and I finally have that done, too. I'll
copy it, do the proof reading on the last chapters, and send them
along.

I had what was for me a very exciting experience. The fifth grade
class that I taught at Shady Hill is now in the 9th grade, and the
other day I read some key passages from these final chapters to
them. Some were bored, but most were very much interested by
what I had to say. As the Quakers put it, I spoke to their condition. I
felt that they felt that here at last was an adult who knew what it was

---

1. Rasmussen is now known for having developed the Miquon Math materials.

like to be in their shoes. I am going back again for further discussion of it.

Also at the class was one of the Shady Hill apprentices, a young woman just out of college or perhaps graduate school. What I have to say conflicts rather strongly with everything she has been told about education, both at college and during her year's work at Shady Hill; but she was so interested in it that she wants me to talk to the other apprentices about it. How we will work out this rather subversive meeting I don't yet know, probably in the evening away from school. But the incident suggests that there may be many people who are ready to hear what I am trying to say, particularly among younger people.

Well, I'll have the concluding chapters in your hands very soon. I am very grateful for your efforts on behalf of this book, and look forward to seeing you when I come to New York—about which I will let you know.

Sincerely,

[TO FRANK JENNINGS]

109 Chestnut St.
Apr. 17 [1963]

Dear Frank,

Thanks very much for calling yesterday. You answered my questions and relieved my mind. I can see that it would be better, in many ways, to be with a firm which was building up a new list and trying to expand into new markets, than with an established firm which would only see you as one author among many, and for whom the book would only be "the item."

To change the subject, in our talk at your office, discussing my future, you mentioned as a possible but not very desirable role for me that of independent critic. I have some thoughts on that, which I'd like to pass on.

I see myself as independent, though I think critic is too narrow and incomplete a description of what I am trying to be and do. I am trying to find out something, which, as I understand the word, makes me a kind of scientist. Specifically, I am trying to find out why the capacity of so many children for perceiving, and learning, and thinking, declines so rapidly as they grow older, and what we could do to prevent this from happening. To put it another way, I am trying to find out what makes intelligence and how we can make more intelligent people—intelligent in the broad sense of being intellectually active, acute, and creative.

The question is whether I could pursue this study more effectively as a member of the faculty of a university. Granting that I may be wrong in thinking so, I am very firmly convinced that a university tie would hinder my work far more than it would help it. I think this would be so for two reasons, one, that a university would require me to spend a certain amount of time working for them, so to speak, for things that interested them, for their concerns rather than mine. If I were attached to a school of education, I would probably have to teach some more or less conventional courses, on psychology or teaching methods or something or other, and I would have to do a certain amount of professional reading, and a certain amount of writing in professional publications. None of this is stuff which I would ordinarily choose to do.

There might be something to be said for spending half my time doing things I did not want to do, if during the other time I could do, with university support, the things I did want to do. But I don't believe this would happen, either. The questions that concern me, in the words of a member of the Harvard School of Education, [are] "not respectable." Neither are my views on intelligence, or the enormous intellectual potential of all children, or almost anything that I know of. For that matter, my way of working would not suit the university world. Universities like to have research projects, with clearly defined goals and methods, and a beginning and an end to them. What I am trying to do can't be done that way. I have learned as much or as little as I have learned about children and their development by seeing them in their native habitat, in my own classroom or the classrooms of other people, and thinking and writing about what I have seen and thought, and then by trying out new ways of dealing with children, either by themselves or in their classrooms, or by getting other people to try out such ideas and talking to them about their results.

In other words, I am working on a very broad front. Broad in terms of material—some of my work is in connection with reading, some with music, some with math, some with sports, some with writing, some with art. Broad in terms of the age of the children—I have learned from teen agers and also from infants less than a year old. Broad in geography—this learning takes place in many different schools and even parts of the country. The way I learn requires that I be free to continue to work on this broad, and in military terms fluid, front. I have recently encountered what seems to me a magnificent way of teaching reading. Fine; I have to be free to try it out, to see how it works and might be improved, to see what effects it has on the children. In such ways I have to be free to pursue promising developments where and when I hear of them.

All this is too vague for a university. I can think of a number of projects that I have carried out in past years, in my own classes or with individual children. From these I have learned a great deal. None of them would have been considered a research project as a university ordinarily understands the word. In none of them did I have a clear idea of what I wanted or expected to achieve or learn; the fact is that all of these projects evolved in rather different ways from what I had expected. You explore, or rather I explore the intelligence of children by creating situations and then seeing how they respond to them and what they make of them. I am truly exploring, and an explorer does not know, when he starts into a bit of unknown country, what he is going to find there. But this is not how most of what passes for educational research is done, or how research proposals are written up.

Aside from that, I would have to say that the business of taking courses and getting a Ph.D. would be as distasteful to me as was for you the idea of working for the *Reader's Digest*. And for that matter, university life itself would be distasteful. I have many friends in it, and from them and from what I read and hear I have an impression of what it is like, and it really is not for me. If, which is unlikely, a university comes to me some day and says that they feel that my work is so useful that they would like to help me do it, well, I will reconsider the matter. For the time being, it seems a matter of spending a large part of my time doing things their way in the hope that they will allow me to spend some of my time doing things my way. I can't see it; life is too short, and I believe that I can learn far more and even have more influence working as I am. Rightly or wrongly, this is the line I am going to pursue for a while.

This leaves me with the problem of earning even the modest amount I need to live on. If my book or books sold well, this problem would be solved; but I can't count on this. There has quite frankly been in my mind the hope that I could eventually persuade a foundation to underwrite, to the tune of two or three thousand dollars a year, the kind of work I have been doing. When I consider what foundations spend, the amount I would need for my work seems like a very tiny investment. When I consider what foundations get for what they spend, the kind of stuff that is being done at Harvard right now, I can't help feeling that an investment in my work would be very productive as educational investments go. I am not teaching pigeons to bowl, or making discoveries which the average classroom teacher could not understand, much less use. I am concerned with the day to day problems of teaching kids and dealing with them, and the suggestions I have made and will make in my writing are in plain English, require no specialized training or ability to understand them and use them, and in many cases do not even cost much money—if any at all. In fact, some of my ideas would save money. Some of them would make teachers' jobs easier, particularly teachers with very large classes. In this sense my work is practical, connected with the small-scale reality of the classroom, in a way that much educational research is not.

So far I have not tried to get foundation support for my work, feeling that if and when my book got published I could then say, "Here is what I have been working on and will continue to work on." Also, I don't know anything about foundations. I have no idea which of them, if any, might be interested in the very personal, small-scale, long-range, and unsystematic work that I am doing. Naturally, any advice you might have on this matter would be more than welcome. But it is the independent line I am going to pursue, cantankerous and quixotic though that may seem—always with the proviso that I am ready to grasp at any opportunity that presents itself and that seems to offer a real opportunity to work in the way that seems most valuable to me.

Thanks for reading this very personal . . . don't know what to call it. I hope you will be in Boston before long.

Sincerely yours,

CHAPTER 2

1964-1976

PREFACE

After the publication of *How Children Fail* in 1964, Holt found himself, as he later wrote to George Dennison, "catapulted into public life." The quiet schoolteacher became an educational critic whose opinions and advice were sought by parents and teachers all over the country.

During this period he spent as many as four days out of five on the road, lecturing, visiting schools, meeting potential allies and friends. He kept up with his growing correspondence by dictating long letters into a tape recorder and then sending the tapes back to his office in Boston to be transcribed. Discussions with writers and thinkers who interested him were continual and extensive, and these correspondences fed and shaped the six books that were published during these years.

In 1968 he wrote to Gary Hicks, "I am meeting a lot of people in education who seem to be thinking in very much the ways I am, or at least seem to be ready to start thinking that way." A few years later this was less true, due to the changes in Holt's thinking, the changes in the educational climate, and perhaps the fact that fewer people than he had supposed had ever seriously agreed with him in the first place. Holt came quickly—more quickly than people realized, then or later—to the belief that schools were not the only way to think about education, and school reform not the only way to think about educational change. Though for years people expected him to speak and write about life in classrooms, by the early 1970s he was already chafing at the "school reformer" label.

The Summerhill Society, inspired by A. S. Neill's
school in England, was a national organization
of Americans interested in freedom in education.
They published a bulletin for which Felix Greene
had written.

[TO FELIX GREENE]

27 September 1967

Dear Mr. Greene,

Thank you very much for the series of pieces you have done for the Society bulletin. I have found them immensely interesting and to the point. I hope you will not be offended if I take a small issue with you on one matter. You say that school should be a place where teachers "will recognize at once the child who needs help, and the help that he needs most is to be loved just because of his unloveableness." I think this is very probably true but I don't think it's very useful advice. The kinds of people who are truly able to love children whom everyone else finds unloveable are exceedingly rare and they don't need to be told to do this. For the rest it is an almost impossible task and it leads them to practice various kinds of emotional dishonesty in the classroom, which are probably at least as damaging to children as anything else they could do. I think enormous harm has been done by the often-repeated dictum that teachers have some kind of an obligation to love children. The effect of this on most teachers is to make them talk to children in affected imitation [of] affectionate ways and to fake smiles. Children soon come to recognize and detest these. Meanwhile the teachers themselves are obliged to pretend to feel what they do not really feel and build up more and more hidden resentment against the children, which the children in turn also feel.

I think there is only one way to break this vicious cycle. It is not possible for more than a few people to genuinely love all children, particularly the unloveable ones. It is possible, however, for all people to treat children with courtesy and respect, to refrain from

31

making snap judgments about their talents or their character and to be willing at all times to reexamine and reconsider whatever judgments they have not been able to avoid making. Out of such treatment a relationship grows, which, because it is honest, may eventually be genuinely friendly, affectionate, and even loving.

There is still another danger in this over-emphasis on love in the classroom. It makes some teachers who on the whole feel genuinely affectionate toward children work to create a situation in which the children are emotionally dependent on them. The fact is that we should be working in precisely the opposite direction. It seems to me that the aim of every good teacher, and indeed every adult who has to deal with children, should be to make them, not dependent, but independent. This is not an argument for callousness or indifference. It may be that the distinction I am trying to make is almost impossible to express in words. It is perhaps the difference between the loving mother or father who is willing to let go of his children so that they may grow up and move freely in the world and those unfortunate parents who, however affectionate they may be, keep their children tied to them through much of their adult lives.

I do not see how we can teach children to accept their own feelings unless we allow teachers to accept theirs. One of the things which makes most classrooms such sick, dishonest places is that everybody in them seems supposed to act as if there were no such things as dislike, jealousy, anger, hatred. Children must be helped to recognize that it is a fact of life that there are times in which we simply do not like other people, do not have kindly feelings toward them, and that it is dishonest and unhealthy and in the long run damaging to pretend otherwise. I think that they must learn to realize that this is just as true of adults as it is of themselves. What is important is not that we always love or like other people but that even when we do not like them and feel angry at them we continue to treat them as human beings and not as some inferior and detestable kind of vermin. This is something that teachers as well as children can learn. If we bend our efforts in this direction I think we may truly accomplish something.

I hope that you will not feel that this argument lessens in any way my admiration for the whole of what you have written. May I say parenthetically that I very much enjoyed your movies about China and hope some day to have the pleasure of meeting you.

Sincerely Yours,
John Holt

Holt wrote to the psychologist Rollo May after
reading his book *Man's Search for Himself.*

[TO ROLLO MAY]

10/23/67

_____

Dear Dr. May,

I first became acquainted with your work when I read an article in
the journal of Orthopsychiatry some years ago, that piece which expressed to me for the first time the most important idea that a neurosis is a defense, a necessary defense, against intolerable outside
burdens or pressures, [and which] made meaningful to me for the
first time much of the behavior I had seen in children in and out of
school.

Now I have just finished your book, *Man's Search for Himself,* and I
cannot deny myself the pleasure of writing to tell you how interesting and important I find it. You will not be at all surprised to hear
that psychology, in the broad and deep sense that you and men like
Erich Fromm understand the word, is a subject of great interest to
teen-aged students, and I am going to recommend most highly your
book to all the young people I know. You might also be interested to
know that in the past two years I asked my eleventh graders to read
Erich Fromm's *Escape from Freedom* and that a very large majority of
them found it absorbing, revealing, and thought-provoking (the reason I did not use your book was that I had not yet read it myself).

I cannot agree too strongly with your contention, and I hope I do
not misstate it, that the most important battles in any person's life, be
he adult or child, are the battles that he is waging right now. I have
never been sympathetic to the strict Freudian position that nothing
could be done about a person's health and strength of mind and
spirit unless we could dig back into his infancy and re-fight and re-
live some of the battles and problems that he met then. In fact it
seems to me, and this was certainly true of my own experience, that
a person has to gain a good deal of confidence and strength from
winning present battles before he will be able to look constructively
at the more traumatic events of his earliest life. One of the reasons
that our memory may repress many painful incidents in our earlier
life is that we are, quite frankly, not strong enough to face them, and
it is only as we gain sufficient strength that these memories are likely

to be revealed to us. Again I know this to be true from my own personal experience.

Let me close by once again thanking you very much for the great contribution you are making to our understanding of ourselves.

Sincerely yours,

During this time Gary Hicks, a former student of Holt's from the Urban School in Boston (where Holt had taught briefly), was serving a prison sentence for resisting the draft. He and Holt wrote regularly.

[TO GARY HICKS]

10/25/67

Dear Gary,

Thanks very much for your letter. It was good to hear from you, even though I wish as much as you do that you were writing from some other address. Under separate cover I will send you a copy of *How Children Fail* and also a copy of *How Children Learn*, as soon as it comes out, which will be around the middle of November.

I'd be very interested in hearing your reactions to them, or reactions of any of your fellow inmates, if they should happen to read them.

I hope you don't find prison *too* unbearable, and I look forward to seeing you and conversing with you before too long.

Very best wishes,

[John]

[TO GARY HICKS]

Dec. 10, 1967

Dear Gary,

Thanks so much for the letters. Glad to know the books arrived, and hope you enjoy them. Another book I am going to send you is called *Richer by Asia,* by Edmond Taylor. (I will have to order it, so it may take some time to get there.) It is about—well, it is about many things, some of which you may not find particularly relevant; but in a very general way it is about conflict, and how one can engage in conflict without losing one's human qualities. This is a subject that doesn't get written about very much, but it's important. So I think the book will be of use to you.

[. . .]

My new book[1] is out, and will receive a very favorable review in the next issue of *Life*—written, as a matter of fact, by Jonathan Kozol. I have just reviewed his book for *New York Review of Books,* so if you were going thru Harvard Square right now you'd see my name in big letters on the cover. If I can send you periodicals, I'll send you a copy.

I'm doing a lot of public speaking these days, and when I come home the piles of paper—you remember how this joint looked—get ever higher. I have about 35 letters ready to drop in the mailbox, and you can hardly tell the difference. The price of fame.

[. . .]

Best,

[TO GARY HICKS]

1/27/68

Dear Gary,

Thanks for your note of January 13th. I came back from the West to find, quite literally, about 300 pieces of mail, so I'll make this note short [. . .] I am working with a small group of people in Cambridge who are interested in prison education. Anything you have to say on this subject would be not only of great interest, but of great value. I would particularly like to hear any ideas you can pick up from your fellow inmates about this. How do they feel about prison education? What kind of study or education would they like to have available? How do they feel about the work you are doing? As I say, anything you can tell me about this will be appreciated.

That's all for now. I hope the time goes by rapidly until you are

---

1. *How Children Learn.*

out. This country needs people like you out more than they do in. If you know what I mean.

Best,

[John]

[TO GARY HICKS]

2/8/68

Dear Gary,

Thanks for your recent letter. Glad you liked *Fail*. I never meant to suggest that the things I was describing applied only to the middle class; my point was to make clear that they applied there as much as elsewhere.

I don't altogether agree with you about what you call society. I think the word is at times a useful abstraction, but we must not let ourselves forget that what it refers to is a large collection of people, doing a wide variety of things for a wide variety of reasons and motives. I don't deny for a second that economic motives play an important part in all of this, but I think they play only a part. You seem to be asking me to believe that when a principal runs a school in a certain way or a teacher says or does certain things in a class, they do it in order that the children may be willing victims of a capitalist society, or something like that. Again, I don't deny for a minute that the way of looking at life of both principal and teacher has been strongly conditioned by life in a capitalist society, but I don't think it follows from that that they are conscious and deliberate, not to say malevolent agents of that society, working for it in everything they do. Maybe you're right but I just don't believe it. Neither do I believe that our society cannot be improved in any details until it is changed top to bottom. In fact, in general, I don't believe in the top to bottom approach to things. I am enough an anarchist to feel that things are improved in general when they are improved in their particulars. And this is not to say that there are not a great many things in our society that need improving. I agree with you that it is both sick and unstable, but the reasons lie less in strictly economic arrangements than in other things.

Well, this is something we could and probably will talk about for a long time. [. . .] I've been going round and round the country and find when I get home a hundred and fifty letters to be answered and the phone ringing half the day so I'm sorry to say I still haven't got around to sending the books but will get after it right away. Hope all goes well.

Best,

[John]

[TO GARY HICKS]

3/26/68

Dear Gary,

Thanks for your letters. Sorry not to have answered in a while, but this is a pretty frantic winter. Very interesting though. I am meeting a lot of people in education in different places who seem to be thinking in very much the ways I am, or at least seem to be ready to start thinking that way.

[. . .]

Don't be too discouraged about losing some of your zip in studying. There's an old quote from Thoreau that I always liked. "The truly efficient labourer will not crowd his day with work, but saunter to the task surrounded by a wide halo of ease and leisure." I can't truthfully say I'm living up to this precept myself these days, but it really is the spirit in which learning must be done. The mind will only take in so much new material; then it has to have some time to work with it and make something out of it, and this process is in large degree unconscious. So if you feel temporarily bored with your studies, it probably means you have a slight case of mental indigestion. Relax with a clear conscience.

I did read *Avatar*. Bought a couple of issues on the corner just to spite the cops. I must say it's a pretty dull paper though. The four letter words don't bother me. I've certainly heard them enough times and used them enough times, so that they have lost most of their shocking power. But speaking as a literary man, a writer, someone with a certain love of and feel for the language, it seems to me that they don't fulfill in print the function that they fulfill in speech. In fact, for reasons that have nothing to do with "morals," they are usually out of place in print. But this is a technical question that I don't want to go into right now.

Once again, give yourself time to think and dream. I suppose the environment is none too good for that, but it is possible to think and dream anywhere. Keep me posted and I will try to do the same.

Best,

Holt visited A. S. Neill and Summerhill, the school Neill founded, twice, and met Neill on one other occasion. A couple of months before the following letter was written, Neill sent Holt a copy of his latest book, *Talking of Summerhill*, with the inscription, "John Holt, A. S. Neill / Couple of bloody pioneers." Later, when Neill was dying, he said that Holt was the one to continue the work—not of running Summerhill, but of making a better world for children.

[TO A. S. NEILL]

September 30, 1968

Dear Neill,

It was lovely to see you the other night at Leila Berg's.[1] I had planned on this visit to England to make a trip to the school to see you, but your being in London made it all the more convenient. Also I was delighted to have a chance to get to know Leila, Harry, Bob and Michael. I am only sorry that I had to run off when I did. The conference at Oxford, except for a lovely Hungarian lady with a wonderful feeling about little children, was not very interesting— much less so than a meeting of teachers I spoke to at Exeter.

I am now on a plane heading for Seattle in our Pacific Northwest, where I will be speaking to some meetings, doing some school visiting. It is evening, and we are going over the Westernmost part of the Great Plains, where they blend into the mountains. The sun is mak-

1. Leila Berg, author of *Reading and Loving* and *Look at Kids*, wrote of this meeting in *Growing without Schooling*, no. 48: "I had just written a book on Risinghill, Mike Duane's school, and somehow I'd got Mike, Bob MacKenzie, John, and A. S. Neill together in my house for a whole weekend—all sleeping on the floor together. Of course, they'd all heard of each other, but they'd never all met in a bunch. They all talked. I cooked. It was quite a weekend." Bob MacKenzie ran Braehead, a school in the Scottish coal-mining district. The "Harry" in Holt's letter is Harry Berg, Leila's husband.

ing long shadows on the ground so that the shapes of the earth are very clear. It is a lesson in geography worth a thousand books, and I wish all children might make some flights high over the earth. From this height my country looks austere and beautiful, and it is hard and painful to remember, every now and then, that a sickness is growing terribly rapidly here that may wipe out the world. I hope not, but it may. [George] Wallace is franker about his aims than I thought he would dare be; he said yesterday in an interview with people from the *New York Times* that he thought only "fear of the constabulary" would restore what he calls "law and order" to this country. When I reflect on what law and order means in his home state, where churches have been bombed, and men and women and even children killed with impunity by white racists, it makes me deeply afraid.

But I didn't write to express such gloomy thoughts. As I write, or rather dictate, we are beginning to meet the mountains. The sun is low enough now so that the valleys are in shadow, and only the mountain tops with a light dusting of snow are still getting the sun. Anyway, when not looking at the scenery, I have been reading *Talking of Summerhill*. It is wonderful, much better, as you say, than the thing they got out in this country. So much better, in fact, that I am recommending to my students at Harvard that they order it from England. By the way, I met my first class today, and have there about a hundred students. Perhaps more may come in later.[2]

The book is delightful and gives a very much better picture of you and your thinking than either of the books of yours published in this country. Here and there are interesting points which, for no particular reason, I feel like remarking on, in the hope that you may find some of these reactions interesting or even in some way useful.

There is a quite fascinating book out in this country called *Stop Time*, in which the author describes, among many things, how he and his fellow students, at an American radical school, voted by strict majority rule that they would all give one generally disliked boy a punch in the jaw. Obviously this is a dreadful distortion of the principle of majority rule, which you would never permit. What makes me think of it is the realization that in a very real sense Fascism, both the German kind and the kind that is developing here, are a kind of unbridled rule of the majority. I don't think there ever was a time, at least until things began going very badly for Germany in the war,

2. The course was called "Student-Directed Learning." See letter to David Zuckerman, 4/11/69.

when even in a free election Hitler would not have been returned to office by an overwhelming majority. The difficult problem of Democracy, in a school or in a country, is to recognize the conflicting ideas of Democracy rule and minority or even individual rights. After all, when in our Southern towns we lynch or murder negroes, an overwhelming majority of the citizens think that is a fine idea—and it might even be that a majority of Americans believe, or will some day believe, that it will be a good idea to do away with all our black people.

I am interested in your story about the girl who complained that she got no education at Summerhill. Not long ago, I saw a former pupil of mine at a college meeting, and in the course of the discussion she announced that her life had been ruined by progressive schools. I did not say publicly what I knew to be the truth, which was that this was sheer romancing. The school she attended as a pupil of mine was in no sense a progressive school, and in any case she came to it in a deep state of psychological disarray as a result of the pressures that she had undergone in a very conventional school, from which she had in plain fact been kicked out in disgrace. She had a difficult growing up, from which she has by no means entirely recovered, but it is sheer romancing, as I said, to blame it on the few people in her schooling who were in any respect considerate or gentle towards her. It is difficult to know how to assess people's remarks about their childhood and education. Sometimes they are profound and revealing, but very often people simply tell lies.

[. . .]

Something troubles me about the notion that people with children of their own cannot teach in a pioneer school. I am not arguing against your experience. But I wonder about places like the Kibbutzim in Israel, where children, who do not have very much exclusive contact with their parents, seem to grow up healthily. Indeed, I think one of the great problems of child rearing these days is that children's family attachments are too few and too exclusive. I think children would benefit from a situation in which they could have fairly close relationships with a much larger number of adults, though I am not sure how to manage this.

You will be shocked to hear that I always say "Who did you see?" I would feel like a fool if I said "Whom." A fool, or what's worse, a pedant. Indeed, well-educated people in this country quite regularly say "Who do you see?" The objective whom is used after the prepositions to, with, from, etc. "To whom did you give the book?" But not in the other instance.

One of the reasons I am very skeptical about Freudian or other analytical interpretations of psychological problems that locate these problems in the relations between children and their parents in the early years is that I had no such relation, or none to speak of. My parents were quite prosperous when I was a baby, and until the age of about eight I was brought up entirely by what you would call nannies, we nurses; one of them, a lovely Scottish lady named Agnes Lesley, was with us a number of years. She was very close to us and was much more a mother than our real mother of whom we saw almost nothing, as she and my father were living the gay social life of rich people in the twenties. Only when I was about nine years old did I begin to have any contact with my parents at which time I discovered, as did my sister, that they had very little use for us, something we accepted with a surprising amount of equanimity though I am sure it left scars on us.

[. . .]

On the subject of morality, one of the things we know about the most hardened and habitual criminals is that they are exceedingly moral, or perhaps moralistic would be a better word. They are censorious in the highest degree.

[. . .]

Enjoyed your remarks about *Lord of the Flies*. May I suggest an addition to that answer. Not long ago, in a large meeting of teachers, someone asked me what I thought of *Lord of the Flies*. I said that it had always been one of my favorite books, and then went on to say, "but of course, you must remember that it is a work of fiction." This seemed to startle people; they take the book for truth. I went on to say, which I believe is true, that Golding has very little first-hand knowledge either of children or of primitive people. He was simply projecting onto a primitive stage his own notions of what people are like. I allowed that his notions may be correct, but they are not proved by that book. It is all made up.

Young people in this country ask me about going to college or staying in college. My answer is a little different than yours. Of course, our young men have to stay in college in order to stay out of Vietnam, unless they have medical exceptions. But where this is not an issue I say to the person, "What do you want to do?" If they know something that they want to do, and I do not accept the statement that they want to be a this or a that, I then say, "Well, go where some-body is doing that thing, and make yourself as useful as you can. Go as far as you can doing this thing that you want to do, until you find, if you do, that you can go no further because of the lack of some kind of academic degree. If you get to that spot, then the task will be to get that otherwise worthless piece of paper as quickly and cheaply and painlessly as possible. If on the other hand you don't know what you want to do, for heaven's sake don't go to college, for you won't find out there. Travel around, see the country, find out what kinds of things are going on, learn something about the ways in which people are dealing with the serious problems of our time." I think it may be more important than you [think it is], particularly in my country, to resist the system as far as one can, without doing damage to oneself. I've been told many times by well-meaning friends that I would be more "effective" if I had a post-graduate degree in education. I don't agree with them. I think the fact that I can do useful work in a num-ber of fields, and that I am invited to participate in a great number of different kinds of professional conferences in spite of not having academic qualifications, is a very powerful argument against the ne-cessity of those qualifications in the first place. In many similar ways I think that one can do a great deal to change a bad social system or arrangement by refusing to take part in it. Thus our large business corporations are already alarmed by the fact that the kind of young men who used to rush to go to work for them are no longer inter-ested in doing so, and they are beginning to ask, with real sincerity and concern, what changes they have to make in their corporations to make the business life more attractive to capable young people. In other words, there may be a great deal that we can do by saying No, and I urge young people to learn how to say it and say it as often as they can. Obviously this matter of where you draw the line is a diffi-cult one. What may be a good place for one person may not be a good place for another. I do say, as you do, that if the lack of a degree really stands between them and something they very much want to do, then they should go get one, but I think it is important for them not to decide a priori that this will be the case. We never know how much freedom we have until we test it out.

Thanks again for a lovely book. I hope you and the school have a good winter and that I will see you again in the spring when I come back to England.

Best,

George Dennison reviewed *How Children Fail* for
Commentary, and after the review came out Holt
wrote to him, saying in part, "More than any
other reviewer you have gone to the heart of what
I was trying to say." When Dennison's book, *The
Lives of Children,* came out in 1969, Holt reviewed
it for *The New York Review of Books,*[1] and for many
years would tell people that if they had time to
read only one book about education, *The Lives of
Children* should be the one. The two
corresponded, and occasionally visited, until the
end of Holt's life.

[TO GEORGE DENNISON]

October 10, 1968

Dear George,

I had a very pleasant surprise the other day. Did I tell you I was
teaching a course this fall at the Harvard School of Education? By
now I have something on the order of 100–200 students, and things
are moving along most interestingly. Anyway, one of my students,
seeing on my reading list your article in *The New American Review,*
asked me if it was the same as the one you published in *Liberation.* I
said it was not. She then told me that another course at Harvard has
been using the *Liberation* piece, and that it is still available in quantity.
As soon as the class was over I went to get a copy—they were almost
out. And now, a day later, I have just finished reading it. I hope you
don't get tired of these letters—being an author, I don't think you
do—but I just cannot find words to say how truthful, revealing,
vivid, profound and important this piece is. Just as it stands, it seems
to me worth more than anything or everything I have read about
education, even (a little hesitation here) my own books. I do a good
deal of talking to "remedial" educators, and from now on I am going
to quite literally require as a condition of my coming, that they order
enough copies of this to distribute to everyone who is coming to hear
me talk. It may not leave me very much to say, except to underline
what you have said, but at least it will clear the bullshit out of the way.

1. Holt's review was published as "To the Rescue" in the Oct. 9, 1969, issue of *The
New York Review of Books.*

It seems a crime as well as a tragedy that the [First Street] school had to close, and also an extraordinarily bad piece of luck.[2] I feel quite sure that if the school was operating today it would be able to get the money it needs. James Herndon's excellent book[3] is a case in point. Three years before Simon and Schuster accepted it he submitted it to virtually every publisher in the city of New York, and all of them turned it down, without even giving him the slightest encouragement. By so much has the educational climate changed. For some reason, or many reasons, there has grown up in the face of a headlong movement towards Fascism an enormous dissatisfaction with traditional conventional schooling. Every radical school that I know of, in almost any part of the country, is swamped with applicants. Not only that, but public school people, teachers and administrators, in a great many parts of the country, are eager to move in this direction.

I have to say it again, and there is really no other way to say it—I *love* this piece. It makes me want to go to Jerry Bruner,[4] who is not a bad cat, really, and say to him, "Jerry, what do you *think* of this?" And yet it is part of the special disability of the man, and men like him, that he would almost certainly refuse to do it. Or am I making an excuse for not asking him?

Do you know who is going to publish your book? What will be the title? When will it come out? I have special reasons for asking. Pitman is going to bring out a paperback edition of *How Children Learn* and they want to include in the back a list of specially recommended reading. I want to have your book on the list, even if it is not out yet, so that people will be looking for it.

Best,

2. The First Street School was the school at which Dennison had taught.
3. *The Way It Spozed to Be.*
4. Jerome Bruner, author of *Toward a Theory of Instruction*, which Holt reviewed in the Apr. 14, 1966, issue of *The New York Review of Books.*

[TO GARY HICKS]

2/24/69

Dear Gary,

Sorry not to have written in a while. I arrived out here[1] expecting to teach two days a week and find myself teaching four, with about three times as many students as I had expected, plus a lot of outside lecture engagements. All this is very interesting but it leaves me working a good deal harder than I meant to, and even then the paperwork gets away from me.

We're in the middle of a big hassle here. The Third World students—black, Asian, Mexican—are holding what they call a strike, but which is really a boycott, trying to get the university to give them a Third World College, with largely autonomous direction. The university, not without provocation, has brought cops on the campus, but about ten times as many as there is any need for, and both sides are working themselves up to a frenzy. I'm not sure what will happen. I certainly sympathize with the feeling on the part of the Third World people that they need an academic institution that will meet their own needs, notably an opportunity to look at their own history without the distorting process of white scholarship. On the other hand, in an effort to meet the fears of the university, they have, perhaps rightly, made their proposal so respectable and academic that I'm damned if I can see how it will be much help to the Third World communities. I wish I could get more excited about it, as I dislike the university and feel that it is not even beginning to deal with them in good faith.[2]

A lot of these young guys seem to me to act and feel like Samson. They don't really have any conviction that they are going to be able to make a good society here, or even substantially change the one we have. What they really want to do is bring the whole temple down with a crash. They talk about a better world rising from the ashes. History shows that things rarely work this way. But the main reason I regret their nihilism is that it ruins their sense of tactics. They have

1. At the University of California at Berkeley, where Holt was teaching during the winter quarter.

2. Holt wrote about the Berkeley student strike in the *Yale Alumni Bulletin* ("Letter from Berkeley," Nov. 1969) and in *The New York Times Magazine* ("The Radicalization of a Guest Teacher at Berkeley," Feb. 22, 1970).

very little idea of where and when to apply the pressure, and when to let it off, or what kinds of pressure might be more effective than others. I understand their rage and despair, but it does not make for effective revolutionaries. A really effective revolutionary has to think that he can and is going to win.

[. . .] Have to stop now. Keep me posted. Did I say my third book is coming out this spring. It will be called *The Underachieving School.* It is a collection of articles and pieces I have already done. Oh, that reminds me; the final issue of the *Saturday Evening Post* has my article in it,[3] which is already kicking up a little fuss, and may kick up more.

Stay well and keep me posted and I'll do the same.

Best,

Holt met Peter Marin, who was then at the Center for the Study of Democratic Institutions, at the University of California Extension seminars on Non-Authoritarian Teaching that Jerry Friedman, a Berkeley elementary school teacher, had orga-nized in 1968 and again in 1969. (James Hern-don, Herbert Kohl, and Paul Goodman were among the other participants.)

[TO PETER MARIN]

3/13/69

Dear Peter,

I am re-reading your piece in *The Center Magazine.*[1] Have not looked at it in the more than a month since I first read it, on the occasion of that conference. It is interesting to encounter it again while the first reading of it has in a way soaked into my bones and in my thinking. There's a sense in which I am quite different reading it the second time from what I was reading it the first time, and the piece itself has made the difference, if you see what I mean. In any case it seems both more familiar and more true. Indeed, there must

3. "School Is Bad for Children," in the Feb. 8, 1969, issue.

1. "The Open Truth and Fiery Vehemence of Youth," in the Jan. 1969 issue. *Center Magazine* was a publication of the Center for the Study of Democratic Institutions.

be much in it that I understand better or in a different way than before.

With the possible exception of George Dennison's new book, *The Lives of Children,* I can think of nothing that I have seen in all the literature about education which seems to me more important, and that I would be more eager to have millions or tens of millions of people read. I do not exclude any writings of my own, good though I think they are. I don't know whether you plan to use this piece in some collection of your own writings, or build a larger discussion of the subject around it, but whatever your plans may be, I think it is of the *utmost* importance that we find as many ways as we can to give this piece the widest possible circulation. I guess, on second thought, that some of our experiences in Berkeley during the past month have contributed to the urgency of my feeling.

I got an amusing note from Ping about it.[2] He said that many of his colleagues were not impressed by it, but were dazzled by its impact on society and on people like myself. He wants me to come by while I am still on the coast, and because I am fond of him—really a good old warrior—and like the town, I will.

I am dictating this from my room in a kind of dormitory for visitors on the campus of Ohio State University. Out of the corner of my eye through the window I see a number of other tall brick dormitories. Both on the outside and the inside they express everything that the young people mean when they call things "plastic." I have often said that I thought that unfinished concrete block was a very handsome interior as well as exterior surface, and it would be in here if they had not painted the entire inside of this room, with cinderblock walls, an awful kind of yellow. The roughness and variability of the original gray would have been interesting. It might even have been possible to paint an occasional random block here and there with a bright primary color. But they missed that boat.

Well, I look forward to your further writings, both the book on drugs[3] and anything else that might follow it, with the greatest impatience. I have decided, for a number of reasons, to reduce very sharply my lecturing during the next year or two. One of the reasons is that I must get out at least two more books in the near future. One

2. Ping is W. H. Ferry.
3. The "book on drugs," written with Allan Y. Cohen, was published as *Understanding Drug Use* in 1971.

of them I suspect you may not like—it will be an enormous list of suggestions or jumping off places in answer to the old question "What do we do Monday?" Indeed, I think I may use this as the title. Not a bad one. I think such questions need to be answered but I'm really getting tired of answering them in meeting after meeting, and want to get them down on paper where people who need such a recipe handbook can get it. And I really think it will make the brick boxes somewhat less awful and start many of the teachers on a road to a very different understanding of themselves and their students. After all, I had to travel such a road myself, and it took some time. [Al]so, I want to have time to get back into the business of making music. I find that people who are busy with the heartbreaking job of trying to make this society into something human and sensible must not neglect their small pleasures and small triumphs, or they can slip into a mood of bitter anger and nihilistic despair, [in?] which the whole damn shooting match doesn't seem worth saving. Also, I want time to talk to many of the people, yourself included, from whom I feel I have things to learn, instead of having to spend all my time talking to people who want to talk to me, if you see what I mean.

Best,

In the Student-Directed Learning course, Holt gave no grades or required assignments, and some of the students found this troubling. While Holt was at Berkeley, one of the students from the Harvard class wrote to discuss the issues that Holt's style of teaching had raised, saying in part, "Those [students] who found some direction for themselves speak fondly of your course, while those who couldn't handle the freedom remain bitter." Holt responded with the following letter when he returned from California.

[TO DAVID ZUCKERMAN]

4/11/69

Dear Dave,

Thanks a lot for yours of 3/15. Please forgive my slow reply—I was busy as hell out there.

I did repeat the same strategy at Berkeley. The courses were nominally somewhat different, being called Advanced Composition, but all my students were prospective or actual teachers; in fact, the course was mostly about education. Again, there was the same spectrum of reactions. A certain number of people went away mad at it, [without?] taking the time or trouble to tell me what it was they were mad at, or what they wanted or expected or needed, or whatever. It seems at first glance a peculiar reaction, but not when you reflect on the kind of schooling they have had.

I refuse to admit for a minute that any students were, as you say, "turned off and lost." If they were turned off, as they may well have been, they were turned off before the course even started. I don't think the cream-separator analogy is well taken. Nobody had to sign up for my course. Nobody suffered in the sense of being flunked or having a black mark put on their record because of not doing what I wanted. You can say that the course was a cream-separator in the sense that any activity in human life is a cream-separator, in that some people want to take part in it and some don't; thus, a movie, a play, a book, a poem, the Boston Public Gardens, are all cream-separators. Some people enjoy them, some don't. I don't see any way in which, in the amount of time I had, I could possibly have undertaken to please everybody in the course or meet everybody's needs, even assuming that I knew, which I didn't, what they were.

You know, Dave, I really have had some experience with this kind of thing. The sort of students who complain because you don't tell them what to do are in about 99 cases out of 100 the students who, when you do tell them what to do, think of all sorts of reasons for not doing it. Read the section in Herndon's *The Way It Spozed to Be* about what his students said about the substitute teacher—all the things she "made" them do. I just refuse to play this cops and robbers game with students. It's degrading to them and degrading to me.

The problem of weaning people from their dependence on authority is indeed a serious, difficult, and important one. I don't mean to dismiss it lightly. On the other hand, I do think it is something that a single teacher in a course like the one I gave can really not undertake to do in a space of three months. Also, I think it is fair to predict that for every student who would have been made happier by the kind of authoritarian regime you suggest, there would have been at least as many who would have been made unhappy. So, what I would have gained in one place I would have lost in another.

As I say, I had the same problem at Berkeley. I agree with you very strongly that a student who feels that he must be told what to do, and can't or won't or at any rate doesn't do anything unless he is told, has a serious problem. But *that* is his problem and when I simply go on doing what everyone else has done for him—i.e. tell him what to do—I am not really helping him solve his problem but only postponing his confrontation with it.

On second thought, I think I have to express a little skepticism about these "turned off" students. It may be true that I was not "telling" them what to do, but I was certainly giving them plenty of suggestions about things that I thought were worth doing. It really is not fair to say that I was leaving them in some kind of vacuum. It isn't as if I made no suggestions, or made no resources or options available to them. I made a great many. If they chose not to avail themselves of *any* of them, that is their right, but I am damned if I can see how I am to somehow be blamed for it.

If I use such emphatic language it is not because your letter or the recollection of the course which it arouses has made me angry, but because this is a question that I meet all the time and which you will meet as you start working in these ways, and I want to state my feelings about it very emphatically. I come back to what I call the submissive-rebellious posture that so many students, like all subject peoples, learn to assume. One of the things they get good at is blaming other people for anything in their lives that goes wrong, and indeed they use this as a kind of emotional blackmail against teachers, and are very likely to use it as kind of emotional blackmail against you someday. So you must be ready for it and not allow yourself to be thrown too much off-balance by it. Yes, when the student says, "You don't care about me, or you would tell me what to do!" the best answer, or an answer as good as any you are going to find, is "Nonsense!"

[. . .]

Best,

[TO GARY HICKS]

7/29/69

Dear Gary,

Thanks for your good letter of 7/19. You make good points about technological education. This raises a lot of complicated questions, more than I will have time to go into in this letter. I find myself remembering a time when, through a friend of mine at Harvard, I was meeting a lot of guys from the about-to-be African nations all rushing to Harvard and MIT to study what they thought they were going to need to develop their countries' economies. I kept thinking, looking at them, "What in the world are you guys doing here? This is a country which, thanks to enormous supplies of readily available resources of every kind, was able to construct the most inefficient and wasteful economy the world has ever seen. You are all from poor countries with very limited resources; any lessons you learn here are likely to be the wrong ones." It seems to me this has largely been true.

What's in my mind is that black people certainly need to know a great deal about economics and technology but that the technology and economics they are likely to be taught at most of our established institutions will be twenty times more harmful than helpful, and I don't know where else they can go. I've been reading some stuff by a man named Schumacher,[1] head of an outfit in England called the Intermediate Technology Development Corporation (or something very close to that—we have his address here). He has a lot of what seem to me very cogent things to say about economic development for poor nations—and the black nation in this country is a poor nation.

Part of my thought is that the black nation has got to find ways to bypass the money economy of the white nation. We have the preposterous situation that millions of black people live in substandard housing, which needs to be extensively repaired or even demolished and rebuilt. At the same time there are hundreds of thousands or perhaps millions of black people who need the work and who would be very glad to do this work. Because of the nature of our money economy there is no way of putting these needs together, so that black people can rebuild their own cities.

1. E. F. Schumacher, author of *Small is Beautiful*.

One of the things that Gandhi did in creating the revolutionary and independence movement in India was to try to persuade as many Indians as possible that they should to the greatest possible degree free themselves from the British economy [by] spinning their own thread, weaving their own cloth, and refusing to buy luxury goods that only the British economy could produce. My rough sense of things at the moment, and I see this as an outsider, is that black people should make a very concerted effort to put as little of their money [as possible] into the pockets of white men. But this is a big subject, which I hope we can continue as we go along.

[. . .]

Have to stop for the moment, but will continue this. The problem is I'm afraid the degree-granting institutions are much less interested in giving you the kind of technological education you want than in preparing you to fit some kind of slot in the university or industry world. But we'll explore this further.

Best,

John

[TO GEORGE DENNISON]

[520 Camino del Monte Sol
Santa Fe, New Mexico]
[ca. September 1969]

Dear George,

I have just finished the review I have written of your book for the *New York Review.* I am sending you a copy because I am afraid they may cut a good deal, and I want you to see all of what I have written—which is only a small part of what I would have liked to write. I am going to ask Bob Silvers, the editor of the *Review,* that if he feels the piece is too long for one issue, he run it in two parts—but he may not agree to this. My fingers are crossed.

Not much I can add to what I have written you before and say in the review. I have by now read the book many times, going back and forth, making the literally agonizing choice of what to quote and what not, since there is not a page that could not well be quoted. I am simply filled with the book; it is in the marrow of my bones; my feeling is that someone who has not read and understood it simply doesn't know anything. A school here, which my niece attends, has asked me to speak to the faculty, and I have exacted the condition that they read my review, and the book itself as soon as possible. I am speaking as literally as I know how when I say that I can hardly think of anything more important to do in education right now than to get as many people as possible—*everyone,* if possible, and why not, to read the book.

However, I am really writing about something else. I can tell you that before long you are going to be inundated with mail, much of it tear-stained—some of the letters I have had from parents and teachers would break your heart—and all of it asking you what to do. I think you are going to find yourself, as I did, as Jonathan Kozol did, and like yourself we are both basically private people, catapulted into public life. I know you won't like this but I have to plead that you not altogether turn your back on it. Just as you want to write, what I really want to do is spend about eight hours a day on the study of music, which I love beyond words—but it is just not to be.

[. . .]

Time to stop. Will be home in Boston in three weeks, and will call you. Hope the book goes like wildfire. At least your publishers are getting it reviewed, which my publishers don't seem to be very good at doing. Let's hope ten million people read it. But it will change your life.

Simon & Schuster sent Holt galleys of James
Herndon's *The Way It Spozed to Be,* and he gave it
an enthusiastic review in *Life* magazine in 1968.
Herndon wrote to thank him and to tell him how
important *How Children Fail* had been to him,
and the correspondence continued.

[TO JAMES HERNDON]

November 25, 1969

Dear Jim,

Wonderful to hear from you. Sorry not to reply sooner. I've been away from the office a good deal, and am only just beginning to dig my way out from under the paper.

I've got an article coming out in the late December, early January issue of *Look* which I think you might like. I enclose an article I wrote for the latest *Yale Alumni Magazine*. I expect it will shake up a few Old Blues.[1]

I know what you mean about feeling that you had thought something yourself, when in fact you hadn't done so. This is exactly how Dennison's new book makes me feel. I'm sending along a review I wrote of it and hope you'll read it (the review) and then the book. I'm also sending along some very important articles by Ivan Illich.[2]

Both these guys have really carried my own thinking forward a little bit, but their thoughts are such a logical consequence of the thoughts I have thought already, that it's really hard to know where my thought ends and theirs begins.

My biggest project is finishing book #4. I have new publishers, and a much better deal than I got from the last one. Herb's agent is now mine—a wonderful guy and enormously helpful.[3] I only wish I'd worked with him sooner. I'm also busily turning down invitations to speak, though I find it hard to turn people away who call me up and say they've come to Boston hoping to be able to see me, and can they come to the office. However. Glad your own new book is coming along fine, and couldn't be more pleased to hear that it is growing all the time, since I liked so much all the parts of it that I know.

My feeling about work is that in the next couple of years a lot of new things are liable to open up, new form[s], new ways of doing things, and some of them are very likely to appeal to you. But if not, it's nice to be doing something that one likes.

[. . .]
Best,

1. The *Look* article was "Why We Need New Schooling," in the Jan. 13, 1970, issue. The Yale article was the one about the Berkeley strike. "Old Blues" are Yale alumni.

2. Ivan Illich's books include *Celebration of Awareness, Deschooling Society, Tools for Conviviality, Energy and Equity,* and *Toward a History of Needs.* See letter to the students at the Center for Intercultural Documentation, 2/19/70.

3. The new publishers were E. P. Dutton, and Herb [Kohl's] agent was Robert Lescher.

Two years after its publication, Dr. J. M. Stephens
reviewed *How Children Learn* in the Winter 1969
issue of the *Harvard Education Review*.

[TO J. M. STEPHENS]

December 1, 1969

Dear Dr. Stephens,

I've been meaning to write you since I read your most kind and
generous review of *How Children Learn* in the *Harvard Education Review*. I only write to make one point. The things that I say I learned
from watching children, I really did learn that way and in no other.
Most of the books to which you refer, I have not read to this day.[1]

One other short point. You say that teachers "may get the idea that
truth in these areas is a matter of free and easy observation." There
was nothing either free or easy about my observation. I learned
whatever I have learned about children by prolonged and careful
observation, and even more importantly, as a result of continued
failures to teach them, in more or less orthodox school fashions,
things people said they should learn. There seems to me a suggestion—forgive me if I'm wrong about this—that in learning about the
world, other people's books are more important than observation.
With this view I most emphatically and strongly disagree. This is indeed part of what I am trying to tell teachers—that the things they
learn or feel they are learning from their direct contact with and
observation of children are more important and what is even more
important more to be trusted than what the theoreticians may tell
them. This is a heretical view, I know, but it is my own.

Sincerely Yours,

John Holt

1. Stephens had not actually referred to specific books, but to John Dewey and
B. F. Skinner, with whom, he claimed, some of the positions in *How Children Learn*
were consistent.

1964–1976

Holt made several visits to the Center for Intercultural Documentation (CIDOC) in Cuernavaca,
Mexico, where Ivan Illich and his colleagues
held seminars about, among many other things,
Illich's concept of "deschooling."

[TO STUDENTS AT THE CENTER FOR INTERCULTURAL DOCUMENTATION]

February 19, 1970

To my student friends and colleagues at CIDOC,

First of all, I want to say that the two weeks I spent among you and
with you were among the most interesting, pleasant, and valuable of
my life. Our talks have strengthened and advanced my thinking in
many ways, and I look forward to seeing as many as possible of you
again as we work to make a more humane, sane, and loving world.

I write mostly for another reason. My short visit to CIDOC has
made me feel much more strongly than before that our worldwide
system of schooling is far more harmful, and far more deeply and
integrally connected with many of the other great evils of our time,
than I had supposed. I have been very critical of what we might call
"schoolism," but I had not thought of it as being anywhere near as
harmful as, say, militarism or modern nationalism, and would have
considered such comparisons overdrawn. They now seem altogether
apt and exact.

This raises a kind of ethical dilemma. You are of course free to
disagree with what I or Ivan Illich and his colleagues have been saying about schooling. But if you agree in any large measure, it seems
to me that you have a duty to begin what we might call school resistance, or credential or diploma resistance, just as those who strongly
disapprove of war in general or our war against Viet Nam in particular ought to express their disapproval in some form of war resistance. In my own case I have been unsure what form this war
resistance should take. For a few years I refused to pay taxes, but as
the result was only that I wound up paying more taxes than ever, I
gave up this tactic, perhaps mistakenly. Though I belong to and con-
tribute to a number of pacifist and resistance organizations, I have
not taken part in active civil disobedience as much as for any other
reason because I feel, again perhaps mistakenly, that the work I do

in education is more valuable, even in terms of ending war, than any witness I might make in going to jail. What is important is that as far as I can I do stay out of positions in which I might *directly profit* from the war.

We can reject out of hand the often heard argument that those who resist an act, institution or government that is inhuman, illegal, or immoral have a duty to "accept the consequences." This is nonsense. If a man sticks a gun in my ribs, law and common sense alike say that anything I can do to escape or outwit him is justified. I am well aware that this argument raises very serious problems, and that it might well have been used as an excuse by those who ran the concentration camps in Germany and Russia, as it would probably be used today by Judge Hoffman or the policeman who murdered the Panthers in Chicago.[1] Nevertheless, in the context of this time and place, as far as I am concerned any young man who wishes has the right and the duty to escape, *at minimum cost to himself,* the government's demand that he take part in our obscene war against the Vietnamese, and anything short of murder he does to that end, *anything at all,* is OK by me. People may be free to sacrifice themselves for the sake of principles, but they are not morally *obliged* to do so. In our struggle to make a viable and decent world, we are all guerillas, and we should as far as we can keep ourselves from being put out of action.

But, to come back to schools, I do not see how you can be a consistent or effective school resister if, knowing them to be bad, oppressive, and discriminatory, you then use them to get a ticket which throughout your lives will give you a great and permanent advantage over all the vast majority who do not have and *cannot possibly get* such a ticket. Many of you feel that the ticket will help you fight schools more effectively. The trouble with this is that the concession you make to the schools, in getting, keeping, and for your own advantage using the ticket, far outweighs anything you may later be able to do against the schools and their stranglehold on men's lives and imaginations. Your example will speak a thousand times more powerfully than your words. You can hardly consistently or honestly urge others to give up the ticket you were glad and eager to take; indeed, you can hardly do other than urge them to struggle with all

1. Judge Julius Hoffman was the judge in the trial of the Chicago Seven, who were charged with inciting to riot at the National Democratic Convention in Chicago in 1968. The Black Panthers was a black revolutionary group.

their might to get the fanciest ticket they can. Which leaves us all exactly where we came in.

We must have by now upwards of 100,000 draft and war resisters. But we have relatively few diploma resisters, people who have deliberately decided to give up their own ticket, and whatever advantages it might give them, as the first step toward making a society and world in which the knowledge, competence, worth and life possibilities of people will not be determined by their school credentials. This is all the more surprising when we see how much greater are the risks and penalties of draft and war resistance than would be those of school and diploma resistance. Most of you overestimate these latter risks. As I said many times in our talks, the people who are doing the kinds of work that will really help to bring about the kind of world we want need all the help they can get, and they are not going to scrutinize the paper credentials of those who come round ready and eager to help. Also, compared to the majority of the young in our country, most of you are in a relatively safe and favored position. There are very few of you whose families are not in the upper 5% or even 2% of the country in income level. Most of your families are now, and will be for many years to come, ready to underwrite your further schooling, even to the tune of many thousands or even tens of thousands of dollars. The option of going back to school will for a long time be open to most of you. Few of your families, whatever they may say in argument, would disown you if as a matter of principle you gave up your diploma. For most of you it is the case that for a good many years to come, if things get tough and you need help, there will be many people able, ready, and eager to give it. You will live your lives, as I have lived mine, and as most people do *not* live theirs, with a safety net underneath you. Whatever else may happen, you are not going to starve. The risks of diploma resistance are for most of you vastly less than they would be for most of the young in this or any other country. If you will not run these risks, it is hard to imagine who will.

One possible compromise might be to get your diploma or ticket, and then refuse to talk about it, saying instead, as I intend to say when asked for biographical information, that I consider my schooling, like my politics or religion, my own personal and private business. In one respect, this compromise is a fair one; you may be able to show in your own life that it is possible to make your way and do good work in the world without a school ticket. In another respect, the compromise is morally weak; others will be able to say to you, and you can hardly help saying to yourself, that you are willing to run whatever may be the risks of ticketlessness only because you know privately that in a pinch you always have that ace in the hole. Still another compromise, perhaps one that tempts many of you, must be rejected altogether, that of saying, "I will get my ticket, so as to get myself in the position where I can give preference to those without tickets." Whoever says this kids himself. Any organization that demands that you show your ticket at the door as the price of getting in will not later allow you to let in people without tickets. Every time you use your own ticket, you necessarily raise the value and price of tickets in general. The only way to downgrade tickets is to do without them.

There I leave the matter. Some of you may feel, and fairly enough, that in presenting this ethical dilemma I have taken unfair advantage, not only of my much more secure position in life, but also of the trust, respect, and affection that has grown up between us. As to the first, until very recently I was the opposite of rich or famous, and in my own life made a good many choices no less risky than those I lay before you. As to the second, I can hardly say to young people in general, as I feel I must, the kinds of things I have said here, if I will not say them to you particular young people that I know and care about. I cannot put before strangers a choice so difficult that I will not put it before my friends.

I do hope that you will let me know any thoughts you may have about this, that you enjoy the rest of your stay in Cuernavaca, and that you will keep in touch.

Thanks for everything, good luck, and peace

[John]

On the lecture circuit, Holt spoke to students as well as to teachers. This letter follows a talk to education students at Boston University, during which Holt had clearly addressed issues similar to those he had raised in the letter to the CIDOC students.

[TO BOSTON UNIVERSITY STUDENTS]

February 27, 1970

To the students at Boston University,

I enjoyed our meeting the other afternoon very much. It started some further thoughts in my mind that I wanted to pass on to you, and this letter seems to be as good a way of doing it as any.

I recall the young lady who said to me angrily that she didn't feel guilty about having a Bachelor's degree. Fine; I don't want her to. Though I am a pacifist now, and have been for some time, I don't feel at all guilty about serving on a submarine in World War II. At the time, in light of how I thought and felt, it seemed exactly the right thing to do, and now I still think of it as one of the important experiences of my life. In the same way, I don't feel guilty about my own schooling. All this misses the point. What I said at the beginning of my letter to the students in Mexico was that *if* you feel, as I now do, that the whole institution of schooling is inherently and incurably discriminatory and repressive, an intolerable burden on the backs of poor people all over the world, a tremendous obstacle standing in the way of any real development of poor nations or communities, and also an obstacle standing between young people and their own lives—*if* you feel this, then indeed you *should* feel guilty if you go on anyway and get a diploma simply for the advantages it will give you over the people who can't get one. If you can't for the moment change or do away with the bad institution, you ought at least do what you can, as Thoreau said some time ago, to get out of positions in which you will profit from it.

I think I disagree very strongly with most people, including most radical people, on the question of the degree to which large institutions are capable of being reformed. I think the position is naive, which may only be another way of saying I disagree with it. My very strong feeling is that constructive change in human affairs does not come about through people clashing with and reforming old institutions, but by their setting up new institutions which because they meet more important human needs gradually displace the old, until they become fossilized in their turn.

One of the things Illich talked about in Mexico, that I did not talk about yesterday, was the degree to which our imaginations have been captured, not just by schools but even more largely by institutions and the idea of institutions. By and large people feel, and this was certainly expressed in much of our meeting, that institutions between them occupy all the life space on earth. Many of the students in Mexico talked this way. Considering the degree to which their lives have been dominated by institutions this is natural. But it [is] nonetheless mistaken. Institutions do *not* occupy all the life space on earth. It is *not* the case that a human being only has a choice between working in one institution or some other institution. There is a lot of life space in between and outside the institutions, in short, there are an enormous number of opportunities, either for starting what I prefer to call new human arrangements, like communes, free schools, cooperatives, artistic ventures, individual consulting, etc. [or] for simply walking away from, deliberately turning one's back on institutions that do not serve one's need. In this connection it is interesting to consider a little bit the phrase that almost everyone at the meeting use[d] to describe this kind of action. They all call[ed] it "dropping out." The metaphor is powerful, and revealing. It suggests that to be outside the world of institutions is to be outside of life altogether, cast adrift in outer space as it were. The suggestion is that if you're not involved with some institution, you're nowhere. My very strong feeling is quite the opposite. It is true that institutions have a great deal of power and do occupy a large amount of the waking hours of a great many people. But they do not by any means occupy all their time. There really is a very large part of our lives which is not dominated by institutions, or at least which might not be if we could break the spell which the institutions have cast over us.

To continue this thought, Illich said and will continue to say that modern man thinks that every human good or human need is or can be the product of an institution and cannot be obtained any other way. This is exactly what Paul Goodman means when in rather different contexts and in different language he says that in our society people can only think of "roles." Practically nobody ever thinks of the task anymore. If I say to young people, what do you want to do, their answer is almost always something like, "I want to be a something or other-ist." When I go on to say, "Well, if you were a something or other-ist, what would you do?" they are usually baffled, but those who continue to answer usually tell me that they will try to work for some kind of institution. If I go on further to say, "OK, if you were working for that institution what would you *do*?" they simply don't know. They never thought in terms of things that needed to be done, and the ways in which they might do them. This is what I meant but did not clearly express, when at one point I said that the reason for getting out of schools and educational institutions was so that you could get to where the work was really being done, and find out which kinds of work you really want to do.

In the context of education, this means that most of you who want to be teachers are in my opinion going about this business entirely backwards. What you really want to do, I suppose, is work with children of certain ages and sizes and at certain kinds of things. I hope this is true. There was of course a time when most people who went into teaching went in for the sake of the "role"—that is, because it was respectable, safe, and fairly easy work, with not [much] pay but long vacations and a certain kind of security if you kept out of trouble. As I say, I assume that you are all looking for something quite different, the opportunity to live with, and relate to and be of use to children in various ways. But you are going about this exactly the wrong way. What you *ought* to do, and what any school of education worthy of the name, and I don't really know of one worthy of the name, ought to be helping you to do, is doing some detective work, trying to find some people who are already living [and] working with children in a way you like. Then, when you've found such a person or a group of people, the next thing you would do would be to say, "I like the way you people are working with children, and I want to work with you. How can I do that?" Now the chances are that if these people are very libertarian, they might say, well, "Come on in and join us right now." It might well be that whatever school this was would have very little money to pay you, but they could probably take you on as an unpaid apprentice, and could probably find or make living and boarding arrangements that would make it possible for you to do your apprenticeship at almost no [monetary] cost to yourself. Then, as you became skilled and valuable to the school, and if you had any luck, this school might be able to start paying you some kind of salary. This is exactly the way I got started. Even if it didn't work out that way, even if you found out after a while that you didn't much like the place, or if the school folded, or if something else went wrong, you would still come out of the experience with a vastly greater amount of real learning and growth than you could get in twenty years of schools of education, and you would be very much better prepared to make your next move, which would probably be to find a place which, in the light of your greater understanding [and] experience, would enable you to do the kind of work you wanted.

It might be that in one of these places, otherwise altogether congenial to you, [someone would say,] "Well, we want very much to have you here, but you are going to have to get a piece of paper in order to satisfy [some] sort of regulation." This is OK. But then they could almost certainly work out with you a way in which you could get that paper locally so that you could continue working with them, and very possibly a way in which your actual work might be given some sort of credit toward the piece of paper. [. . .] To summarize, you begin by finding the *work* that you want to do, and then you dispose in the easiest way that you can, the tactical obstacles standing in the way of your doing that work, which might include the need of getting some sort of credential.

[. . .]

In my talk I talked often about driving hard bargains with institutions. I understand very well that it is necessary to bargain. I talk very often to groups of teachers, and one of the things I say is that it is exceedingly important to keep clearly in mind what we would do if we could do whatever we wanted, to ask ourselves continually, "What would I do if I had my druthers?" At the same time, I say that we are all in varying degrees walled in by circumstances, that we can't have or do everything we want. We then have to consider the tactical problems of getting from where we are to where we want to go. To put this a little differently, we have to push out against the walls of circumstances that hem us in. One of the reasons we have to push is that unless we push we can't really be sure where the walls are. We may find that we are walled in, not so much by a real wall as by a wall that we have built in our imagination, very much like the wall that exists in the minds of most of you, who think that nobody can do anything in the world without a college diploma, in spite of the fact that even in this country the very large majority of our population does not have one. In other words, we have to push against the walls to find out where they really are. The other reason we have to push is that if we do not push them out, they push us in. Our life space is always either expanding or contracting, and it only expands when we try to expand it. So we must be continually driving bargains with whatever circumstances, and they may be institutions, limit our life space. [. . .]

I find myself thinking of something that has happened to me quite a number of times. Often, talking to groups of school teachers, I have asked them to show me, by raised hands, whether they think giving marks or grades generally help[s] or hinders the learning of children. By substantial vote, they almost always indicate that they think this hinders. I then ask them whether they are giving marks, and about 95% of them are. I then ask them, or used to before I realized that it was pointless and embarrassing and perhaps hurtful to them to do so, what they were doing about it. In fact they are doing nothing about it because they don't think anything can be done. You all talk about getting inside the system so you can change it. Let's take a very concrete example, like marks. I dare say that most of you feel that marks and grades are a bad thing. Indeed, I suspect that many of you would agree with a great deal of the things that I say in my article in *Look* about the changes that need to be made in school. You will probably not like the fixed curricula or homogeneous grouping, or the necessity for giving exams, or the disciplinary rules, or the psychological probing, or the making of dossiers on children to give to their future employers. In short, with respect to most of the things that I think are deeply and fundamentally wrong with schools, a large number of you are in a large agreement with me. The question is, do you think that you are going to be able to change this in most of the schools where you are likely to be teaching? What exactly do you plan to do if you say to the principal that you would rather not give marks to your students and he says, "I'm sorry, I understand how you feel, but we have to give grades in this school and that's all there is to it." What are you going to do if he says the same thing about bringing out[side] materials into the class, getting away from the standard text, moving the desks and chairs around, having a little life and activity and conversation in the class. In fact, you're not going to do a damn thing. If you persist—I get correspondence from teachers like these on the average of once a week, sometimes more—you're going to get fired. You may then kick up a kind of squawk as some of these teachers tell me they have done, but they remain fired nonetheless. You simply cannot imagine the number of teachers I have met or heard from that say to me in one way or another, "I've been trying for years and years to find a place in which I can work with children in the way you suggest. Please tell me if there is such a place." There is a thing at the school of education at the University of Massachusetts at Amherst called the Teacher Drop-Out Center, a kind of clearing place for information from teachers who can't stand the schools where they have been working or have gotten fired from them, and are looking for a place where they can teach in a sensible and humane way. The people in the drop out center tell me that they have about a hundred times as many letters from teachers as they have places for them to go. So who is kidding whom about fighting within the system. The thing to do is to find places where you can work in the way you want to work, and if you can't find such places or if they are so full that there is no possibility of getting into them, then make your own place.

Well, this has gone on a long time, and I will bring it to a stop. Perhaps I have made a little more clear the kind of thing I am trying to say. Hope that many of you will keep in touch with me, and will particularly let me know about good schools or school systems as you find them. Good luck to you.

Sincerely,

[TO GARY HICKS]

4/9/70

Dear Gary,

[. . .]

The difference between me and a lot of the radical blacks is that although many of them talk about a Final Solution, gas chambers and the like, they don't act as if they really believed it was possible, whereas I know damn well how possible it is. What gets me is that so many blacks seem *surprised* by the murders of Hampton and others in Chicago. I'm not surprised except that there hasn't been more of it. One of the things I find myself saying to angry young white radicals is, "Things aren't as bad as you *say*, but they're a hell of a lot worse than you *think*." If they want to find out how much worse they could get, they don't have to go any farther than Mexico, where they killed about four or five hundred students with machine guns and threw about four or five hundred more in jail, where they are yet.

[. . .]

Hope you're well. It will be great to have you out of there and to see you.

Best,

[John]

Paul Goodman's book *Growing Up Absurd,* which argued that the troubles of the young were caused by the absurdity of the adult society awaiting them, clarified and stimulated Holt's thoughts about the importance of work worth doing.

[TO PAUL GOODMAN]

July 23, 1970

Dear Paul,

How are you these days? I had dinner with Edgar Friedenberg at Harvard the other day. He is enjoying his work there during the summer. Also told me that he is leaving this country, to live in Canada and teach at Dalhousie in Halifax and become a citizen there. Certainly the temptation to do this is strong. It is a heavy burden on me, as it has been on you, to have to think as badly as I do of so many of my fellow citizens. I keep looking for and hoping to find evidence that they are not as callous and greedy and cruel and envious as I fear they are, and I keep getting disappointed. We still are, in fact, at least compared to a great many other places, a relatively free country, but what scares me is the amount of Fascism in people's spirit. It is the government that so many of our fellow citizens would get if they could that scares me—and I fear we are moving in that direction.

I didn't intend to write about this. I have started reading your new book,[1] enjoying it is as always, and jumping around as is my custom. I find myself moved to write a few words about your quarrel, if we can call it that, with the young—something like a lovers' quarrel,

1. *New Reformation: Notes of a Neolithic Conservative.*

perhaps. I have been at a couple of meetings at which you had arguments with them, and I have gone away distressed, with things on my mind, some of which I may be able to say here.

One way of starting is to say that I fear you take the worst for the whole of them, or the average of them, and also to some extent bring out the worst in them. I have talked with an awful lot of student groups in this last year, both high school and college, and though I certainly run across a lot of the kinds of people you are talking about and indeed know quite a number of such young people quite intimately, I also know a great many others who do not fit into that pattern at all. Not at all. Indeed, I could run off a whole string of complimentary adjectives to say how much I think of them, their intelligence, their seriousness, their sense of where we are.

I went with some young people that I liked in Washington, D.C., to that meeting where you were talking to the—what is it called, National Policy Institute, something like that—and when we left I was very nearly as distressed and angry as they were. I'm not altogether certain that you realize how abrasive your criticisms can sometimes be. In any case, it seemed to me that you were taking that particular group to task for things you had encountered in previous groups, so to speak. In other words, you didn't really give them a chance to show you where they were before you were giving hell. Naturally this aroused everybody's blood. The trouble is that this turns out to be a kind of self-fulfilling prophecy. When you criticize a young person or group of young persons for an attitude or a group of attitudes which are only a small part of the sum of his world view, naturally he rises in defense of what he believes, even if he believes in other things as well, many of them perhaps things you believe in. But the argument gets to be about the things on which you disagree, and you leave the argument thinking that this part is the whole. This distresses me, because you're valuable to them, they need the help and encouragement of sympathetic and wise older people. Also, it may be that in some ways they are valuable to you, and I don't want to see this quarrel go too far.

Also, there is more than I think you are ready to admit in what might be called their philosophical or theological or epistemological position. I remember your saying at the meeting in Washington, "They don't believe there is a world out there." The statement implies a distinction between the subjective and objective, between the world in here, presumably inside the skin, and the world out there—

a position that a great many of the young, but not just the young, reject. Philosophers have been challenging very soberly this particular notion of "objective consciousness" for some time. I have read for years articles in the pages of *Manas*[2]—do you know it?—attacking this very view. [. . .]

I seem to remember we were once having a conversation, perhaps at Jerry Friedman's in Berkeley, on the matter of culture, and I either said or perhaps thought that when you speak of human culture what you are really thinking about is Western culture, that other modes of thinking, other cultures in the world, seem either primitive or initial steps down a road that we have already travelled. At the time this seemed a little parochial, perhaps. Since then, thinking about it more, I have come to feel that it is, if true, quite seriously mistaken. There are many reasons for this, but one will do, particularly as it weighs very heavily with the young. It is not an exaggeration—well, perhaps it is, but at any rate that is how I see things and certainly [how] most of the young [do]—to say that mankind has come to the edge of a cliff. An observer living among us, reporting back home to his distant star, would have to say that the prospects for humanity are not very good, that there is every reason to believe that either through war or through our systematic destruction of our environment we may very soon make the world uninhabitable for us and indeed for all living creatures. Furthermore, this may very well happen within the next hundred years, or generation, or decade. Now it is Western culture, Western science, Western philosophy, Western technology, Western politics etc., and not any other kind, that has brought us to this position. [. . .]

When you defend Western culture you talk as if you thought of yourself, at least in some sense, a more or less typical product of it, and that the mass of technocrats here and all over the world, politicians, scientists, manipulators of men in one way or another, who have led us up to the edge of the cliff were renegades. But it is you who are the exception. As I guess you know better than I, you would probably not be a very welcome permanent member of any university community in this country, and there are a great many in which you would not get hired at all. Why are you any more a true spokesman for Newton than, let us say, Edward Teller or Wernher von

2. *Manas* was a weekly "journal of independent inquiry" published by the late Henry Geiger, with whom Holt often corresponded.

Braun? Or B. F. Skinner? Or the doctors now dosing little children with amphetamines to make them quiet in school?

Another way of putting this might be as follows. You think of yourself as being a true product of Western culture. The young might say, on the other hand, that you deserve a great deal of credit for being as good a man as you are in spite of the culture that produced you, but that the credit is yours, not the culture's. How does the quote go, "By their fruits shall ye know them." The angriest and most alienated of the young are judging all of Western culture by what they see of its fruits, and they are so much more bad than good that they are ready to reject the whole. [. . .]

I've just been skimming through the bound galleys of a book that John Day is going to bring out in the fall, called *No One Will Lissen,* by Lois Forer, who for several years has been trying to get justice for young people in courts in Philadelphia. It is a beautiful book, and you should try to get hold of it. I would be glad to see you review it for someone, if you were so inclined. The story is really horrifying, much worse even than I had suspected, and I keep thinking I know the worst about this country. The degree to which our legal principles, the most profound ones, the ones most deeply rooted in whatever is good in our culture, are daily scorned and violated not just by lawyers but by judges themselves is simply shocking. Mrs. Forer brought great energy to the task, and professional training, and worked hard within the system, within a very small part of the system, to make the law live up to its own principles. Her efforts were almost an unqualified failure. As I read the book, or parts of it, two thoughts struggled in my mind. On the one hand, I thought that we need a great many young people to go into the law to struggle as this woman has, and that if enough of them went in they might in time be able to get things changed around. On the other hand, I found myself thinking, like many of the angry young, that the system is too far gone, too corrupt, too self-serving and self-protecting at a hundred points, too well armed with defensive mechanisms, to be reformable. I'm not at all sure either, that if a considerable number of young lawyers began to work, let us say in Philadelphia, to do the kinds of things that Mrs. Forer was trying to do, and if they grew strong enough to present some kind of serious challenge to the legal and judicial system, that those in charge of the system would not defend themselves by trying to have them disbarred, just as the public schools manage to kick out a great many people if their efforts at changing [the schools] seem to be successful.

In stating these two views I don't mean that I've decided in favor of the second. I am still an evolutionary rather than a revolutionary, and I think that talk about changing this society or bringing it down through violence is just foolish. But I am nowhere near as certain of this as you are. I think it is altogether possible that the professions are so corrupt that they will throw off, like a living body rejecting foreign tissue, any group of people who try to reform them. At any rate, it is an arguable point, and I don't think we can dismiss as simply foolish or misguided people who take that position. I hope they are wrong, and I cling to this hope in every way I can. I am a great clutcher at straws, and I spend a good deal of my time going around trying to plump up other people's courage and faith, and to persuade them that it is still worthwhile working on these things. Incidentally, when I say this a lot of them seem to listen. But it is only really with a kind of ostrich head-in-the-sand stubbornness that I can make myself or enable myself to keep these kinds of hopes alive. [. . .]

Hope you are well, and enjoying life. I am.

Peace,

Everett Reimer, whose association with Ivan Illich dated back to the 1950s, led the Alternatives in Education seminar at CIDOC each year. These seminars, and the discussions that grew from them (of which the following letter is clearly an example), led to his book, *School is Dead,* which was published in 1971.

[TO EVERETT REIMER]

August 28, 1970

Dear Everett,

I'm dictating this letter from Santa Fe, where I'm visiting my sister and her family. We have had, for this part of the country, a rather damp summer, but today is brilliant and cool—the beginning of fall weather, which out here is particularly lovely. I've been having a fine time and getting quite a bit of work done.

I enjoyed your "An Essay on Alternatives in Education" *very* much. There are all kinds of things in it that I want to quote, and if I were to specify all the things in it that I think are interesting and important it would take me almost as long as the book. [. . .] The point about child care getting more and more expensive as children get older is extremely important. This does a lot to explain what we must acknowledge as the hatred which a great many older people feel for the young in general, and their own children in particular. [Whereas] in simpler societies, children got more helpful as they got older, here they get less so. As you point out, this is bad for the kids themselves.

I should say at this point that my thinking about education and the position of young people in society has led me to this position, that I now feel that there should be a guaranteed annual income for all individuals, that people should start receiving this in their own right certainly as young as age 14 and preferably even two or four years sooner than that. I also feel that, beginning at age 14 or even 12 or 10, children should have most of the legal rights and privileges now reserved for what we call adults, including the right to own property, work, travel, live away from home or independently, and so on. I'm not saying anything particularly new when I say that under the law children are non-persons; indeed, their position in the family is almost identical with that of the family dog or cat. They are simply pets. If we gave children a far greater true control over their own lives a great many of what we now consider almost insoluble educational problems would either be solved or well on the way towards solution. Today, almost all independent and autonomous life that a child has is practically by definition peripheral or even illegal. As Edgar Friedenberg has often pointed out, a child has no legal right to *be* anywhere except in school during school hours, and indeed it is not at all far fetched to say that he has a constant obligation under the law to show, wherever he is and whatever he is doing, that he is there and doing it with the permission or on orders of some grown up. In short, he has no *right* to a life of his own.

[. . .]

I find it very difficult to understand or accept as true or important the distinction that you make between learning and education. You say, "Almost no one would call what usually happens in nature or in the learning laboratory education." I most definitely would. [Later] you say, "The ability to learn is itself the best safeguard against uncertainty; this line of thought leads to a definition of education as planned learning for the sake of learning." Planned by whom, in the first place? And what of the child learning to speak? Do we call this learning planned? If not, do we say that learning to speak is not education? I suppose it is possible to say that no, it is not education, but to leave out of our definition of education such a powerful piece of learning, and a great many other kinds of learning which are very similar to this, seems to me to trivialize education more than I am ready to do.

The distinction you make between education and training is clearer to me, but still questionable. A child learning to speak is in fact learning to perform some specified task. The trouble with your three-way division of experience into education, learning, and training is, for me at least, precisely that I cannot fit learning to speak into any one of them, and if I could I would not know in which one to fit it.

I am troubled by your phrase "casual learning." There is something that troubles me about that word casual. It suggests that we can divide learning experiences into casual ones and not casual ones. How does learning to speak fit into this scheme? There is also a hint that casual learning is somehow less important or useful or worthy than non-casual learning. Perhaps you don't intend this. In any case, it is to me a matter of critical importance, because it seems to me that the reason that children are able to master the extraordinarily complicated task of learning to speak is precisely that they do learn it casually, in the process of living, as it were. Paul Goodman is good on this point, I've said some things about it, George Dennison is even better. I find [Dennison's] definition of education and learning, which he does not try to separate, as a kind of growth of a person into the world and incorporation of the world into the person, to be the most useful, and not only do I elaborate and explain this definition and understanding in my new book, of which I will send you a copy as soon as I can, but most of what I suggest in the body of the book about ways to help learning in schools is directed toward blurring or doing away with the distinction between casual and non-casual learning. To put this differently, Dennison says, and again I think quite rightly, that children learn best in what he calls the "continuum of experience," and it is my deepest criticism of conventional schooling that it breaks up this continuum of experience, divides it up into different kinds or classes of experience. I would say this of your three-part division as well. I do not want children to feel, even without words, that their lives are somehow divided into educational experiences, learning experiences, and training experiences.

Now I have really arrived at the main point of this letter. The distinction that you make between training and education is precisely the one that schools make between what they call "skills" and larger activities, or learning. I think this splitting is a profound and deeply harmful error. I think it is possible to say that this tendency to split things that ought not to be split, that are properly joined together, is a peculiar and destructive characteristic of Western thought. Alan Watts in *The Book* said at one point that Western thinkers love to take some part of human experience that is one whole, cut it into two halves, and then torment themselves by asking which is cause and which is effect. I think this is a profoundly true and important observation. Whitehead, somewhere in *The Aims of Education*, if I remember correctly, said that it was a fatal error to separate the skills of an activity from the activity itself. Thus, as I say a thousand times to teachers, children do not learn to speak by learning "the skills of speech" and then going somewhere and using these skills to speak with. They learn to speak by speaking, that is, by communicating about real things to real people who have an interest in them. Here again is Dennison's "the continuum of experience" and "the continuum of persons." A child wants to do and does what advances him into the world, what enables him to grow out into it, to encompass in his own experience and understanding more of the world outside him, the world of geography and the world of human experience.

You say "the child must learn to walk before he can explore the physical world." This is simply not true. The child does a great deal of exploring of the physical world before he can even crawl, let alone walk. Indeed, we have every right to assume that it is an already strongly developed interest in the world around him that provides him with a powerful incentive for learning to walk. He is an explorer before he is a walker. If he were not an explorer he might very well not be a walker. Again, you say that he must learn to read before he can explore the storehouse of human knowledge. Unless you define the storehouse of human knowledge as that which is written down, which is a very narrow definition of it, this is again simply not true.

There are a great many ways of recording and passing on knowledge other than writing them. People knew a lot about the world before men became literate. Literacy is not a prerequisite of human culture. Illiterate men in many parts of the world today, including even our own, can know a great deal about the world around them. Human knowledge is not just contained in books; indeed, I think we could fairly [easily] say that the part of it which is contained in books is only a small part of it. Human knowledge is *exemplified* by the culture around us. Electricity does not just exist in books about electricity; it is what makes the light go on when I press the switch. I do not have to read books about electricity to know something about what it does, and so forth. I belabor this point because I think it is crucial.

Again and again we have this artificial dividing and sequencing of life. You must do this before you can do that. I think in this respect both you and Ivan [Illich], perhaps very traditionally schooled, and well educated in spite of it, are very much prisoners of some of the fundamental assumptions of schooling.

[. . .] As I write it seems to me that this splitting tendency, this dividing of things into training and learning, these skills and activities, is connected somehow with our Calvinist-Protestant notion that life must be divided up into pleasures and pains, that all pleasure must be paid for in pain, and that generally speaking the pain must outweigh the pleasure. This is one of those beliefs of which I think we can say that believing that it is true makes it largely true. I simply don't live my life that way anymore, and hence know that it is not necessary to live it that way. It is a beautiful day outside, the sky is blue, the sun bright, the air clear, the breeze rattling the leaves around. I'm standing here dictating this letter, when I might be walking in the garden or in the streets of Santa Fe, as some people might say "enjoying the weather." I'm writing this letter because I have things to say that I think are important, because I look forward to discussing all of this with you at some length, because I think it has great bearing on our future work, because I hope to develop these ideas later in a book of my own about freedom and the problems we have in thinking about it and dealing with it. Many people would say that I am using my will power to deny myself the pleasure of walking around in the sunshine, and instead compelling myself to do something called "work," so that later on I may get various kinds of benefits from it. But I feel myself connected in space and time, as

I dictate here, with you and Ivan and Dennis[1] in CIDOC, with the other people I've talked to about these things, with the book I will one day write, with whatever consequences may flow from that book when it gets written. In short, I'm not doing something now so that I may do something pleasant later, but I am deeply and fully alive at this moment because I am, as it were, *plugged in* to the whole of my experience, I am much more alive, much more fully experiencing my life, than I was a few hours ago when I first woke up, with quite a lot of hay fever, still feeling a little sleepy, and pondered about whether to get out of bed and do some work or to rest some more.

[. . .]

Cause and effect. Ends and means. The experience is one, the ends and means are one. I like to say to people who are raising this kind of question—I like to illustrate what I am trying to say with some examples that may seem so far fetched as to be ridiculous—but I don't think they are. Suppose you were thirsty. Do you say to yourself that you must go to the trouble, force yourself to open the cupboard, take down a glass, walk over to the sink, extend your hand, turn on the faucet, put some water in the glass, raise the glass to your lips—go through all these time-consuming and arduous steps so you may *then* have the pleasure of feeling the cool water trickling down your throat? No; it is preposterous. You take a drink, which means that you find a glass, fill it up, bring it to your lips, and drink out of it. You don't have to use will power to make yourself get the glass out of the closet door. Do you see? Similarly, a tiny baby, crawling on the floor where he does a lot of exploring, sees a toy or ball or bear across the floor and the thought or feeling invades him that he wants to seize it and play with it. Does there then arise some little conflict inside the baby to the effect that is it worth the effort to crawl across the floor so that he may later grab the toy? No. Babies don't think that way, or even feel that way, which is one of the reasons why they are good learners. To want the toy is to do whatever must be done to get the toy, and he instantly begins to move himself across the floor, probably already feeling some of the excitement and anticipation and pleasure of using whatever it is he wants to use. But we are not as smart as babies, we constantly cut ourselves off from the whole of

1. Dennis Sullivan, who acted as secretary in the conversation between Reimer and Illich.

our own lives. Even my dear friend Abe Maslow,[2] with all his talk about "peak experiences," seem[s] to me to miss the point. It is perhaps true that I have peak experiences in my life but one of the reasons why, in spite of a great deal of worrying about the calamitous stage of our civilization, I am basically a happy man, is that I am *connected* with my various kinds of peak experiences.

[. . .]

Peace,

During this period, Holt's old friend Peggy Hughes—who had encouraged him to make his assorted memos into the book that became *How Children Fail*—was teaching at the Danish Ny Lilleskole (New Little School) described in his *Instead of Education*.

[TO PEGGY HUGHES]

Santa Fe, NM
September 11, 1970

Dear Peggy,

Your nice letter from the campground just arrived. Your description of the children was all too graphic. I've seen a lot of that. I spend a lot of time in public places, and for various reasons I find myself more and more, every time I hear a baby or small child crying really frantically, going over to see what is happening, perhaps as much as for any other reason so that I may understand the kinds of things that make kids cry really hard. A pattern seems to be emerging. I seem to find that when a child is having what is ordinarily called a tantrum, it is because people around him and over him are not simply doing what he doesn't want to do or not letting him do what he does want to do, but treating him as if his wishes and feelings had no importance, or indeed as if he did not exist at all. We saw a graphic example of that just yesterday in a Safeway. As we came in we heard a terrific bellowing, howls and shouts and sobs all mixed together, some little child, as it turned out a girl of about three, shrieking that she didn't want to be in here, she didn't want to be in

2. Abraham Maslow, author of *Toward a Psychology of Being*.

here. Her parents had put her in one of those big shopping baskets, obviously because she had been running around or exploring and they wanted to confine her. We missed the beginning of the crisis. By the time I got there the parents, who were embarrassed by this whole thing, were trying to pass it off by simply acting as if the child did not exist, and this was quite obviously driving her almost crazy with, among other things, fear. I suspect it is true that children get a large part of the so-called proof of their existence from the reaction of other people to them—R. D. Laing says this is true of adults as well—and for a child to be treated as if she didn't exist at all must be really terrifying. Anyway, the screams got louder and louder. I came close to the carriage as if I was moving by and took a long look at the little girl, a long thoughtful look, as if to persuade her that people really could see her. She gave me a rather startled look and for a second or two we stared at each other. A few seconds later, perhaps ashamed, perhaps getting some kind of psychic message from me, the parents took her out of the basket. They then tried to lead her around by the hand but by this time she was really furious and shook that off. In any case, the great storm was over. I can remember a number of times getting into good arguments with little children, including my dear nieces and nephews, and certainly you must re-member many of them too, but at least in an argument a child knows that he is real and is being taken seriously, and this seems to me all important. People really do not know any other way to relate to chil-dren except to indulge them or to shout and yank at them. Indeed, the range of their emotional responses to children [is] not very much greater than their responses to a dog or cat, except that they are more easily irritated at the children.

I'm back in Santa Fe after a very nice trip. This is the first truly fall day we've had here, and it is perhaps of all the seasons here the love-liest. The sky is a mountain blue, of the kind you see around Lake Tahoe, the air cool and dry, a brisk wind, the sun very bright off the leaves of trees, altogether a delicious feeling. I left here just a little over a couple of weeks ago for my camping trip with Bud Talbott. Every year it is the same. The trip, so to speak, catches me in the middle of something I'm doing and enjoying. I was having a lovely time here, playing some tennis with Davey and Alix,[1] and I really didn't want to go. But as always, I enjoyed it. [. . .]

1. Pitcher, his nephew and niece.

1964–1976

From the woods I went to New York City and there read all the galley proofs of *What Do I Do Monday?* It is of course extraordinarily exciting to see one's own book in print. I hadn't looked at it for a while, and once again I have this surprised feeling as I read parts of it that it is really good and did I really write it. There are really lots of things in it that will cause quite a commotion, I think. One of the things that pleases me most is that I am not letting universities off the hook. Everybody is jumping up and down on the poor high schools, and I am making the point that everything that's wrong with education is just as wrong in our institutions of so-called higher learning as anywhere else; indeed most of the ills of education originate there. Dutton is very excited about the book. They tell me that advance book store orders are now about 19,000 copies. Also a small book club has ordered 15,000 copies. [. . .] There is no telling how the book will do, but there is certainly a chance that it may just take off like a big bird. Cross your fingers.

Nice to hear about my books in Denmark. It would be fun, I should say will be fun as I do really want to visit you there, to buy and see them in the window. Even to walk in and say to the man in the store that I wrote them. Did I ever tell you about finding a paperback copy of *How Children Fail* in a very small out-of-the-way London bookstore, going in, and saying to the proprietor, how is that book doing, and when he said that it was doing fairly well, saying that I was glad because I had written it. He was quite surprised. Every so often I see somebody with one of the books on an airplane, and if they look congenial and sympathetic, I do the same thing.

[. . .]

Peace,

Holt wrote frequently to Kevin White, mayor of
Boston from 1968 to 1984, about many of the
city's issues. The reference in the following letter
is to White's bid for lieutenant governor, a race
he ultimately lost.

[TO KEVIN WHITE]

September 25, 1970

Dear Mayor White,

Because I have been in the West all summer and only just returned
in time to vote in the primary, I have only just this minute seen the
broadsheet on education that was distributed in your campaign.

I hope you will allow me the liberty of saying that, like most people
in our country, I think you have equated education with schooling,
and given your own very considerable weight to the idea that the
amount of a person's education can be judged by the number of
years he has spent in school and the kinds of credentials he has
picked up there. I think this is a most serious and dangerous error.
When we define education as formal schooling, and encourage children and their parents all over the country to get into the competitive consumption of schooling, to see who can keep their children in
schools the longest, we bring about a situation in which there is necessarily not enough to go around. The more people who have a
given educational credential, the less value that credential has in
guaranteeing them access to employment and status. When everyone in this country has a high school diploma, the diploma will be
worthless, and the cry will be that you have to go to college to get a
good job. When everyone goes to college the Bachelor's Degree will
in the same way become worthless, and everybody will be told that
they have to go to graduate school to get a good job. It is a never-
ending rat race, and we have got to begin to think of ways to get out
of it.

In this connection, I am also taking the liberty of sending along
two articles by Ivan Illich, who, more than anyone I know, has
thought deeply and profoundly on the subject. I do hope that you,
or someone close to you, will take the time to read and consider carefully what he has to say, and its possible implications for public

policy. I myself am more than ready and willing to discuss these matters further with you or people close to you if you should wish to do so.

Meanwhile, congratulations again for a fine victory.

Best,

Holt began corresponding with Judson Jerome after reading his piece, "The System Really Isn't Working," in *Life* magazine in 1968. Jerome was a poet and professor who ultimately left academia for life on a rural commune, where he became one of the first people Holt knew whose children were learning outside of school. His critique of higher education, *Culture out of Anarchy,* was published in 1971.

[TO JUDSON JEROME]

October 7, 1970

Dear Jud,

Nice to get your letter of 9/9. I'm dictating this in a dining room at O'Hare Airport, looking at the planes. I know what you mean about being addicted to our technology. There are parts of it that seem to me to heighten the quality of human life. I'm an avid fan of classical music and get an enormous pleasure out of hearing recordings on high quality equipment, and indeed think a good deal about how to make this pleasure available to many more people. This seems to me to be a kind of low-pollution way of brightening up people's lives. And in the same way I get a great pleasure out of a well-designed metropolitan transportation system or riding on European rail-roads, and if we ever manage to get in this country a version of the air-support train that the French have developed, you can bet I will be riding it. The problem is that so much of our technology does not fulfill any important human need[s] or wants at all, but is enormously inefficient.

It is not so much a question of going back to the "simple life" as of finding a life which is in some respects simpler. The average person is really very badly served by his automobile and a great many other of his so-called conveniences. I think of something that happened to me just the other day. I was speaking at a conference in a big kind of conference motel. We had our main meeting in a large room. The room was very crowded, it was hot outside, and as happens under these circumstances, the air conditioning system got overloaded and simply stopped working altogether. But then where were we? There was no other effective way of ventilating the room. It had been designed to depend on air conditioning and when we lost that, we were very much worse off than we might have been in some old-fashioned hotel with lots of cross-ventilation, high ceilings, fans and the like. All of which is to say that when a complicated piece of technology stops doing its job well, it leaves us all worse off than before we had it. In any case, I think it is essential that we all recognize that the price of human survival is that we drastically reconsider our notion of human needs and wants, and find vastly more efficient ways of satisfying them. I find myself thinking of the old song, "The Best Things in Life Are Free." This might very well be rephrased, as the young tend to, "The Free Things in Life Are Best." Once we understand that we mean that, then we can perhaps talk about plenty in the world, though given what we know of population and poverty, that may be a little premature.

[...]
Peace,

[TO PETER MARIN]

November 19, 1970

Dear Peter,

[...] It was good to see you in Cambridge and I very much enjoyed our talk. Many parts of it echo in my mind, one part in particular, in which you were talking about Panthers putting their lives on the line. I'm trying and failing to recreate this scene in my memory, but my sense of things was that you felt or at least a great many young people felt that nobody can be taken seriously these days who is not constantly ready to risk his life and indeed [is] risking it. My initial gut reaction to this was rather negative and since then I have been thinking about it further, trying to understand it, which I now think I do.

I'm very suspicious and distrustful of these people who are constantly laying their lives on the line. It seems to me that they are as much as many others preachers of a very bad doctrine, that life is cheap, all life including their own. The man who does not hesitate to throw his own life away will similarly not hesitate to throw my life away if I seem to be standing in his way. The more he is willing to throw his life away for a trifle the smaller the trifle for which he will take mine. I don't think this is good humanity and I don't think it's good revolution. The really good maker of change, guerilla warrior, revolutionary may be ready to sell his life, but he is going to exact a very hard bargain.

To put this another way, I think that Eldridge Cleaver[1] and most of his followers have become much more part of the problem than they have [become] part of the solution. I see, as they do, an extraordinarily sick and twisted society—a world-wide one, which they are not smart enough to realize—headed hell-bent for different kinds of destruction, but I don't think it is going to be saved or changed by them, even if they knew what needed to be done, which I don't think they do.

In any case, as I've said, I distrust the man who is reckless with his own life, because I think he will be reckless with everyone else's. Also, he is likely simply to be a bad soldier, like the soldier on a battlefield who is constantly sticking his head up out of the trench or foxhole. He is going to get himself picked off for no good reason. He is going to sell his life cheaply instead of dearly.

I'm just back in Boston after about a month and a half of almost constant speaking in which I've probably been at over 100 meetings. I have a stack of letters quite literally 6 or 8 inches high to read and pick my way through. If there is something there from you about your West Coast project, which I'm very much interested in, forgive me if I don't answer it in this letter. I'll get to it as soon as I can. When you come to roost let me know your address, and keep in touch.

Peace,

1. Eldridge Cleaver was a black activist and author of *Soul on Ice*.

Len Solo, of the Teacher Drop-Out Center Holt
mentioned in his letter to the Boston University
students, wrote to ask Holt what he would do
if he were put in charge of an undergraduate
teacher preparation program and given a great
deal of freedom.

[TO LEN SOLO]

November 30, 1970

Dear Len,

Thanks very much for your note. Delighted to hear about your
opportunity. I am often asked about the preparation of teachers. I
just answer by saying, first, that I think people who are training to be
teachers or think they might want to train should have a great many
opportunities to come into contact with children of a great many different ages in many different circumstances, and particularly ones in
which they are not bearers of authority, at least not in the conventional school situation. The idea is that unless they see children in
their native habitat, or involved in a much wider range of activities,
they cannot really know much about what children are like.

I also say that it doesn't make much sense to have young people do
a lot of reading or even talking about the psychology or techniques
of the classroom unless they have had a chance to be in some classrooms and had worked with children there. What we do is a little like
having people study books of the theory of swimming and skating,
and then say that when they know everything about the theory we
will take them to a pool or rink. Unless these teachers-to-be come to
their reading with some experience, apprentice teaching, classroom
aid work, etc. before they get very far into academic work, it cannot
be of much use to them.

I also say that teachers are not going to be able to give children
opportunities to do self-motivated, self-directed learning unless they
have had such opportunities themselves. Therefore it seems to me
very important that in their training teachers should have the opportunity to make a very wide range of choices about how they are going
to explore the large field of education—a field much too large for
them to have done more than a little exploring even by the time they
get out of college. In the course I taught at the Harvard Graduate

School of Education I presented my students with a heap of resources, a reading list, many visiting lecturers or discussion leaders to the class, films, plus a number of more or less open schools in the Boston environment that they could visit and work with. I then said that they could use these resources in whatever way they liked. I think some openness of choice is exceedingly important.

Once, talking to a group of people at Northeastern University who had nearly completed their training, I asked them this question: "How many of you have a fairly clear picture, and I leave it up to you to decide how clear is fairly clear, of the way you would teach, of the way you would run your classroom, of the way you would relate to students and their learning if you were free to do it in any way you liked?" In a class of about 60 students, three rather timidly and waveringly raised their hands. The others had simply never thought about this. I later asked how many of them had seen very much of a range of classrooms, to get some idea of the possibilities of teaching relationships [and] styles, and again, hardly any of them had seen any classrooms at all except the one in which they had done their student teaching. This seems to me to be very unwise, and I think we should do everything we can to make it possible for students, even if they have to leave the campus to do so, to visit the widest possible variety of schools and classroom situations.

This more or less sums up my present thinking on these things. I'll be glad to talk about some of these at greater length, but this may give you something to chew on. Once again, I am really delighted to hear about your opportunity. Can you tell me a little more about this college; it sounds interesting.

Peace,

[John]

Pam Dant, who had been Holt's student at Berkeley, was now teaching in Spanish-speaking northern New Mexico.

[TO PAM DANT]

December 5, 1970

Dear Pam,

Just turned up in one of my piles of letters the letter you wrote on Columbus Day, and that I don't think I've read before. Sorry to have mislaid it.

Come to think of it, I guess this is the letter you thought might have annoyed me, and it doesn't or isn't. I often fall into a kind of Lear[y]-ish frame of mind.[1] It seems to me that a very large number of fellow citizens, I don't quite know how many but it must be close to a majority and perhaps much more than that, have thoroughly embraced Fascism in their hearts. Several thoughts come into mind. If we state the problem as [Timothy Leary] does, it becomes automatically and hopelessly insoluble. In other words, if we draw the lines of We and They the way he has drawn them, there turns out to be about 2% on Our side and all the rest on Their side. That is not a very smart way of defining the problem. Also I think it is important to understand that virtually all people, of whatever income level, are oppressed, dehumanized, by what is wrong with contemporary world society—it is a world problem, not an American problem, there are no other societies that are very different from ours in this regard, though they may not show the badness quite as blatantly. Nixon is a perfect victim of America, the perfect homo americanus 1970. I fear him but I feel some kind of compassion for him and without this feeling I simply don't think we can get anywhere. The great pacifist A. J. Muste once said, and we have to remember he was a Jew, "If I can't love Hitler, I can't love anyone." He said this when things like this were not easy to say. What he meant was that for all of Hitler's crimes and wickedness, he was not ready to cast him into some outer darkness, put him outside the pale, treat him as some

1. Timothy Leary was a leader in the counterculture movement and author of *The Psychedelic Experience*.

kind of vermin. He still had to be seen and opposed as a human being. This is the point Leary missed, and it is all-important.

At one point, you say "every time you do anything for the US Government you're killing kids, and mothers, orphans, and boys . . . etc." We have to be careful here. One's responsibility does not outrun one's power. It is a very common piece of angry revolutionary rhetoric to say that every time I put a letter in the mailbox, I am in effect dropping napalm on some kid in Vietnam, but this is quite simply and flatly not true. As there are limits on my power, there are limits on my responsibility. Every single American is not wholly responsible for everything done by every other American.

I see in passing that you scratched out the crest on your family letterhead. No need to do this—I'm not holding it against you.

I remember when the strike was on at Berkeley that there were certain people saying things to the effect that if I did not violently oppose Governor Reagan that meant I was on his side violently attacking the students. In short, you have no choice but to be a killer, and the only question is who do you want to kill for. I absolutely reject this fallacious and profoundly wicked argument, which has always been a favorite of dictators under pressure of any kind—and by the way, if Leary and his pals should ever get control of the US Government, I would head off for Patagonia or someplace about that distance.

[. . .]

Have to stop. Off on another lecture trip tomorrow. Thought I was really out of the [lecture circuit] but the calendar is more full even in December than even I had expected. Hope you're not freezing. Like the deal with the kindling wood. Don't chop a foot.

Peace,
John

[TO PAM DANT]

December 22, 1970

Dear Pam,

Taped a David Frost show the other night and they say they will air it December 30. Didn't get as much time as Cavett gave me, but got in a few good licks.

I am just looking into *Rasberry Exercises*.[1] Did I tell you my niece's baby—this is the niece who is married to Wheeler of Wheeler's ranch in San Francisco, an operation which seems to be turning into a bit of a bummer due to hepatitis widely contracted from people ignoring history's lessons about sewage—now I've lost the beginning of the sentence, but at any rate my niece's daughter is named Raspberry, and is a very cute baby so everyone says. I suppose *Exercises* has been written up in *New Schools Exchange,* but I've been on the run so much I've missed a lot of issues.

Don't knock your writing. It is extra good. Delighted if they used any of your material.

I *love* your stories about Santo Domingo. Made me think "Pam Dam" is perfect, better even than the children know. And what is nice about the love and loyalty of children has nothing to do with sentimental notions about them, but only [that] it is so freely and unreservedly given. Actually we are all looking for people who can be our teachers forever. Here is a part of everyone's proper life work.

Some Mexican Americans—by the way, I don't know about the Albuquerque area, but for some reason around Santa Fe, the word Chicano is bad news and they don't even like Mexican, but prefer to be called Spanish—but anyway, some very good Mexican American people in LA made a proposal to the schools there, which sums up so well the kinds of things that we are talking about that I am sending you a copy. Maybe something like this can begin to do the rounds in Albuquerque.

Listen, it's a pleasure to answer your letters. Feels like a conversation. I'm off this evening to New Haven, to do a thing there. Will spend the night with Bill Coffin, Yale Chaplain and a great guy. One of the nice things about running all over the place—and I went as far north as Edmonton, Alberta, look it up on the map—is that I keep meeting friends and allies everywhere. In a society as bad as ours, and it seems to be getting worse, this is very encouraging.

Don't freeze and have a nice Christmas. I think we're getting some snow here, I wish they'd get some in Santa Fe, for the ski area.

Peace and love,

John

1. The full title was *Rasberry Exercises: How to Start a School and Make a Book*, by Salli Rasberry and Robert Greenway.

A high school student who had been given the
assignment of observing a class of fifth graders
wrote to ask for advice about what to look for.

[TO RON ZAROWITZ]

December 22, 1970

Dear Ron Zarowitz,

[. . .] I don't know exactly what to say about watching those fifth
graders. On many occasions I have said that one of the reasons I was
able to see what I did see in my classes was that I didn't go in with
some preconceived notion about what I was looking for. What is important is that you watch the children. But don't make up your mind
about what you think you are going to see. Be open to whatever
occurs.

[. . .] One of the things I found myself doing when I was observing 5th graders was to observe a certain child or group of children
over an extended period of time and try to get some sense of where
their attention was and how they perceived the class situation. Also
you have to remember that your own presence in the classroom
somewhat changes it, and may also somewhat change the teacher's
way of working. Perhaps as the children get to know you better, you
can talk with them about all kinds of things. Remember to them you
look just about as grown up as the teacher. Another big person.

I don't know if this is going to be much help, but feel free to write
and ask further questions. Good luck and thanks for writing.

Peace,

California State Superintendent of Public Instruction Max Rafferty, who wrote one of the
"against" pieces in the book *Summerhill: For and
Against,* was openly critical of what Holt and Neill
were advocating.

[TO MAX RAFFERTY]

December 28, 1970

Dear Max,

Hope you had a smooth trip home.

I thought of you the other day when I was in Edmonton, Alberta. The temperature was about 10 degrees below zero and as I walked on the snow, it gave out a very brittle, high-pitched squeak, which I remembered from old days in Colorado. I found myself wondering why snow begins to do this around zero degrees, what there is about snow crystals that makes them act that way. It occurred to me to wonder whether anyone else had wondered about this, and if so, who, and where he might be found. I realized that he would probably be found among the ranks of physicists and here I saw once again the thought I want to share with you, which is that what we call physics, chemistry, biology, and the like, are not separate hunks of something called the Body of Knowledge, but different ways in which living men look at the wholeness of the world and the human experience around them. There is no physics out there in front of us, only snow, but the physicist asks himself a certain kind of question about it, or looks at it in a certain way, while someone else might think about it quite differently. Chemists might examine snow to see whether there was any dissolved matter in it. A biologist might look at it to see whether any microscopic life forms were attached to it, and so on. Perhaps the trouble with the traditional notion of the Body of Knowledge is that it makes knowledge dead where it should be alive, and that it divides it up into parts where it should be a whole. This is part of what I am trying to say. The other thing I would like to say is that there is nothing in books but print. There is no knowledge in books; the knowledge only comes when I have read the print and, *in my mind,* changed or added to my view of how things are. We like to say that we get knowledge from books; it would be more accurate to say we *make* knowledge out of books.

Have a good holiday.

Best,

[TO PAM DANT]

February 23, 1971

Dear Pam,

Just read your wonderful letter. Glad you survived the cold. I really think you are getting something a bit extra along that line; I've known people who have lived for years in Santa Fe, and they don't usually have that severe winters. Maybe Bernalillo is a little different, being more out in the open, sort of. Anyway, I really am sure that 24 degrees below is quite exceptional for that part of the world and hope you don't get more of it. Winter is usually quite a lovely season there—spring, oddly enough, isn't so hot, lots of wind and gusts blowing around. Anyway, glad you are making it. It is nice to know that one can.

Busy these days working on another book. By the way, just read the galleys of Jim Herndon's newest book, *How to Survive in Your Native Land.* It is just wonderful. He is a most natural comic writer. I wouldn't try to write funny. I can write clear, but not funny—except occasionally, perhaps by accident. But he can do it all the time. The book is just as good as his first and I can hardly wait for it to come out. Anyway, I think there is a lot of good stuff in what I am working on. It has mostly risen out of questions that people ask me all the time about freedom, discipline, things like that. Not so much a book of nuts and bolts ideas as a book about attitudes and hangups. I was just off at a lecture gig at Wagner College in Staten Island and Allegheny College in Pa. Enjoyed them both—the usual scene, many meetings, lots of nice students, some interested faculty. Talked a lot about deschooling society in Illichian terms. Am going to CIDOC first two weeks of Feb. Thought I might be able to come down to Santa Fe for a two or three day visit in January, see my sister, see my parents who are there too (bugging my sister out of her mind) and pay you a little visit, but it didn't work out. I have not done as much on the book as I would like; the correspondence comes in waves. I promised an article on "Sesame Street" to the *Atlantic,* and lots to do. But I'm really looking forward to CIDOC—it is a mind blowing place, and Illich is one of the really great thinkers of our time. I am absolutely delighted to hear, though I was sorry to miss him, that he was for two straight days on the "Today" show.

The *Times* review of [*What Do I Do*] *Monday* was a slash job, really very poor, personal, sneering, not saying anything about what the book was about.[1] I was disappointed but don't worry about it much. I guess I have gotten to the place where people can get their names in print just taking swipes at me, but as you say, I don't really mind, or at least not much. One guy who sprang into print this way is a teacher from Reed College named Samuel McCracken. Some college asked me if I would come and speak in a kind of public debate with McCracken. I told them I was busy. What I didn't tell them is that I'm damned if I'm going to be the bait to attract audiences so he can talk. If anybody is interested in hearing what he has to say about education let him crank up his own leading. In general, I am going to refuse to get involved in those kinds of public debates.

Also, I am interested in much other stuff. As you know, I am a classical music freak. I have been associated with a small orchestra here in Boston called the Philharmonic, of which I have become a trustee and am now a vice president. I am interested in finding ways to get a whole lot of people to go to concerts who have never been. Also, the conductor of the Indianapolis Symphony[2] is a dear friend of mine and an absolutely wonderful man and musician, and I am concerned how to help him and his organization grow. I expect I'll be more into this in the next couple of years, trying to broaden the audience for classical music and indeed others of the arts. All of this seems to me to fit very closely with what Illich is writing about. The liberation of learning—actually that's my phrase—from the confines of schools. One of the reasons I think Paul Goodman has gotten so bitter is that, so to speak, he has stayed in one place saying the same thing over and over again to the same people, and getting very angry when they didn't respond the way he wanted them to. I certainly

1. The review was written by Leonard B. Stevens in the Nov. 29, 1970, issue of *The New York Times Book Review.*
2. Izler Solomon.

don't plan to keep saying the same thing forever, being naturally more restless.

Peace,
John

[TO JAMES HERNDON]

April 30, 1971

Dear Jim,

Hope this finds you well settled in your new house and enjoying it. Delighted the book is doing so well.[1] The reviews have been terrific. I hope S[imon] and S[chuster] are keeping it on the bookstore shelves—that's what makes the difference. I also hope it sells a million copies, at least.

Came across a letter of yours that I guess I haven't answered. You say not much point in talking about doing without schools because we *got* schools. Yes, but we also *got,* among other things, cancer, dope addiction, the Viet Nam war, J. Edgar Hoover, pollution, and god knows what else. Universal Compulsory Schooling is a comparatively recent invention. It doesn't work, for reasons you yourself have pointed out, among many others, and it cannot be made to work. We'd better start thinking about what might work. I'm not indifferent to the plight of people trapped in schooling, teachers and students, and therefore expect to spend a considerable amount of time talking and writing about how to make these places somewhat less bad. But I can no longer accept the idea that you would have a good educational system if we could just make enough changes in enough schools. Fundamentally we have to go in another direction.

Love to all the family,
John

1. *How to Survive in Your Native Land.*

Holt wrote to Ronald Dworkin, professor of law,
after reading his "Taking Rights Seriously" in
The New York Review of Books in 1970, and they
continued to correspond.

[TO RONALD DWORKIN]

July 14, 1971

Dear Mr. Dworkin,

Thanks so much for your letter. As it happens, I've just returned
from England and was in Oxford for a day or so visiting my very
dear friend Strobe Talbott, who is completing his Rhodes Scholarship there. You may possibly know him as the translator and editor
of *Khrushchev Remembers*. A most interesting and delightful young
man, and one of my dearest friends.

I would have liked very much to have had the opportunity to talk
with you on this trip, but my time got gobbled up by school people.
Strobe seemed to feel that you were going to be at Oxford for quite
a number of years. Is this the case, or do you plan to be back at Yale
in the fall?

I don't know whether you are familiar with the writings of Ivan
Illich, whose first book, *Celebration of Awareness*, has just come out in
England, and whose second, *Deschooling Society*, will soon come out
there. The point he is making, and I and others with him, is that
what is really wrong with education and our society is that the societies themselves are not educative. Indeed, anti-educative—an obscure collection of mysteries and monopolies. Everything takes place
behind closed doors, so to speak. We speak of a de-institutionalized
society in which people will be able to move much more directly to
meet their own needs, instead of always having to go through the
medium of a Black Box called an institution, be it corporation, government, or profession.

I [have] felt very disturbed for some time by the fact that for most
people the law seems to be a mystery, the private property of lawyers
and judges, and I feel very strongly that when this happens the
country becomes lawless. If law cannot be understood, if it is not
accessible and reasonable, people will feel very little compunction to
obey it, and what is perhaps worse, will not understand the rights
and privileges they have under it. So when I think about some kind

of hypothetical good society for men to live in, one of the things I ask is how we can de-mystify the law.

One friend of mine suggests that a very good case can be made for a legal system which is not based on precedent, since this is what piles up those whole wall fulls of law books in lawyers' offices. The idea seemed startling to me at first, but I can see something to be said for it. One might say that basing law on precedent kept a certain continuity [in] human affairs, but it seems to me to put the dead hand of the past fairly heavily on our shoulders.

In other contexts I am beginning to have more and more reservations about the whole notion of adversary law. I think there are times when an adversary situation may be helpful, but I don't think an adversary situation is the best way to determine in a given situation what happened. One might say that in a court we are concerned first with truth, the facts, what happened; then with law, what the law says ought to happen; then justice, what ought to be done. I suspect in many cases the adversary system does not help us answer these kinds of questions. In any case it certainly creates a situation in which the law belongs to and serves those who can afford to pay for the biggest legal guns. I've not lost the astonishment, horror, and dismay I felt when the Milwaukee Fourteen[1] wrote me to say that they had to have $70,000 in order to pay to defend themselves against charges brought against them by the government. Why should a man accused of a crime by the U.S. Government have to pay to defend himself?

Such questions are [perhaps] a very long way from the things you are most concerned about or interested in, and if so, feel perfectly free to let them drop to the ground with a thud. But if they strike some spark of interest, I would be very glad, at your convenience, to hear some of your thoughts about them.

Most lawyers or people in the law would, I think, say with some surprise and scorn, "What business do you, without any legal training, have concerning yourself with the law?" Well, I stick my nose into everybody's business, regardless of training; but it is just exactly this sort of attitude, which we encounter in almost all fields, that I want to combat.

Have a pleasant time in Oxford—certainly a pleasant place.
Sincerely,

---

1. The Milwaukee Fourteen were religious activists who burned and destroyed draft files. Holt wrote to their defense committee in 1968 asking for an explanation of

[TO PAM DANT]

September 30, 1971

Dear Pam,

I'm so absent-minded these days I can hardly believe it. Either that, or just plain feeble-minded. I thought when you told me the name of the town where your land is that I would surely remember it as far as Santa Fe, but as it happened it had slipped right out of my mind even before I got to the front gate. So do let me have your next address. Meanwhile I will have the *Mother Earth News*[1] sent to the Bernalillo address.

Off on a lecture tour tomorrow. I will be talking to a number of groups of teachers on this trip and don't exactly know what to talk to them about. In one way, I agree with what you say about making schools better, and in any case I am always in favor of making things better, not believing in the notion that the way to make things better is to make them worse. But on the other hand, I think that any small-scale changes and reforms that we make in schools are perilous and likely to be short-lived as long as the fundamental mission of the schools is inhumane, as I think it is. That is, as long as schools are primarily in the jail business, the indoctrination business, the business of separating children into winners and losers, there is going to be a very real limit to what can be done to make them really helpful places. We are in trouble in schools because we are working at fundamentally cross purposes, and until we get our real priorities and purposes straightened out, I think our progress is going to be limited.

Anyway, I'm getting to the point where I can no longer think of education as something that primarily concerns children—why should it, after all?—or that takes place primarily in learning institutions. I'm concerned about the total educational quality of a society, for all the people in it. I don't think we can have good education for children in a society where life in general is stupid and stupefying. And I very strongly suspect that, even in the case of children, the society as a whole educates far more than does any particular school.

---

the enormous legal fees, and he received a reply from the national coordinator of the defense committee.

1. *The Mother Earth News* is a magazine about self-reliant, rural life.

In any case, regardless of what people like me say, I think schools are in serious trouble. On the one hand, they are being rejected in larger and larger numbers by the students themselves. On the other hand, they are beginning to be questioned by more and more of the adult members of the population. We have here an 80 plus billion dollar a year industry which is not really producing anything that anybody wants—neither courageous, confident, life-loving human beings, [nor] even, on the other hand, docile and skillful workers. Nothing in the future is certain, but one thing seems to me as certain as any, and that is that 25 or even 10 years from now schools will not be anywhere near as prominent in American life as they are now.

Well, I don't mean to preach a long sermon. I do hope by now you are settled on your land and hard at work on those adobes, and that the winter holds off long enough for you to get the walls of your house up, or at least some of it. Anyway, keep us posted here and do let me know your new address.

Peace and love,

John

Benjamin DeMott, professor of English at
Amherst College, had just reviewed Herndon's *How
to Survive in Your Native Land* in *Saturday Review.*

[TO BENJAMIN DeMOTT]

October 13, 1971

Dear Ben,

I enjoyed so much seeing your fine review of Jim Herndon's new book, and I'm so glad that you reviewed it.

I write to say that it is not altogether clear to me from your review that you fully understand how bleak and bitter Jim's position is. When he writes about "how to survive" he is writing about surviving without hope. It is easy to miss this message in the jollity of the book, but it is what the book is about. Jim thinks the schools are not better but worse than they used to be and he expects them to get worse than they are now. He does not think that our cities or indeed our country is going to get to be a better or a more human place to live in. He does not think that we are going to be able to change things. His concern is how we can live without going crazy in a country and world in which everything gets steadily worse.

When I look at the earth as if through the eyes of a visitor from another [solar] system, I tend to agree with him; a galactic observer would be crazy to do other than put heavy odds against humanity, but since I live here and have no other place to go, I am a straw clutcher.

Incidentally, Herb Kohl writes in the latest issue of a West Coast publication called *The Teacher Paper* that there is considerable likelihood that Jim may be fired this year from the school in which he has been teaching. I don't know what moral we can draw from this if it proves to be true.

Peace,
John

P.S.—I have only just started to read Dan Fader's new book and it looks wonderful.[1]

A mother wrote with some concerns about her son's education in a free school, particularly about the "subculture" present among the school's teachers.

[TO JOAN PITKIN]

October 22, 1971

Dear Joan Pitkin,

Forgive my slow reply, but I have been out of the office on lecture tours and various travels and have been spending most of my other time writing my fifth book.

I have come to believe more and more strongly that it is society as a whole, and the general quality of life in it, that educates all of us, including children, much more than school, and therefore that to the extent that the general quality of life in society is poor, there is not very much that we can do in school to make up for that.

One problem with many free schools is that they attract as staff

1. *The Naked Children.*

people who, for the most understandable of reasons, are profoundly alienated from the larger society around them, and use the school as a kind of refuge. This is okay for them, but not very interesting for the kids, who need to be associated with adults who are very much involved with life.

Another way of saying what is on my mind is this. I think children need much more than they have of opportunities to come into contact with adults who are seriously doing their adult thing, not just hanging around entertaining or instructing or being nice to children. They also need much more than they have of opportunities to get away from adults altogether, and live their lives free of older people's anxious attention.

About reading, children learn something much more difficult than reading without instruction—namely, to speak and understand their native language. I do not think they would or could learn it if they were instructed. I think reading instruction is the enemy of reading. However, I do think it is important for kids to be around people who use writing and reading and enjoy using it. That is all the example and encouragement they need, and I suppose such people are often not in free schools.

Thanks again for your letter and for[give] my taking so long to reply. The questions you raise are common in the alternative school movement. I think we have to understand why many young people break away from the culture they grew up in, and here I have to say that I entirely agree with them, that the prevailing culture is exploitive, unjust, inhuman and above all suicidal—to break away from this takes so much strength and energy and leaves so many psychic injuries that there's not much left over to make something different. All of which makes problems.

Hope your Davey is enjoying himself. Try not to worry too much about his learning. Living is learning, and when kids are living fully and energetically and happily they are learning a lot, even if we don't always know what it is. Do, if you feel the inclination, write about your and his further adventures.

Peace,

[TO JUDSON JEROME]

December 6, 1971

Dear Jud,

I finally finished my manuscript for *Freedom and Beyond*. I am excited about it and so is Dutton. We hope to have it out in the spring. The first part of the book takes up in detail questions of authority, freedom, structure, choice and so on—the sorts of things people are worried about when they think of noncoercive education. The last part of the book extends a good bit further the case for the deschooling of society, already very well stated by Ivan Illich and Everett Reimer. By the way, do you know the Reimer book *School Is Dead* (Doubleday)? It's very good.

These are certainly difficult times to live in. Everything I read about the environmental crisis and the slowness of people and their institutions to respond to it, makes me feel that from some kind of objective view we would have to say that prospects of humanity's surviving are fairly slight. It's hard to know how to live with this.

[. . .]

About electric lights, I don't think it's important that Mr. Average Citizen have them, but if he hasn't got them, he ought to have something else, be it only candles. He ought to know that he is not going to have them. The electric light was a kind of metaphor. We are not going to be able to persuade many people to give up one way of life unless we can show them in such a way that it seems real, possible, and desirable, something else. Any so-called revolution that seems to the average man to threaten or destroy his present way of life, leaving nothing in its place at all—no electric light, no kerosene lamp, no candles, no matches, nothing—is going to be fought by him as an unendurable threat.

Perhaps the example of light is not well chosen. Perhaps we should have talked about heat or food. The fact is that one of the first things that any "revolution" has to do when it takes over is keep these kinds of services running—in your words, keep the trains running on time. That is what all the people demand of it and what usually happens then is in its need to keep things running it falls back on running them just the way they were run before because nobody has thought of any other way of running them. How do we get the food from the farms to the markets?

I may be reading something into your words that is not really in your thoughts but I know very well it is in the thoughts of many counterculture people so I will mention it. When you speak of there being fewer people alive, you make me think of a notion which many counterculture people have said already, that the big cities, the big population centers, and all the people living in them, will somehow just disappear or die or go away, leaving the earth to those few pure souls left in communes out in the countryside. Interesting in this connection to note how much the counterculture has inherited an earlier rural American fear and hatred of the city.

In other words there are more than a few counterculture people who think and say that it would be a very good thing if most of those millions living in New York or Chicago or wherever, froze or starved to death in the breakdown of contemporary society—a consummation devoutly to be wished. This is not your thought but it is or was the thought of many young people I know. Perhaps this is changing now, but my very strong sense was that the counterculture people were not proposing or offering a way of life that more than a few people could reach out and take, and that they knew this. There is not enough woodland in America, to say nothing of its distribution, to make it possible for 200 or even 100 million to get their heating needs satisfied by wood-burning stoves. Thus, the transition we are going to have to make [is] from a wasteful use of fossil fuels and atomic energy to an economical use of solar or tidal energy. But this requires inventions and social organizations that on the whole counterculture people don't think or talk much about. Again, a large amount of raw physical *shelter* that now exists in this country or other developed countries, places where human beings live or could live, is concentrated in the cities and their suburbs. But if people are going to live there, they are going to have to depend on various more or less complicated food gathering and transportation systems. Part[s] of these could be much more organic, decentralized, efficient, much less wasteful and luxurious and chemical infested than the arrangement we have now, but arrangements we will need, unless we are going to say that it's just too bad for most of the people who now live in or near big cities, they will just have to go and the world will be better off without them. This is not a loving doctrine or indeed a very sensible one. If there was any such massive breakdown in society and economic arrangements, the surviving people in the cities would flood out into the countryside, in search of whatever it might have to offer in the way of shelter and food and they would take it away from those who had it or compel them in some way to share it with them. Well, you can imagine that scenario; I don't need to get into it much.

I would agree with Illich that the problem is to redefine human needs and the ways in which people can go about meeting these needs in such a way that there is at least a reasonable chance that large numbers of people now existing will in fact be able to meet these needs. No more than he, am I talking about ways in which everybody can have Cadillacs or ride jet planes to Las Vegas or whatever. But this is very far from defining as the good life a kind of life which excludes necessarily and inevitably large numbers of people. Indeed, it seems to me about as heartless, heartless because impossible, to say that the good life requires that everyone live on a subsistent farm as to say that the good life requires that everybody have a Cadillac and their own speed boat.

Or to put this a little differently. There will be a long and difficult and delicate transition period between where we are and where we think we ought to be. I would hope *someday* to see a much more decentralized, communal, self-sufficient kind of life here and everywhere on the planet. But, it seems to me that if we are going to talk seriously about this alternative way of life we have to talk about There in place of Here. We have to talk about ways to get from here to there. You must see *Mother Earth News*, probably knew it long before I did. Rather like it, and one of the reasons why I like it is that in some ways it seems to be thinking about transitions. Also, it puts a heavy stress on competence and skill, things which many of the early commune people rather neglected. We ought to remember that New England was once covered with farms and that those farms were abandoned by men who were on the whole vastly more skillful than almost anyone today, because the land simply would not support that many people. We are going to have to be not just kinder but very much smarter than men have ever been before and that's an interesting challenge.

Though the tone of this letter may be gloomy I am actually enjoying myself enormously. Tremendously pleased to have finished the book and am much involved in various projects of all kinds. Hope to see you again before too long.

Peace and love,

[. . .]

1964–1976

Holt wrote to Jim Dillon after reading his book
Personal Teaching.

[TO JIM DILLON]

December 15, 1971

Dear Jim,

Sorry not to have written sooner about your letter of September 28 and your book. I have been thrashing around this fall trying to finish a book of my own, *Freedom and Beyond,* which Dutton hopes to get out in the spring. It's finally done and I finally got around to reading your book. I am bowled over. I think it is one of the two or three best books about teaching and being a teacher that I know—indeed, I don't think I know anything except Jim Herndon's two books that compare[s] with it and for me this is about the highest praise I can give. Incidentally, do you know his stuff? I think you would like his books, and if you met him you would like him.

I wanted to take a few words here to talk about a point you make on page 144, about changing the system and the structure. I have said, I think in *What Do I Do Monday?*, that if a teacher wants to teach in a certain way, it is important for him to find a school which will let him do it. I hope you understand that there are *very* few schools in the United States which would allow a teacher to do the things you describe in your book. In fact, I think I can safely say that in about 99% of the schools in this country, a teacher, even with tenure, would be instantly and summarily dismissed even for allowing the students to give their own grades or for allowing the students not to come to class—to say nothing of the others. I think you would be making a serious error if you did not understand that this was so.

I agree very much with Jim Herndon in saying to young people that you must not make the possibility of making change in a school the reason for your being there and teaching there. To go into any institution only because you want to change it is to court not only ineffectiveness, but madness. I say all the time to teachers or teachers-to-be, that what they must do is strike a good bargain with circumstance to find a place in which they can do pretty much what they want and not too much what they really don't want. But this is not easy. There are, in fact, not many schools in which it would be possible, in which one would be allowed to teach humanely and lovingly, as you describe so well how to do, and beyond that I see no possibility that there will be many such schools in the foreseeable future. The institution itself is not and was not designed to be humane. To talk about trying to make all our schools humane or to teach humanely in them is like talking about modifying a submarine and making it into an airplane. It can't be done.

You say "no one can legislate that I cannot listen to a student or that I cannot love him." Oh, yes indeed, they can. Many teachers, some of whom I have known personally, have been fired for no less than exactly this. I went once to a high school, as it happens near Chicago, to testify on behalf of a couple of teachers who were being fired for just that reason. My testimony, as I suspected, did them no good—they did not get their jobs back. We must not fool ourselves about this.

To young teachers who say they should go into the worst possible school systems because those are the ones that need humane teaching [most], I offer a metaphor. Like all, it may be misleading, but here it is. I say that a friend of mine is a noted open-heart surgeon. If I were to ask him to do an operation at 5:00 in the subway during rush hour using an old rusty Swiss Army knife he would simply refuse. He would quite rightly say that he requires certain conditions to do his work, and in the absence of those conditions he will not take responsibility for doing it. I think this is the proper view to take. I think it is possible that a repressive school system, if shrewd enough, might be willing to tolerate and use a few teachers like you (or me), to pacify the students and give a certain sheen of legitimacy to a bad system. But by the very support we gave that system, I suspect we would be doing more its work than our own. You mention the example of the concentration camp guards. I think it's well-chosen. Could one be a humane and loving person in such a place? Could you be a humane and loving prison guard in Death Row? I think it is a contradiction in terms.

I push for alternatives to schools, escapes from schools, and to a large degree elimination of schools, certainly of compulsory schooling, because the schools look to me like a burning building. If you see someone in a burning building you know that the longer he stays in there the worse he's going to get hurt, and you want to get him out and provide ways for him to get out. This is what I am trying to do. I think, since there are many schools and teachers, it is legitimate and helpful to talk about making them better or at least less bad. But no imaginable series of school reforms could by themselves influence and make up for the educational deficiencies of modern society or counteract the forces which make it so difficult for young people to grow up healthy and whole. And so to some degree I think we must think about larger structures.

[. . .]

You don't have to have schools in order to have teachers and learning. There will always be a need and a demand for people who can help other people learn. But in my opinion for the most part schools get in the way of teachers and teaching, prevent teaching, and therefore this obstruction should be cleared out of the way as fast as we can. But a lot of this is in my new book so I won't try and rewrite it here.

Where are you now? What's happening to you? How is the book doing? Can I help it in any way? I am going to add it to my own list of recommended readings, and will mention it a little in the new book. As I say, it really is wonderful. Thank you very much for writing it and do write some more stuff. Good luck to you.

Peace and love,

John

Holt wrote to Gloria Steinem just after the first
issue of *Ms.* magazine was published.

[TO GLORIA STEINEM]

January 13, 1972

Dear Ms. Gloria Steinem,

I enjoyed the first issue of *Ms.* magazine and look forward to further issues.

A number of people have written about the need of a pronoun to take the place of he/she. Some have suggested "ta." I find it not very satisfactory because it looks and sounds too different. It occurs to me that "se" might be better. I can feel myself slipping more easily into writing it and more particularly saying it. For an objective I can imagine combining "him" and "her" into "herm," though it might trouble some people that this sounds like the man's name, Herm. I am not quite sure what to do about the possessive, "his/hers"; it could easily be combined in writing to make "hirs" but this would sound exactly like "hers." Perhaps someone else can work this out, but I do want to make a strong plug for "se."

I think the "Women's Liberation Movement" is of enormous importance and I hope it grows and succeeds. In this spirit may I say that I don't think it will have much chance of doing either unless it can, as it has not so far done, speak effectively to a large group of women, of whom my own sister is one. She is and would most unashamedly admit to being "a housewife." Comparing the work she does with the work most men do and that many women in the movement seem to be eager to do, she has said to me many times that her work is more interesting, more varied, more purposeful and that she has vastly more control over when and how she does it. If someone were to tell her—I'm not saying that the Movement is—that she had to give up this work in favor of some kind of office job (and I add parenthetically that she had a number of New York jobs before she married), she would probably pick up a gun.

I suspect that among women she may represent a minority and perhaps a small one; still it is a minority that a great many women would like to think of themselves as joining. So at some point you will have to be able to talk to her.

Once again, best wishes to your magazine.

Peace,

P.S. I'm dictating this on a jet. The stewardess has just made an announcement saying, "Your pilot is Captain Stone and serving you in the cabin will be Linda and Candy." How come last name only for the captain and first name only for the stewardesses? Not an original observation, I'm sure.

Holt corresponded a few times with the linguist and social critic Noam Chomsky.

[TO NOAM CHOMSKY]

April 4, 1972

Dear Noam,

A thought is beginning to sprout in my mind, and I want to share it with you.

In the past few months I have reached a couple of decisions. I've decided to get off the sawdust trail, the nation-wide college lecture circuit, for at least a year or more. And I have decided to stop writing about schools, school reform and so forth. My newest book, *Freedom and Beyond* (a title I thought of before I heard Skinner's),[1] starts out talking about children and learning but moves in to a discussion of politics and economics, and from now on that is what I expect to do all my writing about.

I used to think that working for change in schools was an effective way, perhaps the most effective way, to work for changes in society. I no longer believe it—it seems to me an extraordinary roundabout way, like one of those old Rube Goldberg inventions.

The other part of my thought is this. I begin to suspect that radicals must get themselves much more strongly involved in politics— even to the extent of running for office. There seem to me a couple of reasons for this. The first is that outside of a political campaign there is hardly any way in which we can reach the large numbers of Americans whose minds we most need to influence or change. These people do not come to our meetings, and do not read the books and articles we write. I thought for a while it might be possible to reach them on television, but I am coming to agree more and more with Ivan Illich who says that the medium itself trivializes everything that is said upon it.

I am coming to feel that for a certain class of people in this country, hearing more or less big-name figures talk about controversial issues is a kind of entertainment—not really very different in seriousness or spirit from the entertainment that other people get going to pro football games or the Roller Derby.

When we talk about the kinds of things we are interested in, care about, in the context of politics, two things happen. One is that we have a legitimate reason for talking to people that we could not otherwise reach. If I stop a stranger on the street, or go ring his doorbell and say that I want to talk to him about some kind of political issue, he is as likely as not to offer me a punch in the nose. If I say that I am running for office, or working on behalf of somebody who is, this very much increases my chances of being able to talk to him.

Perhaps more important, it increases the seriousness of the conversation. Certainly committing civil disobedience, nonviolent or otherwise, is a way of putting oneself on the line for one's beliefs, of

1. Skinner's title was *Beyond Freedom and Dignity*.

putting one's money where one's mouth is. But I think we must realize that it is a way which many or most Americans see as profoundly
illegitimate, and which may have exactly [opposite] effects on them
from what we had hoped. But somebody running for office must be
presumed to be serious. He is putting a lot of his time and effort into
it, and if he takes a licking, he is going to take it right out there where
everybody is going to see it.

I think electoral campaigns show us more clearly than anything
else can what is in fact the strength of an idea. Every time some ex-
treme right-wing character runs for office and gets elected, it increases the legitimacy of his kind of thinking. But this can work just
as well in the opposite direction. Certainly the strength of the Mc-
Govern campaign to date has pulled many of the other Democratic
candidates more to the left, where in the absence of such a campaign
they might have been expected to move to the right in an effort to
soak up Wallace votes.

What I am saying is that radicals have perhaps not sufficiently considered the possibility of the political process as an educational device. The candidacy of Shirley Chisholm is for this reason extremely
important. A radical running for any office tends to pull a more
moderate and conventional candidate in this direction—at least if he
has some worthwhile issues and runs an intelligent and vigorous
campaign. The strength of his support shows the moderate candidate how much support there is for his ideas. And the moderate
candidate has to move over in his direction in an effort to catch some
of his votes. Another way of saying all this is to say that it is not necessary to win an election in order to have a profound influence on
the election.

I don't write this to persuade you to do anything, but simply to
plant the germ of an idea. I'm not sure where my own thinking on
these matters may lead me. God knows, I have never been attracted
in any way to politics, but the idea of politics as serious education,
and indeed the only kind of serious education, is beginning to work
on me. One thing standing in the way is a feeling, which may change
in time, that a person ought not to run for office unless he really
wants to win. In short, I think if a candidate tries to use the electoral
process only as a device for pushing ideas he will not push them very
effectively. It is only as he is seen as someone who really wants to win
and means to win that his ideas will be taken seriously. Sometimes
when I play Walter Mitty games I can imagine that I might be

persuaded to run for some office if I can only be sure that I would lose—but I don't think this is the spirit in which it has to be done.

One reason why I am *determined* to get off the lecture circuit is so that I will have some time to see and talk to the interesting people in my own backyard, and you are certainly one of them. I have gotten myself pretty well tied up through the middle of May, but after that things begin to open up a little, so I'll probably be in touch soon.

Interesting article in *Esquire* on *The New York Review.*

Peace,

John

[TO IVAN ILLICH]

April 19, 1972

Dear Ivan,

Back home again after another lovely stay in Cuernavaca. I can hardly say how much it meant to me.

One result of my visit, and of my conversations with you, is that I too have reached a firm decision to get off the lecture trail for at least the next year or two—though I might make an exception to this in order to speak on behalf of the candidacy of George McGovern. But like you I am distressed by my ever stronger feeling that the people with whom or to whom or at whom I talk have put a kind of label on me that I do not want to carry; that they want to talk about things, or hear me talk about things, which are no longer of primary interest to me; that for the most part they have not taken or will not take the trouble to acquaint themselves fully with what I have already said in print; and beyond all this that they are using me as some kind of entertainment figure or hero-symbol or I don't exactly know what. It does seem to me that for certain people to be titillated with new ideas by "name" speakers is a new kind of entertainment, in many ways less serious and honorable than what, let us say, a comedian or singer does, who does not pretend to be doing anything but entertaining.

When I was right in the middle of all that lecturing and enjoying it very much—indeed I still do enjoy it—I used to say to myself and other people that reading someone's books was not the same thing as hearing the living person. But now I wonder about this. If the kinds of changes that you and I and others are talking about are ever to come about, these ideas must become familiar to a great many millions of people—more than we could see or speak to, even in large meetings, if we were to spend a lifetime doing nothing else.

What astonished me most about a lot of the reaction I sense to your announcement that you were not going to speak any longer at the Wednesday morning Ciclos[1] was the feeling on the part of many people, which they often stated quite explicitly, that you had no "right" to do this. This proves more clearly than anything else could, if any proof was needed, that your decision was and is a wise one.

There's something very wrong with the whole idea of a celebrity, though I'm not sure what it is. It is, I suppose, a kind of consumption, [being] a packaged commodity, among other [things]. It suddenly occurs to me as I write that intellectuals, the kind of people who like to come to hear people like you or me lecture, are very scornful of the kind of people who read movie or TV fan magazines. It is easy to see that such people are living their lives vicariously, are pretending to themselves that they really do know and take part in the lives of this or that popular entertainer. But there is probably not very much difference between that kind of vicarious living and what those people who come to hear you or me or someone speak for an hour or two at a meeting [think when they] go away thinking to themselves that they "know" who we are and what we think.

I have not sworn some mighty oath never to get into this business again. For quite a while my lectures were very useful to me. They did for me what your Ciclos did for a long time at CIDOC. They gave me a chance to [bounce?] my ideas off many people and get reactions from them, find weak spots and so on. They generated much of the writing. But like you I am now at a point at which I am getting nothing of that kind from the meetings. What I want to do is get enough new material written so that people will stop type-casting me as somebody who is interested in changing primarily what goes on in classrooms.

Change of subject. I want to make a number of comments about *Institutional Inversion*,[2] which I find extraordinarily interesting and thought-provoking—and for which I hope you will find another title, at least if you plan to get it commercially published, which I hope you will.

1. El Ciclos was the daily free lecture at CIDOC.
2. Probably an early draft of the essay published as "Political Inversion" in the book *Imprisoned in the Global Classroom* by Ivan Illich and Etienne Verne.

Indeed, I have to note that, though I can't think of a better substitute, the word "deschooling" seems to be unfortunate, in that it creates more confusion than understanding. I am distressed and discouraged to note how little even those people who spend many weeks or months at CIDOC understand what you are saying and how little their own lives or ways of thinking are touched by it. They go to Ciclos and lectures and discuss all of these things. Then, in the Cucaracha, they sit around discussing their various colleges and universities. It is as if these ideas did not have and could not possibly have any effect on their own way of living.

But then, in all fairness, the same remark might be made of me. As it happens, I am dictating this into a tape recorder, which I suspect wouldn't be a part of any reduced technology which you envisage, as I ride along in a jet, which I'm sure would not be. And yet I think I can fairly say that my own life has already been considerably changed, and will be more changed, by my contact with you.

One way of introducing some of the things I want to say about *Institutional Inversion* is to say that, in working for the kind of changes we want, for a convivial society and a nonsuicidal technology, you and I may have slightly different functions. You may be somewhat more of a prophet and I somewhat more a tactician. I've often said to people that the process of making important social change seems to me to have three parts to it. Part one is to illuminate the present state of affairs in such a way that people will see it for what it is—to de-mystify and de-mythologize reality. Part two is to suggest an alternative and very different and better way which things might be. Part three is to suggest ways in which we can get from where we are to where we want to be.

I have tended to say in the past and would still say of many people that it is not enough to talk only of part one and part two. Unless we can suggest to people possible ways of attaining the better reality we hold out before them, we may be simply creating anxiety, frustration, perhaps doing more harm than good. There seems to be no point in telling people that they have to go to a certain place unless one can suggest at least a possible way of getting there. But now I am not so sure that this is true, at least of you. I sense you are impatient with what I call tactical questions, how-do-we-get-there type questions, and you may be right to be so. There are at least two very great dangers for the excessively tactical person. One is that in dealing with immediate problems he will simply lose his way. One of the very important things you have done and surely will continue to do for me is to help me keep my compass adjusted, so to speak. The other more serious danger is that because we cannot see at first *how* to get to another place, we may decide all too quickly that it is not worth getting to. I have in mind here the extraordinary reaction of many people to your suggestion of limiting speed.[3] They simply cannot imagine how it might be done, how people might be persuaded to do it, and hence refuse to consider, or are unable to consider, the question of whether it might be worth doing, or something that someday we will have to do.

Another difference between us is that I look at all these questions and problems, not just with the eyes of a tactician, who asks how do we get there from here, but even more particularly through the eyes of an American, who asks, "what sorts of changes or series of changes in American political and economic and social life might take us to the desired place?" I would guess that you get rather impatient with all these people who come down from the United States and act and talk as if the United States was the whole world, or as if anything that couldn't be done in the United States couldn't be done anywhere and wasn't even worth talking about, or as if every American problem was ipso facto a world problem. And I should think you might get quite impatient with the many American students who come to CIDOC and then complain about being asked to pay money to support an institution which in turn supports a number of Mexicans who are vastly poorer than any American who could afford to come to Cuernavaca. It is almost impossible for Americans, black or otherwise, who think of themselves as radicals, to understand that most of the people in the United States who are there considered poor, and often quite rightly so, are by the standards of the world as a whole definitely middle class.

It would be in some ways easier for me if I could say, as I think you are inclined to, that the United States, and perhaps along with it the highly developed economies of Northern Europe, are a lost cause, as good as dead, and that the rest of the world must think how to escape being poisoned by these societies while waiting for them to choke themselves to death. But I can't do it. For one thing, as I keep

3. Illich believed that the speed of transportation should be limited to the speed of a bicycle. Greater speed, he argued, created distance between people and dependence on a technology that exceeded appropriate, or "convivial," limits. See *Tools for Conviviality.*

discovering over and over again to my surprise, I am really an American (it must annoy many people to hear citizens of the United States use this word to describe themselves, which equally applies to anyone in the whole hemisphere—but anyway, that's common usage, so I'll go on using it). As much as I dislike and fear and disapprove of our society in a large sense, I have enormous numbers of ties to it. Like Gulliver tied down by the Lilliputians I am tied to a great many people and places in this country. I can imagine a time when living and working here would become so impossible that I might become an exile, but I realize, like the young men who left the country to avoid having to take part in the Vietnam War, that it's a hard thing to be an exile, that a person who leaves his own country, turns his back on it, abandons it, gives it up for lost, loses a great deal of himself. I'm not ready to do that yet.

But a more important consideration is this. It would relieve my mind a good deal to be able to believe that it might be possible for the United States to collapse as a country, society, civilization, without bringing the rest of the world down with it. I don't think this is true. I think if U.S. society collapses, it will collapse into some kind of fascism, some sort of violence-worshipping totalitarian government, and I think it is almost certain that such a government would get itself involved in a Third (nuclear) World War, which very few people would survive. [. . .] I'm terribly afraid of fascism for my country and it seems to me that there are certain places, much more than others, where fascism is learned—in school, in front of the television set, and almost above all at the wheel of a car. I am horrified to find what happens to my own character if I do very much of the kind of driving that most people do all the time.

Forgive this rather abrupt stop right in the middle of what will surely become a much longer letter. I will continue it as soon as I can.

Meanwhile, a question to ponder between now and your seminar. How do we use the machinery of law to bring about the kind of society you envisage when the law itself is deeply corrupted, an instrument owned and controlled by those who have the greatest interest in resisting and preventing the kinds of changes you suggest?

Peace,

John

[TO A. S. NEILL]

June 12, 1972

Dear Neill,

Thank you so much for your letter, for news of the school and yourself, and for your very kind and perceptive remarks about my new book.[1] Your words to Dutton were and will be most helpful to us. We hope to get an edition published in England before too long.

My father is within a couple of years of your age, has a gadget in his heart called a Pacemaker, and is in a way re-learning to walk after an operation to replace a badly eroded hip joint. I feel in him the same flagging of energy. But there is a great difference between his life and yours, which I think makes it harder for him to face death. Whether through bad luck or bad management, he was never able to do work that seemed to him worth doing, and I think he must often have the painful feeling that the world is no different for his having been in it. As a matter of fact, I do not think this is true for anyone, but it is certainly not true of you. I think, in the words of who was that old English Cardinal, that you have helped to light a fire that will not be put out. "Be of good cheer, Master Gridley, for today we shall light a fire in England as, by God's grace, shall never be put out." Cardinal Woolsey? Burnt by Mary Tudor? No matter, the words are what are important.

I share your view that in a personal sense death is simply the end of life. I don't know whether I will have your toughness of character at your age, or whether, like my father, after a long lifetime of not believing in Christianity, or at any rate in the notion of Heaven and life after death, I will at the last minute try to find comfort in such a belief.

But I have a feeling that the very early Christians did not mean the idea of immortality to be taken literally, but metaphorically. What they were trying to say about the soul or spirit was that it remained among living men when the individual person was dead, that we do not leave the world exactly as it would have been had we not been in it, that every person who lives, by the fact of his living, makes a difference. They were saying to their first humble and downtrodden

---

1. *Freedom and Beyond.*

believers, "You are not nothing, you will change the world forever for having lived in it, you will not be forgotten, the traces of your being here will in one way or another endure forever." But this notion—if I am correct—became corrupted into the idea of a personal Heaven.

It is difficult for me to imagine what it would be like to be near the end of my life. Not as difficult as it once was, but difficult. What bothers me most is just what bothers you—not knowing how it is all going to come out. So many things are going to happen, and I won't know about them. I think of this when I see my youngest nieces and nephews. All the things they will see that I won't see. But then, I have seen some things that they won't see.

[. . .]

I have read only a very little Reich.[2] [I] plan and mean to read more. I have been very much on the lecture trail for the past few years, stopping every so often to try to clear away the tons of paper that come through the office. When the campaign is over, and McGovern (I hope) is President, I plan to get off the lecture trail for a while, do more reading, thinking, writing, playing the cello.

I am pleased that you find my style readable. I work very hard to make it that way. Nothing annoys me more about the academic-intellectual community than their notion that an idea is important in proportion as it is obscure. I feel a moral as well as aesthetic duty to speak as plainly as I can.

I know I join a great many other people in saying that I hope you will be with us yet for quite a while. You have made a great difference in the thinking and living of many people. We'll certainly do all we can to keep the work going, and to keep alive the fragile notions of freedom and joy.

peace,

[John]

2. Wilhelm Reich, author of *The Function of the Orgasm.* Neill had written, about *Freedom and Beyond,* "I wonder why you didn't mention Reich and his views on kids' freedom."

Holt corresponded for a while with Arthur Pearl,
author of *The Atrocity of Education.*

[TO ARTHUR PEARL]

June 14, 1972

Dear Art,

Thanks for letter. My question: do I have the right to define my
work, or does someone else have the right to define it for me? If so,
who, how, and why? What gives someone else the right to tell me that
of the things I feel are worth doing and need to be done, some are
"work" and some are not. What gives someone else the right to decide whether what I do, to use your words, contributes to the quality
of life of others, or does not? Why is my judgment on this question
not as good as another person's?

Most of the work I do in this office, including writing this letter to
you, and including answering letters from thousands of people a
year, I do not get paid for. I am able to do it only because my books
happen to make money. But this work, for which I do not get paid,
seems to me at least as useful and valuable, if not a great deal more
so, than much or most of the "work" for which many people do get
paid.

In a country short of, say, food, I can see the justice in a social
agreement that says, in effect, if you do not help us produce the necessities of life you can't share in them—though even this is by no
means the whole story, and primitive societies are usually or often
not that grim. But in a country which could produce necessities and
amenities for all with a fraction of the available manpower, I can see
no reason why people should be required to do ridiculous, unnecessary, wasteful, shameful or destructive work in order to eat and have
a roof over their heads. If A wants to say to B, "I'll make an electric
comb for you if you'll make an electric hairbrush for me," that is OK
by me. If a whole lot of people want to band together in an agreement whereby they spend half their time making junk for each other
so that they may spend the rest of the time buying it from each other,
again, they have a right to. But I don't see why anyone else should
be bound by the terms of that agreement.

I'm afraid that the society you envision—not the one described
above, although maybe not so different—"You cure my neurosis and

115

I'll cure your headache"—seems to me a nightmarish society. I see it as a society in which every human need is defined as a "job" which only a "qualified" person on one or another career ladder is entitled to carry out. It is now a crime for anyone other than an M.D. to practice medicine. May we look forward to the day when it will be a crime for anyone other than a certified teacher to teach anyone anything? When parents can be prosecuted under the law for teaching their children, or allowing them to teach themselves, to read?

Mind you, as I said, I think there should be more ladders than there are, and enough space on them for everyone who wants to be on a ladder. But not everyone needs to define himself or his work in this way, and those who do not wish to should have the option not to.

We cannot have it both ways. If we believe that people find meaning and dignity in their lives by doing work that is obviously necessary, then we cannot have more and more labor-saving economies. On the contrary, we must find ways to devise more labor-intensive economies, with only the most backbreaking and intensive work done by machines. We can't with one voice preach the beauties of leisure and the need to supply more and more of it, and at the same time preach the virtues of work.

Beyond all that, God save me from living in a country in which everyone is a Professional.

I suspect this gap between us will be bridged, if it is, by time rather than by words. We will probably find ourselves allies on many matters of detail. But I think our visions of a good society are in important respects hard to reconcile.

Peace,
John

Holt exchanged several letters with Marcus
Foster, who, taking over the job of Oakland Public
School Superintendent in 1970, became the first
black superintendent of a large school district
in California. Foster was killed by members of the
Symbionese Liberation Army in November of
1973.

[TO MARCUS FOSTER]

June 27, 1972

Dear Marc,

It was good to see you and to have a chance to talk with you at
Aspen; if nothing else had happened there (and other things did),
that would have been worth the trip.

[. . .] Let me amplify one point, about the pool of talent that a
child is likely to encounter in school. Most elementary school classrooms are self-contained. This means that by the end of sixth grade
a child will have had fairly close contact with only about six or seven
adults. Not very much, even if they all happen to be good. By the
end of junior high and high school a child may have known a dozen
or so more. Again, not much, even if they are all good and concerned people. Even a poor community has a lot more to offer than
that. And the hard fact is that a good many teachers that a poor child
meets in his schooling will not be people of much knowledge or talent, and will not be very interested in or concerned with the child.

Most of the children I have taught, except for working with inner
city and ghetto kids during four years of summer school teaching,
have been white, upper middle class, so-called high achieving kids.
My very strong belief, indeed conviction, is that most of what they
know they did not learn in school. As I described in *How Children
Fail*, for these children, even their "quality" school was an almost
wholly negative experience. Fortunately, most of these children had
other things to make up for it. If their brains were not completely
knocked out by fifth grade, it was because they had other resources
outside of school.

All of which is to say that if black people want their schools to help
their kids, they *can not and must not* make them into copies of the
schools that the rich white kids go to—which, I fear, is what many of

117

them want to do. They must find ways to do in their schools things that are better than what is done in middle class white schools, things that are not done there at all.

Anytime you and some of your colleagues and teachers want to talk with me about what such things might be, I am at your service. [...]

I read in today's paper that there is by now all over the U.S. a flourishing black press—many newspapers and magazines. Same must be true, on a lesser scale, for Chicanos. These newspapers, from all over the country, should be in minority group schools. They could be a vehicle through which black kids in one part of the country could get in touch with, and write to, black kids in many other parts. This would be worth 100 basal readers or high-powered reading systems (Sullivan, SRA, etc.).

But we can talk more about this later. Hope to see you again before long. Good luck in your work.

best,

A friend from the Colorado Rocky Mountain School wrote saying she hoped Holt felt satisfied with what he had accomplished thus far, rather than frustrated at what had not yet happened.

[TO JO MITCHELL]

July 20, 1972

Dear Jo,

[...]

I am enjoying life very much, and am pleased with the new direction that my book sent me off in. That isn't a very good sentence. What I mean to say is that writing that book and its successors changed my life, and in ways I like. I'm often asked whether I think I have had an effect. I answer truthfully that I really don't know. But I do feel sure that along with a number of other writers I was instrumental in getting large numbers of people to take a second look at a whole lot of things they'd been taking for granted. In short, though I don't know how much I may have changed schools, I think I have changed a lot of people's consciousness, which is as much as any writer can ask for. And in spite of all my worries about the state of the world and country, I am most of the time happier than I have ever been in my life. Who can ask for more than that?

[. . .]

Peace,

[TO JUDSON JEROME]

September 27, 1972

Dear Jud,

So good to get your latest letter. Delighted to hear about your ingenious solution to the school problem.[1] I've had in mind for some years the thought that something like that might be possible, but it's nice to know it's working. I suppose, the way things are going in this country, or the way I think they're going when I'm feeling a little gloomy, that someday some school bureaucrat may get the idea of making a computerized file of all children in all schools in the country, so that at any minute somebody can check to see if some particular child is in some particular school. But we don't have any such arrangement yet, and who knows, considering the incompetence of most school people, [maybe] by the time they do get such a thing going they won't know how to work it. So I suspect there will be loopholes for some time to come. I suppose when enough people start escaping through the loopholes the government people will start looking for ways to plug them up. This presents a bit of a problem. How much talking should we do about the loopholes we find? On the one hand, we want to help other people find them who are looking for them and need them. On the other hand, we don't want to make too much noise about what we're doing. I don't quite know how to work this one out.

Much amused, touched and reassured by your most perceptive and tactful remarks about me in communes.[2] I guess you're quite

1. Jerome had written that his daughter was enrolled in but not attending a private school in another state.

2. Holt had written, "Even within a fairly small community I would want to have some say about the degree of intimacy between myself and other people—and it may very well be that just this statement contradicts your definition of community." Jerome replied, "You protest too much, I think, about wanting to join a commune! I certainly

right. It isn't everyone's cup of tea. By the way, since I last wrote I spent a day at a reunion of my old submarine. There were about 22 or 23 men there, the Skipper and I the only officers, one former chief, the others all enlisted men. It was a most interesting occasion. I had a lot more fun than I would have expected, found at least some of the people there more interesting and varied than I would have expected, and learned an immense amount. It is a hard experience to write about. Most of the things I could think of to say about it sound more like putdowns, and indeed there was a great deal about the experience that is disheartening. But it was greater than the sum of its parts, if you know what I mean. If I had to gather all the things I could think of to say about it, I still come up with something far short of the experience. And people themselves are more complicated than what we can think of to say about them.

For one thing, practically everyone there was some sort of gun freak. An awful lot of them were deeply into shooting things. They talked with enormous relish about the number of ducks they had bagged on this hunt, or the number of some other kind of animal they had gotten somewhere else. And yet, though all the things that are said by non-gun people about gun people are probably true, they add up to a good deal less than the whole truth about these men. Mixed in with their love of hunting is a real love of and feeling for at least certain kinds of nature and wildness. And so on. I suppose most of them are for Nixon, support the bombing of Vietnam, are pretty strongly against blacks—though I am mostly guessing here, and may simply be projecting my own Archie Bunker type stereotypes onto them. And yet, though there were some I didn't like much, in a great many I found a lot of warmth and vitality, lots of energy and humor that made them good companions and shipmates on a submarine.

I am on the lecture trail much less, and it is a relief. I have started to play the cello a little more. My hands are barely working themselves into shape, but it is exciting even in the few days that I have been playing to feel how quickly they become stronger and more flexible. The first day I could hardly play five minutes at a stretch without their becoming tired and exhausted and painful. Now they are tougher. I am collecting thoughts, quotes, and ideas for my next book, for which I have at the moment the title *The Prison of Childhood*. Have I talked to you at all about this? What I have in mind is that the

don't think it is the life for everyone, and from the little I know about you I think you would be much happier living as you do."

institution of childhood, all those laws, customs, and attitudes which lock young people into an extended condition of dependency and subserviency, and put a great wall between them and the larger society around them, is very harmful and needs to be done away with. More specifically, the legal barriers that we have put between young people and many of the permitted activities of adulthood should be lowered, so that young people, when they want to, should have the right to work, own property, take part in political affairs, vote, travel, manage their own learning, live away from home if they like and perhaps make quasi-familial relationships with other young people and/or adults of their own choosing—a kind of re-creation of the extended family. All this is exciting to me. I have told the lecture people that I will talk to audiences if they want to talk about this subject. But I am on the whole bone-weary of talking to teachers about what goes on or ought to go on in classrooms. I have lots of sympathy and affection for people who are working on the reform of schools, but I have put in my own time on this venture and am ready to move on to other things.

[. . .]

I know what you mean about being older than your father ever became. My context is of course a little different. I'm thinking of my submarine skipper, who as long as I live will seem a kind of father figure to me, as to everyone else on that boat. Indeed, he was in a real sense the center of our reunion. He could not have been any older than his early 30's when he was in command of that submarine. Here I am getting on to twenty years older than that, and I still think of that mythical figure in the past not as a young man but as some sort of patriarch. And in a similar way when my sister and I think of our relations with our mother when we were, let us say, between ten and fifteen, and she was between 30 and 35, it slays us to think that we are now 15 years older than she was then. Time is indeed an odd thing. I don't *feel* older but people younger than I am *get* older. Not an original observation.

[. . .]

Have to laugh about the public Jud rising again. I get the most extraordinary quantity of mail in this office from people, often total strangers, demanding insistently that I do them some kind of favor, which in many cases requires quite a bit of time and effort. Often they get furiously angry if I don't hop to it. But I suppose the answer is that people look for help where they think help might be found.

One young man just sent me a letter only the other day saying why did I endorse so many books—the implication being very clearly that I did it for some nefarious reason.

[. . .]

Thanks again for your letter, and a joy as always. Love to everyone there.

Peace,

John

After meeting him at CIDOC, Holt kept in touch with Hartmut von Hentig, who had started an experimental laboratory school in Germany.

[TO HARMUT VON HENTIG]

October 9, 1972

Dear Hartmut,

[. . .] I'm reading on in your interview. You say, "Push the system as far as you can until they kick you out of the place you're in, then go to another place. Because you're a qualified person and have the skills and credentials to get another position, you can do that."

It may be true of Germany but it is certainly not true here. We have various ways of blacklisting people. This was true even before we got a big teacher surplus. Most of the people I know, admittedly not a very large number, who were kicked out of teaching for in one way or another pushing against the system, have *not* been able to get another place somewhere else. After all, you have to say where you worked last, and when your new employer or possible employer asks them what kind of person you were, and is told that you were a troublemaker, he doesn't give you a job. [. . .]

I have to say that when people talk to me, as they do all the time, about working "within the system" or "outside the system," I honestly do not know what they mean. I do not know where the boundary lines of these "systems" are, or how to tell whether I am in or out. I am as often criticized in this country for working within the system as I am for working outside it. Talk about "inside / outside" the system is simplistic, two-valued, and a great distortion of reality. What we need to discuss are far more concrete and practical questions.

Given a certain institution, what are the possibilities of making certain kinds of reforms in it? What are the possibilities of achieving the same objectives in other ways, or making other human arrangements which would work more effectively? If both are possible, which is likely to yield the best results for a given amount of effort. This sort of cost-benefit analysis, as they say in business, is what any tactician of social change has to think about. But inside / outside talk, I'm afraid, just muddies the water. Hope you won't think that's too harsh.

[. . .]

I don't mean by the quarrelsome tone of much of this letter to suggest that there are not a great many things about which we agree very strongly. If that were not so, I would not have taken my time to write or your time to read such a letter.

Until we see each other again,

Peace,

John

Holt corresponded about publishing for a while
with a former Berkeley student who had written a
book about motherhood.

[TO BETTY RIVARD]

October 20, 1972

Dear Betty,

[. . .] The titles of four of my books have been mine. *The Under-achieving School* was Pitman's, but I had not been able to think of anything I liked at all, let alone liked better, we were in a hurry, I didn't mind their title, so we went ahead with it. I had to battle with them a little over the first book, which they wanted to be *Why Children Fail.* I felt strongly about the *How,* and won out. My first thought for the title of the newest book was *Summerhill and Beyond,* but my editor quickly persuaded me that we could do better. For a while we thought of changing our title because of [B. F.] Skinner's book, but we finally agreed to stay with the title we had. We are arguing a little now about the title for the next book, but I think I can win them over. This is partly a matter of friendly argument with your editor, and partly a matter of feeling so strongly about it that you are willing to say, "Do it my way or I won't let you have the book." But that is an ace in the hole that one ought not to bring out too often—save it for major issues.

As for jacket design, I never asked to do anything about this. Dutton showed me the jacket of *What Do I Do Monday?* and I made a minor change in it. Otherwise I have had no objections to anything done along those lines. Unless you are good at this I would let the publisher take care of it—they have commercial artists and designers who do know what looks good on a book cover. On the other hand, if you have some ideas about design, whether or not you want to use a photo, etc., by all means make them known. If the company likes your book they will almost certainly listen to you on such matters. I don't think you need anticipate a lot of heavy struggles over such matters. Some of the biggest arguments I have had have been not so much about the contents of the book as over their organization. The initial form of *How Children Fail* was somewhat different— I had all my journals or letters in pure chronological order, without any organization as to subject. My initial idea about the book was that it would record my own mental journey, so to speak. My editor thought that this made it too hard to follow, that the various things I thought of were connected in my mind in a way they would not be for the reader, and that it was hard from the inside to recognize how fragmented the book would seem. On the whole I think he was very right. Other suggestions made to me by Hal Scharlatt for the two books done by Dutton have been very sensible—and I must say that I resisted them at first. When you finish a book you can't imagine it in any other shape than the one it is in; it is very hard to look at it through the eyes of a reader who has not gone through the process. This is one of the things an editor does. It doesn't mean that on all the points on which you disagree he will be right; there are places where I have stood firm and am glad I did. What I am saying is that this dialogue is a reasonable and natural part of the process of doing a book. It is not (I am not suggesting that you think it is) a struggle over the integrity of the author vs. the money interest of the publisher, etc. It is an argument about how to make the book as good as possible and how to make it have the best possible impact, etc. All of which is to say that good editors love books and like writers, and care about their work, so any arguing that goes on should go on in that spirit.

[. . .] On the whole I think you have to trust them, and I think the kind of publishers that I believe will be interested in your book are trustworthy. They are business people, they are not of the counter-culture, but they are far less rip-off artists than (let us say) almost any rock groups you could think of. You won't see eye to eye on every-thing but I think their positions are basically decent and reasonable. And there is this to be said, that the more money they make on your book, the more eagerly they will receive another when it appears— and the next time around you will be in a stronger bargaining position.

Will stop here. I loved your letter, and portrait of the principal. I mentioned Pam Stoloff [1] from my class at Berkeley (another wonder-ful writer, tho she writes only letters). She too is teaching in a little school in a little town way up in Northern New Mexico, in an almost entirely Spanish speaking community, and, with her husband, hav-ing not the problem but the task of getting known and accepted by their very different neighbors. Love to all there.

Peace,

[TO MARCUS FOSTER]

October 25, 1972

Dear Marc,

Interesting story in one of the local weeklies about the death of a famous local bookstore. The writer points out that when he was growing up, he learned, along with a lot of other young people who had very little money, to love books and reading by hanging around a bunch of old second-hand bookstores that used to line Huntington Ave., hidden away in basements and run by various oddballs. This may be an institution we need to bring back, I'm not sure how. I keep saying that it's not going to do much good to help young kids learn to read if, after they've learned, there's nothing around for them *to* read.

I recall a meeting about something or other in San Francisco at which a black parent asked me, with some asperity, why I had learned to read. I said then and repeat now that I sure as heck didn't

1. Later, and in this collection, Pam Dant.

learn because I thought I was someday going to get a good job, or get into a good college, or even to please my parents and teachers— I learned before I went to school and my parents didn't even know I was doing it. I learned to read mostly because I wanted to figure out what all that written stuff said and I figured I was smart enough to do it.

I suspect that almost [any] other kind of motivation defeats itself. The trouble with saying to poor kids, whether white, black, or any other minority group, that if they only learned to read well they would do well in later life, is that it leads them, perhaps only inside their heads, to ask a couple of questions. Looking around them at all the adults they know know how to read they must think, "Well, all you guys know how to read, and it obviously hasn't done you so much good, so what makes you think it's going to solve anything for me?" Or if, conversely, they look around and see some adults who don't know how to read or read very badly, or even very seldom, they might ask, "Well, if this reading is such hot stuff, and the cure for all our ills, how come you're not doing more of it."

Children, in whatever community, get their sense of what is important and also possible from what happens around them. All of which is to say, and this only underlines what I've written before, that if we want to make education or schooling or whatever it is look important to black kids, then it has to look important to everyone in the community. But it's very difficult to get kids to swallow a kind of medicine that they can see very few adults around them are willing to take.

I hasten to add that though it may sound like it, what I'm saying is not at all that the reason that poor kids don't learn is because of the community they live in, and I think [you] already know me well enough to know that is not at all in my mind. I want to see the poor and oppressed people of this country get a hell of a lot more knowledge and skills than they have, because if they get it and use it, and use it wisely and rightly and for their general good, they can do a lot to improve their condition and the whole society. People who know what the score is are harder to push around, and the more kids come into [contact with] adults who, knowing the score, are hard to push around, the [more they] will want to know the score themselves.

I don't know what happens to magazines when they go off the newsstands, that is when the new issues come in and the old ones go out. There are in this city a certain number of back magazine stores where you can get old issues, usually with the covers torn off. But all of these put together would account for [no] more than half of one percent of all the magazines published. Obviously a lot of this paper with valuable print is floating around somewhere if we can find a way to lay our hands on it. I expect it might be possible to equip a lot of mini-libraries and store front libraries and neighborhood centers with these back-dated periodicals, at next to no cost, if we could find the right connections. And you or people close to you might be in a position to find out what some of those connections are.

Hope all goes well.

My old friend Herb Kohl, whom you may very well know, now living up in Berkeley, has a book coming out this fall called *Reading: How To*. I have only seen parts of it, but I suspect it may have a lot of good stuff in it, and in any case Herb may be somebody worth making a connection with—that is, if you haven't already.

Best,

Holt's correspondence with Edgar Friedenberg, author of *The Vanishing Adolescent* and *Coming of Age in America*, began in 1962 when Holt wrote to praise Friedenberg's article about Erich Fromm that had just been published in *Commentary*. Having emigrated to Canada in 1970, Friedenberg was, at the time of the following letter, teaching at Dalhousie University in Nova Scotia and thinking about becoming a Canadian citizen. A letter from Friedenberg to Holt in 1983 indicates that he ultimately chose to retain his U.S. citizenship.

[TO EDGAR FRIEDENBERG]

October 25, 1972

Dear Edgar,

Thanks for all your excellent and kind words over the phone, and your most interesting paper about the Citadel, which I just read.

Given your life, work, needs, temperament, etc. I think you have made a very sensible choice. Oddly enough, your article made me feel that it might not be the right choice for me, at least not yet. What

127

I miss in America is the sense of being at home, a citizen. Or, to put it the other way, what troubles me most is the feeling I've had for a long time that I'm an alien, like somebody in a science fiction story come from another planet and wandering around in disguise, whom the locals would tear apart if they knew he really came from Arcturis or somewhere. For probably over 25 years I've been acutely conscious that if they knew what was going on in my head, a large majority of my fellow citizens would be happy to put me in jail if not kill me. This is oppressive, and when I think of moving, I think of moving to a place about which I would feel much less that this was true. What you have conveyed to me about Canada is that it is about as honky as the U.S. is but that its honky-ishness is less likely to be translated into government policy, i.e. that the honkies are more likely to leave you alone. Well, the time may come when this may be all I need to make me move. But if I moved now I think I would want to get more out of it than that.

I may really be kidding myself—it may very well be that in every country of the world, even the suppo[sedly] peaceful and gentle Scandinavian countries, there is a big streak of honky-ishness waiting to burst out. I would not have guessed, for example, how quickly and violently the supposedly reasonable and law abiding society of Great Britain would become racist—and it is at least as bad in that respect as we are. It may very well be that it would not take more than a small influx of, let us say, low-wage workers from Southern Europe and the Middle East, to arouse in the Scandinavians just as much ugliness of spirit as we see in so many of our own people. Beyond that, I suspect that they all have a fairly good dose of the American disease, a belief in unlimited progress, unlimited growth, unlimited greed, which has largely corrupted whatever good there may have been in this society and will if not carefully checked corrupt theirs. Also, the information that I get from you makes me realize that it's going to be harder to get tax dollars away from the Pentagon than I thought. Also, I'm a little less low in spirits than the other day. McGovern came to town and we had an immense rally. Crowd estimates range anywhere from 35,000 up to 100,000—it was hard to tell because they filled a whole lot of back streets and there was no place from which you could see all the people. The police were estimating 100,000 and they have no particular reason to be kind to McGovern. Anyway, it was an immense and enthusiastic crowd. He may be beginning to turn things around, and indeed the press is saying so. I suspect the apparent Nixon majority is unstable, that a lot of people are saying they prefer him in the polls because the last poll they [saw?] said the same thing. So there is some possibility that [McGovern] may win. I entirely agree with you that this would not make this country into the kind of place that you or I would feel at home in, but it will I think prevent or slow down something else, an increasingly fast move in the direction of the corporate-military-police state—which, by the way, I think we have a worse dose of than ten years ago, if only because its instruments are perfected. Perhaps the most important difference between McGovern and Nixon, outside of the matter of ending the war, will be in the matter of court appointments. What I fear will happen if Nixon is elected again is that he will pack the Federal judiciary at all levels with the kind of people who will in effect let our municipal and state legislatures write laws as oppressive as they want. To put it a little differently, I think the people of this country are much more fascist than their government, and that on the whole local governments are far more repressive than the national, and this will be very much accelerated. Indeed, it seems to me that there really is no particular need for a national machinery of repression and terror; it could all be handled quite effectively on the local level, with agencies like the FBI fingering certain people for local police harassment, framing, etc. I think that will probably be the mechanism, but it will require a compliant judiciary and this McGovern may somewhat prevent. But you're right—he has already lost the mandate we once hoped he would have. If he is elected, it will clearly be as a regular if somewhat eccentric Democrat. But he will not be able to say to the Congress, as I once hoped he might, that his election shows that there is a majority of people who want a very different kind of society here, including at the very least an end to poverty and misery.

Part of my problem is that I really do have a lot of connections here with people and places. Also, I had a vision or notion which may be unrealistic, that it might be possible for me to be a citizen of another country, or at least a resident, and spend only about five or six months of the year over here, during which time I would still do a lot of my lecturing and writing work. That may not work out.

So my thoughts are as confused as ever, but altogether. That is, they are confused in somewhat different ways, on the basis of better information, and in all of this I'm very grateful to you for your help. Wherever I live, I think I will want to try to make my living as an independent writer and lecturer. I am not really an academic person, don't like universities on the whole, and wouldn't much want to be associated with one, even if they would have me on my own terms, which is exceedingly unlikely. But all of that may change. Meanwhile, best to you.

Peace,

As the previous letter reveals, Holt took a great interest in the presidential candidacy of George McGovern. He gave several speeches on behalf of the campaign, and often wrote to McGovern with an idea for campaign strategy or a suggested reading. McGovern wrote back regularly, often responding to comments Holt had made about his campaign speeches. In one letter he said that he carried Holt's *How Children Fail* around in his briefcase. (Later, after Holt had died, McGovern wrote an introduction to a new edition of the book.)
Holt wrote the following letter just after McGovern lost the 1972 election.

[TO GEORGE McGOVERN]

November 12, 1972

Dear George,

Well, it's over, and it already seems like a long time ago. You certainly gave it everything you had. To keep your spirits, courage, and resolution for such a long time and in the face of so much discouragement took about twenty times more guts than I have. The day may yet come when the people of this country will really realize that they are in deep trouble, and if so, they may call on you. [. . .]

A great many people will be counting on you to keep a spotlight on the doings of the Nixon crew. By dint of all your hard work you are the leader of the Democratic Party, and will remain so until someone else can prove he has a better right to the job.

Four years may be time enough, as six months was not, to educate the American people to understand that we can't go on indefinitely as we are—in short, to put over the ideas you were talking about last spring.

Arguments will rage for years about whether you were wise to moderate and down-play your original positions on many issues, or whether you should have continued to push them as hard as you did in the spring. We will never know, but on the whole I think what you did, you had to do. The California primary made it clear, certainly to me, that the constituency for your original ideas was not large enough to win the election.

What I think we may have learned from the election, or at least, what I have learned, is not only that fewer Americans than I would have supposed are concerned about war, militarism, poverty, racism, and so forth, but that many more Americans than I would have suspected are violently opposed to the raising of such issues. Not only were your supporters fewer than we thought, but their enemies were numerous and determined. But I don't think there was any way to find this out except by waging the campaign you waged. If the results show that the American people are much further to the right than I would have thought or hoped, then that is something we must know.

I still think it is of the greatest importance that we find a way to work the bugs out of your tax-credit or income maintenance plan, and get it into the stream of practical politics. The basic idea is sound, if the details can be properly worked out.

I, and many friends of mine, were very moved by your concession speech.

Thanks again for a great effort. You're certainly always welcome here in Boston and in Massachusetts. We half expect Nixon to mine Boston harbor. And in fact there probably will be political reprisals.

Best wishes to you and all your family. In a way, it must be a kind of relief for all of you.

Peace,

John

1964–1976

A college student who had been given the assignment of writing about elementary education in the twenty-first century wrote to ask for Holt's ideas, saying he was looking for "an accurate prophet" of the twenty-first century.

[TO TIM ROWAN]

November 15, 1972

Dear Mr. Rowan,

Thanks very much for your letter of Nov. 12 and kind words about my books. You ask an interesting question, and my reply to it may surprise you.

You show by your letter and your request that you share with most of the people of the world, or at least the country, a view about the future which is not only wholly mistaken but extraordinarily dangerous. Like most people, you seem to believe that the future already exists, that it is already *out there* somewhere, waiting for us to come to it, borne along on the current of time. I can't blame you for this; practically everything you read in the public prints support[s] this superstition. The woods are full of what are called Futurologists, busily telling us exactly what the future is going to be. Of course, no two of them agree with each other, but that is all right; they still persuade us, and we still profoundly believe, that the future really exists somewhere, and if we could just know which stone to turn over we could find out what it was.

Now the hard fact, an obvious fact when we think about it for a little while, is that the future doesn't exist. *It does not exist.* It is not waiting for us, like a station down the railroad track, which we can only guess about but will finally see when the train pulls into it. The future will be what we make it, by our acts in the present. Nobody knows, or can know what it will be. The question you are asked to write about is absurd, pure science fiction. If you want to treat it as such, let your imagination roam freely; you don't need me. You say that you "don't know where to go to find an accurate prophet of the twenty-first century." Forgive my language, but your statement is absurd. There is not, nor can be, any such thing.

Since the future does not exist until we make it, since we cannot know what is going to happen, the only thing that is important, that is worth spending time on, is to consider what kind of future we

132

would like to have, and then how we may most effectively work to get it.

As I read on in your letter I see that you are looking for "a realistic authority on the subject whose opinions I can justify." Once again, talk about the future is simply science fiction. This is not changed by stating these guesses in terms of "probability." When I am feeling gloomy, I think that the "probability" is that [in the] next 50 years or so we will destroy ourselves in a series of more destructive wars and/ or ecological disasters. When I am feeling good, I think we may smarten up in time and find a way to prevent this. But there is no way to justify either of these opinions.

The best word on this subject was spoken by G. B. Shaw: "Be sure to get what you like, or else you will have to like what you get." Tell that to your professor; I'll bet a nickel none of them ever heard it. And indeed, I would be grateful if you would communicate the contents of this letter to as many as possible of your fellow students and professors, particularly the one who gave this assignment.

The belief that the future already exists and that the right experts can tell us what it will be or is, this determinist, fatalist superstition, is at the same time both one of the symptoms and the causes of our rapid slide into totalitarianism. I hope you will join me in doing whatever you can to prevent it. Thanks again for writing—and do let me know your response to this letter.

Sincerely,

[TO PEGGY HUGHES]

November 29, 1972

Dear Peggy,

It's snowing outside today, though a little sun is shining.

Had a terrific experience a couple of nights ago. Ronald Laing[1] came to town, and Margot, Terry,[2] and I, along with about 2,500 people, went to hear him at the gymnasium at Tufts. Then afterwards Margot and I went to a small reception in the Alumni Lounge. It was one of the great evenings of my life. It's hard to describe the scene. I don't know if you know that gym. There are banks of seats

1. R. D. Laing, author of *The Politics of Experience, The Divided Self*, and others.
2. Margot Priest and Terry Kros, on Holt's office staff.

on two sides, a couple of high balconies at one end, and then the floor. People were sitting all over the floor. Because I had spoken there earlier they let me sit in the reserved seats at the side. The place was absolutely mobbed, jammed. There was an extraordinarily expectant kind of hush in the air. Most of us had never even heard Laing's voice. All we knew of his looks was that crazy picture they have on the front of his books, which I now think he uses as a bit of a joke on the world. The meeting was supposed to begin at 8, but crowds kept pouring in. Finally a little blue curtain behind the dais parted, and a slender man in brown slacks and a brown turtleneck shirt slipped through, sat down in a chair and began to talk—in broad Scots. I'm such a sucker for Scots accent that I'd be happy to spend my day listening to a Scotsman reading the telephone book aloud. He spoke without any notes, just rambled along, which was his plan. He spoke rather slowly, often pausing to think about what he would say next, as he explained later, and very much as has been my experience, in order to keep from boring himself he has learned to speak without any notes and without even making up his mind about what he is going to speak about. As he later said, it is what is called "a rap," which he also said is one of the American expressions he likes best, and it's fun to hear him say it in Scots. He's an extraordinarily funny man. He said at the beginning of his talk that he was going to talk about how he had come to write his books, but his talk led him into another direction, mostly a discussion of the circumstances of birth as it is carried out in most hospitals, and how hard this is on the mother and the child. He was absolutely delightful. But what reassured me most—it's no exaggeration to say I was overjoyed by the evening, and still am—was to find that this man, who seems to me one of the wisest men in the world, and from whom we have so much to learn, but who I had feared might be something close to a madman himself, was on the other hand the sanest and most rational of Scotsmen. From the public prints we have received an image of Laing, that he lives close to madness all the time, that he likes to wander in and out of the territory of insanity, that he really thinks that madness is better than sanity, etc. All such doubts were set aside in his talk, and even more in the smaller session afterwards. Though he is enormously critical of our society, and above all the medical profession—I wish you could have heard him on the subject of doctors, and since what he said comes out of firsthand experience with them it is frighteningly true—he has not abandoned this world for a kind of preferable world of madness or delusion, but is instead extraordinarily sane, practical, feet on the ground. I just can hardly say how relieved and happy I am to find that this is so. I thought, as was once the case with Wilhelm Reich, we might have learned from Laing all that he had to teach us. But now I can see that this is not so, that we are going to go on learning from him for a long time.

In the small meeting afterwards he said, among a great many other good things, one thing that I am going to have to try to remember during the difficult years to come, and that I think, if I can remember it, may more or less save my sanity. Someone asked what he thought personally of Nixon. He went on to say that in his travels he had not met one single person who had a good word to say about Nixon, but that he understood that his audiences were not representative. But then he said that one of the things he had learned in his life, and written about, is to reserve his "pairsonal" feelings for people he knew "pairsonally." He added that this is what he had been trying to tell people in all of his writings, to make a distinction between those things that were projected on to them, told to them by other people, and the things they knew from their direct experience. He said, as a matter of fact, that he would rather like to meet Nixon, as he was curious to know what the man might be like who has such a bad image, but that until he did meet him he was not going to have and could not have any personal feelings about him.

Well, of course, this is something we have heard before in other kinds of words. I guess this is part of what A. J. Muste, pacifist and Jew, meant when right in the middle of World War II he said, "If I can't love Hitler, I can't love anybody." And yet there is something about Laing's way of saying it that makes it seem much less abstract and saintly. Nothing in Laing's remark implies that he expects to like Nixon if and when he does meet him, or that he approves in any way of anything he does. It is just a calm statement of a sensible point of view.

[. . .] Hope you are all well. You must have a pretty firm plan about coming home. When do you think you will arrive?

Peace and love,

John

1964–1976

[TO JUDSON JEROME]

December 20, 1972

Dear Jud,

Wonderful to see you the other weekend. I'm so glad you called me and got me included in. [. . .]

Some later thoughts on our meeting—perhaps somewhat prompted by my re-reading of a wonderful book, of which I may have spoken—*The Changing Nature of Man,* by J. H. van den Berg. I re-read the book because it has much to say about the origins of the present institution of childhood, but I realize now that, written in 1961, it says a great many things that were to be said later by the philosophers of the counterculture. It is a very timely book.

At one point he says that happy married couples don't talk much, and that couples who do talk a lot use words to box each others' ears with. Much truth in that. I am in some ways a word-pusher, a word-smith, but in other ways I often like not to have to talk. I would hate to be asked to talk about any experience, artistic or otherwise, that had a strong emotional effect on me. Sometimes the event may make me feel like talking, but often I need time to soak it in and digest it. And this reminds me that at one point, as we were sitting around, Rosie asked me what I was doing these days. I felt a great heaviness inside; so many people ask me that, it is so hard to answer; there is so much, and so much of that so vague. I was trying to think of words to begin when she, very perceptively and sensitively, caught a lot of my feelings and said that I didn't have to answer if I didn't feel like it. I thanked her and I guess I said something.

This reminds me of something I thought about at one point in the discussion, but did not mention. I once spent a weekend at a conference in St. Louis—as a matter of fact, you were going to come, but like many others invited, could not. For me, it was a bummer, and this in spite of the fact that a couple of good friends of mine were running the affair. It was supposed to be a meeting about communication (one of the things no meeting should ever be about), the idea being that if we change-makers or would-be makers of change knew how to communicate better, we would be more effective. The guy more or less in charge, an interesting man that I like and respect, was a kind of communications expert, a psychologist whose business—and I think he is probably good at it—is working with people

136

who are in some sort of conflict and who are having trouble because they can't hear each other talking. So we were talking about many things, but all along he was talking to us about how we were communicating. I realized after a while that though the meeting was small, I was in a state of very high anxiety, that I was being judged not only on what I said but on the way in which I said it. That is, both my ideas as such, and my way of putting them out, were subject to criticism—and also, since there is always a kind of infinite regress in these things, my way of responding to the criticism. My hands were sweating, my heart was pounding—at one point I could stand it no longer and said to the expert running the show, "My God, I feel like a little kid in school, I haven't felt this anxious in years." This, of course, since he thinks of himself as a specialist in reducing anxiety, made him anxious—what have I done wrong, etc.

[. . .] I don't believe in openness as a duty. It is surely a right, and probably a blessing, but it is not something that anyone ought to be compelled to do. Everyone has a right to his secrets. I am not obliged to tell anyone any more of my feelings than I wish.

It may be hard to believe, but you have no idea how much I enjoy being in situations in which I don't have to talk, don't have to hold forth, where there is a kind of easy relaxed flow of talk, jokes, etc., none of it terribly consequential, going around people, with a much stronger current of things unsaid. What fun it is, as last night, to be with people I like and just soak in the pleasure of their company. [. . .]

An odd memory. Two years ago, when I was last in Norway, visiting my dear friend Mosse Jørgensen, she took me one evening out into the country to a little dinner party of some of her closest friends, and there we were, from five until after midnight, in that lovely Northern summer night (I think I am a true Northerner, maybe in a kind of exile). Everyone there spoke English, and now and then there would be a little flurry of English, to catch me up in the conversation and give me an idea of what was going on. But 95% of the talk was in Norwegian, one of the prettiest of languages, of which I know not a word. And I can't tell you how much I enjoyed the evening, a valued and cherished guest, friend of their dear friend, sitting in the midst of these nice people all enjoying each other, and by association, me— like a loved child sitting at a party of grown-ups of whose talk he understands not a word, except that he is somehow not excluded from it. There was no pressure on me to produce anything, wisdom, knowledge about schools, or whatever. I could look at the faces, and

hear the voices, and listen to the sounds, and try to catch the meaning, and look at the house and the pretty surroundings, and go off
in my own thoughts, and come back when I felt like it—I did not
even have to pay attention, did not even have to listen, though I
could if I wanted to. It was lovely.

And wasn't that fun, relaxed, joyful, when we were in the kitchen
painting. People were talking; you could listen if you wanted to, join
in if you wanted, but not joining in didn't convey any messages; you
could walk in and out. Whereas when the more formal discussion
was going on it was hard to leave the room, hard even to be silent,
without seeming to make a statement about the value or lack of value
of what was being said. [. . .]

Most of those people in our society who talk very much, probably
talk too much. And badly. I felt over and over again, in our meeting,
as we groped toward a better understanding of each other, how
much we were handicapped by our training and habits of thought,
how hard it was for us to speak directly, plainly, unselfconsciously,
without making judgments about our own talk or worrying about
what judgments others might be making. Hard.

I guess we can learn to do better. Anyway, we have to.

Peace,

John

Holt left Pitman Publishing Company for E. P.
Dutton in 1969, when he began working on *What
Do I Do Monday?* He stayed with Dutton through
Instead of Education (the "book #7" of the follow-
ing letter; #6 was *Escape from Childhood*). *Never
Too Late, Teach Your Own,* and the revised editions
of *How Children Fail* and *How Children Learn* were
published by Dell.
"Hal and Bob" of the following letter are Hal
Scharlatt, his editor at Dutton, and Robert
Lescher, his agent.

[TO HAL SCHARLATT AND ROBERT LESCHER]

1/14/73

Dear Hal and Bob,

I want to pass on to you my thoughts on the subject of book #7—
or #4 in our association.

As I have been working on the new book, I have been writing a number of letters and essays, either in reply to letters I have received or things I have read, or simply because of what I have been thinking and doing.

A lot of these are beginning to coalesce in my mind into a book called *Teachers and Learners,* which will be about, among other things, the relationship of teachers and learners in a proper learning setting, the kinds of things that one person can do to assist the learning of another, the meaning of de-schooling, more thoughts on the relationship between de-schooling, schools, poverty, more thoughts on black and minority group education, more thoughts on the act of learning, and so on.

Since much of this stuff is already down in fairly good shape, I think I should be able to get it together into a book before too long after #6 comes out. Later on in the spring, when I am further into #6, I'll send you some of the materials that I think will go into #7.

As I may have told you, on my travels I now and then run into young people who tell me they want to be writers, but who, when I ask what they write, tell me they haven't written anything. My answer to this is—writers are people who write. Properly understood, it may be a terrible disease. But I seem to have caught it.

Peace,

[TO HAL SCHARLATT]

[January 16, 1973]

Dear Hal,

Been working frantically on the book.[1] I'm in the brainstorming stage, just sitting down at a typewriter and letting ideas pour out as fast as I can. After being a bit stuck, I think things are beginning to move. I think yesterday I actually wrote on the order of 12,000 words, which I think may be a new North American record—perhaps even world record. Now this is not even first draft; it is rough; much of it may not be used, and much of the rest heavily squeezed. The hardest part is still ahead. But this is a useful exercise. It has clarified a lot of my thinking, and generated some new thoughts. And as the body of rough notes gets larger and larger, I believe more

1. *Escape from Childhood.*

and more strongly in the reality and worth of the book. And this can be a problem for a writer, at least for me. Between the time when you first think of a book, and the time when it's done, there are times when you wonder whether the idea was anything more than an idea.

I've been thinking about the title, and the following ideas are in my mind at the moment. I think of Jencks' book[2]—and I have to add that it irritates and frustrates me to some extent that he should get so much public notice for saying rather weakly what I said earlier and more strongly. When I say weakly, I simply mean that his case rests on interpretation of statistics, whereas mine does not. Even if it could be shown that incomes correlated 100% with success in school, it would remain true, and for the reasons I state, that the schools cannot make everybody a success, that however good we make the schools and however hard everybody works in them, we're still going to wind up with a few winners and lots of losers.

But I was going to say something about his title, which makes it clearer what his book is about. I now have second thoughts about the titles to my last two books, and if there is blame I blame only myself, since I thought them up and was very proud of them. (They still don't seem to me like bad titles.) The trouble is that neither of them say clearly enough what the books are about. *How Children Fail* and *How Children Learn* had the advantages of not only being catchy titles, but of saying very directly what the books were about. There is nothing in *What Do I Do Monday?* to show the casual looker that it is a book about education and schools, and in the same way there is nothing about *Freedom and Beyond* to show that it is a discussion of freedom in the learning situation, and beyond that a discussion of the relationships between schools, society, and poverty. I now wish I had put in a subtitle making this clearer. Indeed, it occurs to me as I write that it might not be a bad idea at all, if we get into additional printings, or when Dell puts out a paperback, to have a subtitle. Even something as long as "Why Education Is Not Schooling, and Schooling Cannot Cure Poverty."

At any rate, I feel very strongly that I do not want to make the same mistake (if, as I believe, it was a mistake) in the next book. If we begin with a title like *Out of the Prison of Childhood,* or *Escape from the Prison of Childhood,* I would want to follow with something like "The Case for Making Full Citizenship Available to the Young" or something as explicit as that. In short, I want something that will tell

2. *Inequality: A Reassessment of the Effect of Family and Schooling in America.*

people, even if they only see the cover of the book in a bookstore or ad, a little more what the book is about.

By the way, I'd love to know, if you can tell me without too much trouble, what the sales of *Freedom and Beyond* were in the most recent months. I believe you said that as of October it had sold about 18,000 copies; I wonder where we stand now.

I will close here and get back to the brainstorming. If all goes well in this stage of the work, and if making these rough outpourings into a working draft does not take too long, I would love to get the book finished in the spring, so that we might think of having it come out in the fall. I won't promise this, but I will work very hard to make it possible.

Peace to all,

Holt often wrote to Nat Hentoff, author of *Our Children Are Dying*, about his column in *The Village Voice*.

[TO NAT HENTOFF]

January 16, 1973

Dear Nat,

Some thoughts on your recent piece. I agree, we have to keep what pressure we can on Nixon. I am not at all sure that large street demonstrations are the way to do it. Sometime during the last year there was a poll which made a great impression on me. Perhaps I wrote you about this before. Anyway, the people polled said by some convincing majority that they considered *any* large-scale demonstration against government policy to be "violent," whatever the demonstrators did or did not do. Conversely, they would not apply the word "violent" to any action the government took to break up these demonstrations, including clubbing and shooting. Seem hard to believe? Not to me. We have to keep reminding ourselves of where we are.

I think there is a very real possibility, though we must be wary of jumping too quickly to conclusions about this, that Nixon is already losing or has lost a lot of the credibility and support he had on election day. I think at least a certain number of people are disappointed that the promised peace has not come; a somewhat smaller number perhaps feel cheated; and a still smaller number feel and share the horror you and I feel about these bombings. But I very much fear that any large-scale program of street demonstrations, even if they remain nonviolent, which is far from certain, indeed very unlikely, would make large numbers of Americans feel that the government was under some sort of attack, and so rally to Nixon's support. I think we have to feel our way very cautiously and carefully here, lest we strengthen his hand.

I hate having to write this. I hate believing, as I do, that very large numbers of American people, and very possibly a majority, are ready for, and would indeed welcome a very much more Fascist society and government than we yet have. I keep looking for signs that the American people, as a whole, are more sensible, generous, and humane than I fear, but the signs don't appear. If you know of some, do let me know.

I read the *Times,* the *Voice,* and many other liberal-radical-protest publications from all over the country. The cumulative effect of these, as you must know, is exhausting. From every side I hear reports of injustices, cruelties, and outrages that demand my immediate attention. If I had 240 hours in the day instead of 24 I could not do all the things that need to be done in these matters, or that I would like to do, or that various people, often friends, urge me to do. I have to find some ways to limit my intake of bad news, and even to limit my indignation at the bad news I hear. I am learning to greet much of this news—by no means all of it—with gallows humor, a cynical laugh, a what-do-you-expect? Otherwise I begin to go crazy with indignation, rage, and frustration. At least some of the time, I have to find other things to think about and do.

There is more to this than just self-preservation. People like you and me, and many of the people we write for and talk to, seem to me like people trying to pump water out of a boat. They pump and pump frantically; they call on other people to join them pumping, and others do; they pump and pump and pump. But the level of the water in the boat gets no lower; in fact it gets higher. At some point I have to start asking myself, maybe we are trying to pump out a boat that has holes in it. Maybe we should stop to find out where these holes are and find out how to plug them up. Of course, a certain amount of pumping has to go on even as we do this, or the boat will sink before we find the holes. But the pumping seems not to be enough. Or maybe it is more than just holes that can be plugged up.

Maybe the timbers out of which the boat is made are rotten, or have sprung loose; maybe the whole design is wrong. Maybe there is nothing we can do to keep this particular boat from sinking, and in such time as we have left we have to think about using as much as we can salvage of the materials of the boat to build another one, a better designed one, that will not leak and sink.

It's not easy to know how to divide one's time and energy among these priorities. But I know for myself that I have to spend at least some of my time trying to find an answer to the question, what is fundamentally wrong with human (not just American) society in this year 1973? Why is it leaking everywhere? And I have to spend some of my time reading and thinking and talking about what might be the design of a better boat, a better society, and in trying to help build that one even under the shadow of the old—to switch the metaphor for a second.

Some people might say all this is illusion, self-deception, a retreat from the rigors of the struggle. They might say that the idea of finding and patching up the leaks in the boat, or building a better boat with many fewer leaks, is impossible, that all boats by definition are full of leaks, and that life is just an endless struggle to keep the water level down a little bit lower, to keep the boat from sinking. They might be right. But this diagnosis seems too gloomy and too hopeless to me. And in any case, if only because of lack of character, I can't live that kind of life. I have to win a few now and then; I have to feel that we're making some headway somewhere, and not just being forced back on all fronts. Also, I do think that modern society is a boat built out of rotten timbers and unworkable design, and I do think I have some ideas about what is fundamentally wrong, and I can begin to see, if only very dimly, what the design of a much less leaky boat might be. So I have to do some of that.

No particular thing has prompted this outburst, just an unusually large bunch of bad news in the papers and magazines these days.

[. . .]

Peace,

John

1964–1976

Catherine Roques translated *How Children Fail*
and *What Do I Do Monday?* into French, and
worked to spread Holt's ideas in France.

[TO CATHERINE ROQUES]

February 13, 1973

Dear Catherine,

Thank you so much for your good letter. It seems like ages ago
that we had the election. It is difficult for me to describe the state of
my own mind. I am enormously busy and enthusiastic about a number of projects in my own life and writing, about which I won't talk
at great length here, saving more news for when I see you. I've done
a lot of work on the new book on the institution of childhood and
hope, though this may be unrealistic, to get it finished in time to
come out sometime next fall. Beyond that, I am getting more and
more interested in and involved with music and music education,
and in finding ways to make what I am learning in my own exploration of music available to more people. I find that music teaching
here is as bad as teaching everything else, and suffers from about the
same defects, so I may be in a position both to talk about what is
wrong and to suggest very specifically what might be done better,
and what is even more fun, illustrate it out of my own experience. So
I think that I should have two other books out within a couple of
years of the arrival of the book on childhood. All of this, as I say,
keeps me excited and energetic most of the time. I simply don't think
much about the state of the country and in a larger sense of the
world, and when I do, it is often with what we call gallows humor.
The news about the cease fire in Vietnam leaves me surprisingly indifferent. I neither believe in it nor disbelieve. I am ready to thank
heaven for small favors, and we are at least killing fewer people than
we were a few weeks ago, but I am not in the least convinced that we
may not start killing them at almost any second. I simply don't know
whether the few people who rule this country and who obviously
care very little about what the people think have decided to let events
take their natural course in Vietnam, which means that in time
Thieu will be overthrown and the country unified, or whether they
are determined to pursue their old objectives by new means, in
which case the war will continue and we will before long be em-

144

broiled in it in one way if not another. I just don't know, so I don't think about it very much.

Nixon has recently announced enormous cuts in the budget, cancelling all kinds of programs that Congress has voted. This has caused a storm of outrage which will probably continue for some time. Still, I don't think Congress is going to be able to reverse him. I don't know whether Nixon has correctly judged the popular temper or is simply using this opportunity to act out his long-standing fantasies of what he would do in this country if he could. I'm less outraged than many of my Democratic friends about the cancellation of these programs. They did almost nothing to solve the problem of poverty while they were in effect, and I don't think their being cancelled will make the problem very much worse. They may force a lot of our minorities and poor people to understand something about their condition that they would have to understand anyway, that there is no hope for them except in much more cooperative forms of action than they have been interested in. I hope that blacks, Puerto Ricans, and Mexican-Americans, and similar groups, will give up their notions about making it to the suburbs, and realize that this could never have been an escape for more than a few, and that they must now address themselves to the terribly difficult problem of making livable the communities in which they live—and doing this with almost no outside help. It will be a cruel task, but at least there is no reason for putting it off any longer in the hopes that some deus ex machina will save them. Obviously here I am clutching for what comfort I can; I would be much happier if this country had the kinds of policies about employment and social welfare that are taken for granted in much more civilized countries, such as the Scandinavian. But there are much deeper senses in which the highly technocratic, growth and progress oriented, science and efficiency worshipping societies of the late 20th century are simply not viable, and we may come to that understanding rather earlier than, say, Sweden, where they have been able to make this society work well enough to prevent most people from thinking about its fundamental faults. Well, here I am trembling on the edge of a long discourse which will have to wait until we see each other.

Part of my feeling is the resignation of the impotent. There are all sorts of terrible things about this country that I am not going to be able to change in the next few years, certainly not by griping about them. Furthermore, most of these things are likely to get worse rather than better, and again there isn't much I can do about that.

Though I have to concentrate on doing what I can do, like the juggler of Notre Dame, and perhaps out of this exercise may come things that will be useful in other ways.

[. . .] I never liked the doctrine, popular among young radical or revolutionary friends of mine, that things have to get worse before they can get better. I always say 'n reply, worse is worse, and the sicker somebody gets, the harder it will be for him to get well. But there is this much truth in what they say, that things may have to get fairly bad before people will begin to recognize that they are [bad]. It is the beginning of something when a sick person recognizes his sickness. All over the world, in countries of every kind of political and economic persuasion, there is increasing evidence, harder and harder to deny or ignore, that our present form of civilization or society is not working and cannot be made to work. As more people realize that, they will begin to ask in more fundamental and searching ways, what is wrong, and as they do that I think they will begin to hear what people like my friend Ivan Illich, whom I will see in Mexico this week, and a few other people are saying, that a civilization based on the idea or the myth of constant growth and progress, that the new must always be better than the old, is not only ecologically destructive but psychologically unstable because it must always promise vastly more than it can deliver, and must make people dissatisfied with even those promises that it has been able to keep. I will send you a xerox copy of an article which illustrates this. The man in the family being described owns a three bedroom house, has a fairly secure job, in short, is rich and secure beyond the wildest dreams of most of the world's inhabitants, and yet he is driven nearly frantic by fear, worry, frustration, humiliation, and the conviction that his whole life has been a failure. As I keep saying to my businessmen friends, to convince 99% of the people that the most important thing in life is to be a winner, and then to define winner and loser in such terms that you have to convince 99% of them that they are losers, is to create an extraordinarily explosive psychological and social situation.

But I am well into this discourse I promised to avoid, so will apply the brakes.

[. . .] I will most definitely come to Europe around the end of April, probably stay for six or seven weeks and certainly plan to visit you. Meanwhile, I hope you are all well, and I do look forward to seeing you.

Peace,

At the sub base in New London, Connecticut, 1943

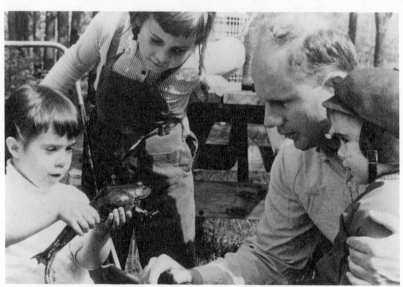

With students at the time of *How Children Fail*

With students, 1960s

George Dennison at the time of *The Lives of Children* (Photo by Karl Bissinger)

Ivan Illich (Photo by Claude Deffarge)

Overflowing paper, circa 1967 (Photo from the *Boston Globe*)

At work, circa 1970 (Photo by Lee Lockwood)

Giving a radical commencement speech at Wesleyan University, 1970 (Photo from Associated Press)

With George McGovern at Copley Plaza, Boston, 1972

At the time of *Escape from Childhood*

Clowning around with the cello, circa 1982

Posing, 1980s (Photo by Kelly Wise)

[TO IVAN ILLICH]

February 22, 1973

Dear Ivan,

It was wonderful to see and get a chance to talk with you in Cuernavaca. I went to Mi Inchito and had the mixiotes, as you advised. Was very good, though I think not as interesting as the food we had in the Yucatan restaurant. But the Mi Inchito was interesting as a scene and a spectacle, and I enjoyed it very much.

I walked up the long hill to the place where the road turns off to the Yucatan restaurant, and there turned to the right and walked over to the road on which Mi Inchito is located, and then walked down to it—quite a walk. I was tired when I got there. Later I walked down the hill in the center of town. On the way I passed the Go Cart track. I went there with Everett Reimer a couple of years ago to watch the spectacle. At the time it seemed to be very comic. These people driving these ridiculous small machines around the track were obviously what our young people would call on a fantasy trip, very much like the stories that James Thurber once wrote about Walter Mitty. They took their ridiculous activity so seriously that it was amusing. This time I didn't really get any such feeling for it; it seemed to me quite a terrifying ritual. Very expressive of much of the sickness of our times.

Thank you very much, too, for allowing me to attend that session of your seminar. I fear that as one who had participated in it I should have spoken much less, if indeed at all. I hope my contributions were to the point and useful. I certainly did enjoy the discussion. As soon as I can I will find in *Novel on Yellow Paper*[1] the section in which the narrator or protagonist, a young English woman between the wars, describes how and why, if she had children, she would talk to them about suicide, not as a cowardly act at all, but as a way of mastering and owning death. I found that part of the discussion immensely interesting, particularly the bit about the care which the state takes of those people which it has decided to execute. It is very much as if the state was saying to them, "Death belongs, not to you, but to us." I want to stress again how important it would be for a convivial society, and how powerful a weapon against tyranny, and the fear of pain

---

1. By Stevie Smith, published in 1936.

and subjugation which is one of the great weapons of tyranny, if people did in fact have that ultimate control of their own lives, the ability to end them even if totally helpless, bound hand and foot. I said that perhaps we should do research on such matters, and one person quite sensibly asked who might be the subjects. At the time I had no answer, but it occurs to me that people ill with terminal cancer might be interested in and willing to take part in such research. I have no idea how to pursue this further, but I think it needs a lot more thought, study, and discussion.

[. . .]

On the question of technology I think we may have to take a more radical position than we now seem to be taking. To put this a little differently, I think that you may be finding yourself forced into compromises on the question of an industrial base of technology which under scrutiny are not really tenable. For example, I think of your small electric reading light. I think you may underestimate the size, complexity, the non-conviviality of the industrial base which is required to produce even something as simple as a light bulb. The incandescent bulb was invented somewhere around the turn of the century, but I suspect strongly that it is the case that if someone had had the idea as little as a hundred or even fifty years earlier there simply would not have existed the supporting technologies to make it. Thus the incandescent bulb required a machine which, having blown a glass bulb, evacuated all the air from it and then sealed it off, and this machine was a good deal more sophisticated and complicated than the bulb itself. It also required that we have ways of making very fine diameter tungsten filaments; surely this technology did not exist even as much as a century before.

[. . .] All of what I am saying here may perhaps be summed up thus, that what we are proposing, difficult and radical as it may sound, and certain as it is to draw all sorts of the most contemptuous criticism, is on further examination far more difficult and radical than we may even suspect. I am just not sure that a truly convivial society will be or can be anywhere nearly as technological as we presently imagine. Man may have to declare his independence of machines far more radically than supposed.

Continuing this on board an airplane on the way to Chicago. Spent the night in Mexico City. Came in about 7:30 or 8 P.M., when the traffic was unbelievable, worse than I think I've ever seen it, certainly in Boston, though that is a much smaller city. Something about

Mexico City rather terrifies me. It is so flat, it has so little geography, there are so few reference points, and the taxis and buses take so many seemingly meaningless turns this way and that that after a while I get the feeling that the city is 900 miles wide and that I will never get out of it. The smog is unbelievable. Perhaps if I had time to know the city better I would feel more at home in it, but as it was I was glad to get out of it.

On the way to the airport I found myself thinking that those of us who talk about a convivial society may be open to the charge that we are opposed to change, and it occurred to me that we need to make an important distinction here, that we are interested in recovering the possibilities of change on a human and interpersonal level. And these words began to pop into my mind, that we have created a world of dynamic machines or tools and institutions, and static men; or living tools and dead men. Almost all of the change, growth, creativity that people would ascribe to our civilization takes place at the institutional level, but within these giant and rapidly changing institutions live many millions of people who are terrified of and paralyzed by this rapid change, by uncertainty, by the impossibility of knowing or influencing these institutions. I think a case can be made that we cannot have, and certainly do not have, rapid growth at the institutional level without giving up the possibilities for growth at the human level.

In this connection we really cannot say too often that institutions like the General Motors Corporation or Harvard University or whatever they may be are themselves, quite literally, machines—only machines whose parts are human beings. Like all other machines, they depend for their swift, smooth and sure functioning on the reliability, precision and interchangeability of these parts. The part must fit its place, it must be properly shaped, smooth surface, hard finish—it must stand up under various kinds of stress. As you have pointed out, it is the function of education in the modern state to turn people into serviceable parts for their institutional machines, which means killing in them the possibility of change so that the institutions themselves may change and grow more freely.

I think we may have to take account of a point raised by one of the members of Dennis [Sullivan]'s seminar, that what some of us might call convivial and others might call primitive societies have often, or at least as it appears to the eye of the outsider, bound people in very tightly and not allowed much possibility for human growth. I found myself thinking as she said this that we don't in fact know this to be true; it is very difficult for a visitor from one culture to get any feeling of the inner or personal lives of the members of another, and it may very well be that within societies which appear very stratified, rigid, role-defined, people lead rich and varied emotional and personal lives. But it is at least possible that the opposite is true. So it may very well be worth saying that a convivial society is not just opposed to rapid institutional growth and change for its own sake but sees the possibility for individual and personal change and growth as a value to be cultivated, encouraged, and so on. We are not only against one kind of change, but very much in favor of another.

Though I was at first, and somewhat unreasonably, quite put off by his way of delivering it, I found the report of your colleague on happiness and the limitations of the concept of happiness very interesting, and even more striking your six point summation of it. But it occurred to me as he spoke, and has many times, that happiness is not a notion or a concept or a feeling that occupies a very large place in my mind. Just as I said in Dennis's seminar that when people were really very much more different from each other and prized their differences, they probably did a lot less talking about "individuality" than people now, so it seems to me very likely that the fact that we talk so much now about happiness is a further evidence that there is something very wrong with [our] lives. Certainly "the pursuit of happiness" is a disastrous metaphor; I have often said in conversations with young people that happiness, like a great many other values in life, is not found or caught by pursuing it, it comes sideways, unexpectedly, as a result of other things.

Here I think we may profit from some of the vocabulary of the younger American generation. They don't talk much about happiness, but they do talk quite a lot about levels of energy, and if I am not often conscious of being or not being happy—though there are moments when I experience a kind of all-embracing joy which couldn't be described any other way—I am very conscious of the level of energy at which I am living. During the late parts of the Presidential campaign and the early days afterwards, I was at a very low level of energy, I needed a lot of sleep, I got up late in the morning and didn't get much work done. Now I'm conscious of living at a much higher level of energy; I have all sorts of ideas and projects that fire my imagination, and that I'm eager to get to work on. Now this has relatively little to do with the presence or absence of my worries or concerns about the state of my country and the world, or with feeling pessimistic one moment and optimistic the next. These worries and concerns are always with me, and I never feel what you could call optimistic. What makes the difference for me and my internal state is whether I feel that there are, or are not, things that can be done about it. It is a sense of possibilities still open that heightens my energy, while a sense that all hope is lost lowers and destroys it. And this is one of the reasons why it does me so much good to talk with you and Dennis, and to others of the seers and prophets of our time, whether they be Doris Lessing or Ronald Laing or Thomas Szasz,[2] or whoever they may be. Even in a situation of desperate emergency such as we find ourselves in, it is no small comfort to feel that one understands what the trouble is. It's something like the difference [between] being in the woods 20 miles away from the nearest habitation and not having the faintest idea of where one is, or being in the same place and knowing exactly where one is and what kind of a journey one has to make to get out. The journey may be difficult, but knowing what has to be done adds a great deal to energy.

[. . .]

I remember that one of the last times I saw you you were very interested in the whole question and history of measurement. I don't know whether this is still one of your active concerns, but it occurs to me that one of the ingredients of the psychological and spiritual sickness of our time is a belief that practically everything is measurable, including things like happiness. I find myself thinking of utilitarianism, and the notion of the greatest good for the greatest number. Some such notion is strongly linked with the idea of progress that afflicts our world. It is as if something like happiness were one of the elements of the Gross National Product. We need to understand better than we do that a great many things are not quantifiable, not comparable, that it makes no sense to keep asking ourselves whether we are happier than we used to be or as happy as we might be or whether some people are happier than others or what sorts of things we can do to *make* other people happier. This does not mean of course that I am indifferent to suffering, to real pain and want.

I remember when we were having dinner the night I arrived in Cuernavaca that you showed signs of acute distress on thinking, because of some impression I had given, that I wanted to be a better cellist than anybody else. No such notion is in my head. I would like to play the cello better than I do now, but by this I mean something

2. Novelist Doris Lessing, and Thomas Szasz, whose critiques of the psychiatric profession include *The Myth of Mental Illness.*

quite concrete—I would like to be able to play a lot of pieces of music that I can't play now. Specifically, I would like someday to be able to play, quite competently, let us say, the chamber music of Beethoven and Schubert, though not a great deal of what has been written since then attracts me very much. I would also like to be able to play, if not in a professional orchestra, which probably requires a greater degree of technical facility than I will ever have time to acquire, in a reasonably good amateur orchestra, so I can have the experience of playing some of my favorite pieces of music. But whether someone else or a great many other people play the cello better than I do or not is of no concern to me. And here I remember in your summary your pointing out that happiness was not competitive, a very important point.

In that opposition of machines and people, I have also these words—organic institutions and inorganic or mechanical people.

We have just landed in Chicago. The ground is lightly covered with snow. I'm back in the middle of winter again, and Cuernavaca seems a long way away. The stewardess has just given her usual landing speech. They make this little speech about having enjoyed serving the passengers and so forth, but the speech is canned, it never changes from airline to airline, it is almost always delivered in a kind of school teacherish voice—a perfect example of a ritual empty of meaning—and I should say that I think rituals empty of meaning are worse than no rituals. Odd, I've only been out of the United States about five days and it seems like five months. I find myself wondering what has happened here.

Looking forward to reading the proofs of the new book and will send you any pertinent comments as soon as I can. Now I have to get to work hard on my own book, which I hope I can complete this spring. Hope the rest of your seminar is as interesting as the session I attended—I really hated to leave it. Best to all.

Peace,

[TO IVAN ILLICH]

[undated postscript from the same period]

Some other thoughts about death come to mind. I said that people tend to think of their lives as a piece of property. Perhaps it would be more accurate to say that they think of their life as they might think of a house on which they had a 99 year lease. They understand that it is not theirs to keep forever, but they think there is a contract somewhere saying they are entitled to keep it for a long time, during which time it is as if it is their property.

There's a colloquial expression in English about getting a new lease on life—I don't know its origins, but I suspect they are a bit different.

The thought I am extending this letter to write is this—there seems to me to be a contradiction between the very proprietary feeling people have about their lives, that they are a "thing" which, for a while at least, they own, and are entitled to own, keep, protect, and the fact that so many citizens in modern societies constantly do or fail to do things that will shorten their lives. That sentence is not clear. They do things like smoking; they fail to do things like eat good food, exercise, get enough sleep, or to be more specific, fasten the seat belts in their cars. All the figures we have show that properly fastened seat belts will prevent people from being killed, or even seriously injured, in auto crashes all the way up to 60 miles per hour. These figures are well publicized and known. Yet in this and all other auto-dominated countries, only a very small percentage of people use seat belts. The new American cars have buzzers to remind people to fasten the belts—the buzzers don't stop until the belt is on. But most people go to great trouble to find ways to defeat this reminder, even to the extent of sabotaging the seat belts altogether, so that they can't use them.

Why are people in some contexts so careless about protecting what in other contexts they seem so eager to save? My own hunch is that most people find their lives so little worth living that they aren't much worth protecting. It is interesting to talk to young people who smoke a lot—when told that smoking may shorten their life, they say they know it, but that they don't want or expect to grow old anyway. I have heard people in their late teens say that they did not want to get to be old—when asked what they mean by "old" they say, 40.

Is it possible that this new fatalism about life, or the state of the world, may usher in some new attitudes about death, and thereby undermine traditional medical practice?

On the other hand, I don't know how widespread may be the hopeless and apocalyptic and fatalistic view of the world taken by young people in the counterculture. Perhaps the ordinary Westerner feels as he has for the past few generations. But there is the matter of smoking and the seat belts. Perhaps, since you don't spend much time in cars, the seat belt thing doesn't strike you as it does me. But I know so many intelligent people—both my sisters, for example—who never use them, but who will admit if asked that they know how dangerous it is not to.

For what it may be worth, I insist on using them, and am very reluctant to ride in the front seat of a car that does not have them. Some people say to me, "If you're going to die you're going to die, why worry about it?" My feeling is that if I can put off dying for a while, so much the better—life is a gift, I enjoy it, I have lots of things I want to do. Perhaps I am the aging lecher at the desk. Now and then on a plane I wonder what I would think if the plane caught fire or was obviously going to crash, and I usually think that I would think sadly of all the things I wanted to do that I would never get a chance to do.

My father is in his mid-80s, almost sure to die within the next year or so, kept alive by the miracles of medicine, though still with his wits and senses and not, I think, in very much pain. But when I see him and my mother (15 years younger) the subject of death does not come up. No one knows how to bring it up—I certainly don't. I think—and I may be wrong about this—that both of them would be horrified and offended if I were to mention it. Yet is this true? Perhaps it is I, not my parents, who shrink away from the subject.

In England I saw A. S. Neill, almost 90, and almost sure to die before I see him again. We did talk quite a bit about death—or rather, he talked about how he felt about it, and where it felt appropriate I made a comment now and then. But his death was very much the topic of our long conversation. I would like to have such a conversation with my father. On the other hand, though I have only seen Neill a few times in my life, I am much closer to him than I ever was to my father.

[TO PEGGY HUGHES]

April 5, 1973

Dear Peggy,
  [...]
Reading in your first big letter about your discussions in the [Ny Lilleskole] about politics and the way the teachers feel about society,

I have an odd feeling that whatever we do in environments we share with children, we ought to do because they seem like the most sensible, interesting, and humane things to do in the here and now, without hoping or expecting too much that this will cause the children to grow up to be this or that kind of person or to do this or that or the other thing. In other words, I think free schools make a great mistake if they think of themselves as incubators for later world changes. They may perhaps turn out to be such, or they may not; the experience of Summerhill has certainly been that the people who come out have not been politically active in any way, though I'm not offering Summerhill as an ideal and it is probably not as good an environment as the Lille Skole. But, like George Dennison, I've been troubled by much of what has been written in the free school movement in America about the kinds of people these young people were going to be. They might turn out to be in many ways rather conventional people, we would perhaps hope easier in their skin than most. I know a lot of people, including my dear friend Jud Jerome, who are living in rural communes of one kind or another, at least partly in the hope that this will help their children be very different kinds of people. I suspect that the time is going to come, and I suspect it will be a traumatic time for many of the adults, when a lot of the kids, having grown up happily in these places, will split for the big city and the wide world to see what it is like. No doubt they will find many things about it that they don't like, but I doubt whether the children of communards will necessarily be communards, if you see what I mean.

The school really sounds so lovely. I look forward so much to visiting again, and I think I will remember all of my life the day I spent with them going out in the harbor for a picnic on that little island. I think of other wonderful days, but none really any better than that.

I know just what you mean about ideas in the early part of the morning—that's when a lot of them come to me, in just that funny mixture of waking and sleeping. Sometimes I get one so good that I have to wake myself up enough to jot it down. If not, it sometimes happens that an idea that seems so vivid that I can't possibly forget it turns out an hour or two later to have disappeared, which drives me absolutely frantic. Fortunately, usually much later in the day or even a day or two afterwards, something will bring it back.

I find myself thinking that I will be coming to Denmark in a somewhat different frame of mind, eager to see it again and to see more of it, but perhaps a little less romantic. My deepened interest in music, my clearer idea of what my work will be, my closer connections with my own town of Boston, and in general a greater sense of purpose and cohesiveness in my life have made it a lot easier for me to live here at home, and I am resigned to a lot of things that I can't change, so I will really be looking much less at Denmark as a possible place to move to, though that is not ruled out if things get bad enough. Also, partly from my greater association with Ivan [Illich] and the development of our thought, and partly just from things I read in the newspapers, I realize that all societies suffer in one degree or another from the diseases which afflict us. [. . .]

Well, I will cut this short, though that hardly seems the word, and we can talk about all these and many other things when I see you.

Peace and love,

John

With publication of his book *Teaching as a Subversive Activity* in 1969, Neil Postman joined those who were criticizing the educational system. The "new book" of the following letter was *The School Book*, an overview of the people and issues that had characterized the educational reform movement in recent years.

[TO NEIL POSTMAN]

August 30, 1973

Dear Neil,

Some time since I've seen you. Your new book just arrived. I took a quick skim through it, and read the chapter on reading. Like what you said there. I wrote someone not long ago that perhaps the main reason why some people in society want other people to be able to read is so that they [can] more easily give them orders and tell them lies. You make the same point, a good one.

People don't ask me as much as they used to what I think about Marshall McLuhan,[1] but when they did, I used to say that for someone who thought that the printed word was outmoded he sure wrote a lot of books. I still feel that way.

1. Marshall McLuhan, author of *The Medium Is the Message*.

As I have often said and written, I am no worshipper of the printed word, and agree wholeheartedly with much [of what] you say about it. For all of that, it is a very compact, cheap, and widely available way of putting out a lot of a certain kind of information to a lot of people. In that respect not even magnetic tape can compare with it, and television is not in the running. The two media do different kinds of things.

Why do the schools not teach critical thinking (assuming, which I am not sure of, that it can be taught)? Because they don't know how to? Because they never thought of it? No. Because they don't want to. Their assigned task is quite the opposite—to convey a set of conventional beliefs, attitudes, and values. Can this be changed? Perhaps, *but not in and by the schools.* No use asking school people to reform the schools. Might as well ask soldiers to become pacifists. The schools, like the Army, are what they are because of what they do, and are given to do, and told to do. To change this is a political task (which like all political tasks has an educational component).

Not sure whether you've seen Illich's *Tools for Conviviality.* Would like to urge you to read it. I don't think one can understand what he is saying, even about schools, without reading it. It also says a good deal, more than any other book I know, about the social and economic and political context—well, that sentence isn't coming out the way I want, so I'll give it up. The book is worth reading.

The reason George Dennison did not do a lot of lecturing, etc., about *The Lives of Children* and education in general is that he did not want to. At one time I urged him to; I said we needed his voice. He said, among other things, "The difference between you and me, John, is that basically you're a teacher, and basically I'm not." What he really likes doing, and is doing, is writing poetry, plays, and novels, or fiction. Incidentally, he has written a wonderful book for kids called *And Then a Harvest Feast* which Random House published but is doing nothing about.

The matter of freedom is not irrelevant to the matter of critical thought, for obvious reasons. May I quote again the Harvard student, magna cum laude, who told me just before he graduated that he and his fellow students were careful to tell the professors what they thought they wanted to hear. As they say (or used to), it figures. A is not going to be able to teach B critical thought while he holds some kind of metaphorical club over his head, the threat of the grade, the diploma, the job. If you and other teachers want to get into the critical thought business, in any large way—most modern institutions like to have a couple of mavericks around, it's good for the image—they are going to have to get out of the grading-labeling-ranking-credentialing business. But the public and its lawmakers have put the schools into that business; they alone must get them out. Which leads us to the critical issue: people who feel no freedom in their own lives do not want it and will not tolerate it for their kids. A slave society will have slave schools, will demand slave schools.

Your book looks interesting and when I finish the one I am working on I will read all of it. Hope it does well.

Peace,

[John]

[P.S.] This spring I testified in the Mass. legislature on behalf of a bill, introduced by a legislator, to require the schools of Mass. to make available, on request, all their records on any student to the parents of that student, or the student himself if he was over 18. (The bill passed.) As I recall the hearing, no professional educator testified in favor of the bill, and a whole raft of school principals took the day off to testify against it. This is a very small-scale example of effective school reform. I expect to spend much more time talking to legislators and much less talking to educators—who usually wind up telling me that they would like to do some of the things I (and you) suggest, but can't.

[. . .]

After reading the novelist and critic Elizabeth Janeway's review of Richard Hughes's *The Wooden Shepherdess,* Holt wrote a letter to the *New York Times Book Review* saying in part that he was "surprised and distressed to find" in the review "the old canard about the infant psychopath—the 'roaring infant' who thinks 'he could and should have what he wanted just because he wanted it' . . ." and that a mother he knew, "who raised seven babies, most of them without help and many of them in somewhat trying circumstances, put the case well when she said, 'Babies are nice people.' Almost all of the many babies I have seen seemed so to me. Their wants are simple, natural,

basic, reasonable, limited, and easily satisfied.
They cry (not 'roar'—a semantic low blow) not in
rage and hate but because they are in pain or
discomfort, or are hungry (which hurts), or are
tired, or lonely and feeling abandoned, or frightened. . . . If a baby's cries turn into cries of rage
and hate, as they sometimes may, it is usually
because his earlier cries were unheard, or misun-
derstood, or deliberately ignored. . . ."
Elizabeth Janeway sent Holt a copy of her response, which read in part, "I read Dr. [sic] Holt's
letter with interest, for I find his work most illu-
minating. But honestly, two generations of experience with some highly estimable infants has
taught me that even the nicest babies roar, at
times, with rage. For example: Daisy Janeway, age
three, recently formed the opinion that, if she
wore her new party dress, there would be a party
for her to attend. By the time I had her clothed
in the overalls and sandals more suitable for a
trip to a Central Park playground, she was roaring. In life, the reality principle frustrates us all at
times, but this frustration is, I believe, a way in
which human beings learn to accommodate themselves to reality. . . ."
Holt responded with the following letter.

[TO ELIZABETH JANEWAY]

September 11, 1973

Dear Ms. Janeway,

Thank you for sending me the copy of your ltr to the *Times*, with
kind footnote. Think you might be interested in some of what I
have to say about discipline in *Freedom and Beyond*. Bears on our
discussion.

Was really thinking of babies in what I wrote, rather than three
year olds. By the time a child is three he has had plenty of experience
of living as a powerless and dependent person, and it may in many
cases have filled him with more anger than he can deal with.

A friend of mine went with wife and three year old child to a hotel.

When time came to take a bath, the three year old said he could not, because there was no bathmat—and there always had been one. The logical error called post hoc, ergo propter hoc. Things that go together must be causally related. Not a bad way to begin trying to make sense of the world, particularly when we consider that most of our researchers never really get over it—that is, they don't generally seem to understand that correlation cannot prove any sort of causal relationship.

Indeed, the whole notion of causality is an interesting and peculiar human invention—but this is a subject larger than I want to take up.

For a three year old, who has gone to a party every time she put on a party dress, it is not an unreasonable assumption that if you put on a party dress you will go to a party. If someone says, "No, you can't wear the party dress," it will sound as if they are saying, "No, you can't go to a party," not, "No, there isn't any party." I think reality could have been encountered more directly if the child had worn the dress and then found that there was no party—that the two weren't necessarily connected. Though this may have had its problems. But from a three-year-old view, it might have looked as if a perfectly reasonable wish was being arbitrarily denied.

What I am saying is that if you and I lived in the reality situation of a three year old, in which we were subject at every moment to the whim of someone of superior power, who more often than not did not understand what we wanted or if he did, did not care—in that situation we would be angry. In short, I don't think children are more prone to rage than most adults, or that the things they get angry about are any more irrational. Where they are at a disadvantage, and also often a nuisance, is that they are poor at controlling their anger.

But it was mostly about babies that I was talking when I said that when they cry it is generally because they want or need something important. This doesn't necessarily mean that the parents have done something wrong; I would say it rarely means that. But it is a signal for them to do something, take some sort of action. I believe that it *is* wrong, and beyond that stupid and harmful, for people to let babies cry, without making any attempt to find out what they want or need, on the theory that they will get tired and stop.

Many of the other points you make are excellent. I don't want to increase parents' guilt, because it so quickly turns into resentment and hatred; parents will usually find a way to take their guilt out on the child. But it is hard to see how people can take credit for all the good things a child does, which most parents like to do, without at the same time taking the blame for the bad. The real problem is not guilt but that we think we can play God, or at least Pygmalion, with our children. There's a comment on this in the book I am just finishing, *Escape from Childhood*.

If it is a burden to think of one's child as a lump of clay and oneself a sculptor with the task of making that lump into a human being, it is an even worse burden to feel oneself a lump of clay that others are shaping. Young people these days often make the bitter comment, "I don't want to have any children; I don't need them as an extension of my personality." The remark shows that they sense, quite accurately, that their parents saw them as extensions of their personality. This feeling is what produces much of the guilt you mentioned.

Reality. My editor cut out of *Freedom and Beyond* an example I wanted left in. Let's say a robber puts a gun in someone's back and says, "Give me your money or I'll shoot." If the victim resists, and the robber shoots, and is later caught, we do not allow him to say, "Well, I told him I was going to shoot, the only reason he got hurt is because he didn't face reality." We would reply to the robber that he had no right to force that choice on his victim, to structure reality in that way. But much of the time the reality we impose on children is not the Out-There reality of nature, but simply the fact of our own wills and desires. We say, "If you don't do what we want, you are going to be punished," and then, when the child doesn't do it, and we punish him, we say that he has to learn to accept reality. The only reality is that because we are bigger and stronger than the child, we can hurt him if he doesn't do what we want. He may accept this reality in the sense of knowing that it is a fact. But he has every right to be angry about it.

In The Wizard of Id,[1] the king is one day telling his subjects that they have to obey the Golden Rule. One of them asks his neighbor what is the Golden Rule. The other says, "The man who has the gold (power) makes the rules."

I have learned that when most people talk to me about Reality, the way things are, they are really talking Philosophy, the way they would like things to be.

1. A cartoon strip.

But I am beginning to wander. This letter is long enough.

And I am not Dr. Natural, perhaps, that you should assume I was. But a funny comment on our times.

Perhaps I will close by saying that we must be careful what sort of reality we demand that others accept.

Sincerely,

P.S.—Terrible of me to go on, but I just had to return once more to the three year old and the party dress. The point I want to make is this. If we grant, as I think we must, that it is not at all unreasonable for a three year old to assume that if she puts on a party dress she will go to a party, then it becomes important *how* we deal with this notion. If we convey to such a child that we think it is silly or ridiculous to want to put on a party dress, the child may be really angry. My own experience is that what makes children most hurt and angry and insulted is not being told that they can't do what they want to do, but being told (explicitly or implicitly) that they were foolish or wrong or bad to have wanted it in the first place. This is a very great discourtesy, and a needless one—and one to which children are very sensitive.

One of the reasons three year olds may be difficult is that they are smart enough to have generated some very reasonable notions about how the world works, and not experienced enough to know that in fact the world does not work that way. A baby doesn't know much of that kind of disappointment, because he hasn't been around long enough to develop many theories, and hence can't be disappointed.

[. . .]

[TO PEGGY HUGHES]

December 3, 1973

Dear Peggy,

Sunday afternoon, about 3:30 pm, quite pleasantly warm outside, about 55 degrees, gray sky, occasional few gentle drops of rain, really a balmy afternoon, sort of English-type weather. [. . .]

I've been playing the cello more and more, and this afternoon am interspersing playing with dictating letters. I don't usually dictate to you, but am this time in the interest of saving a little time. In some ways it might also make more sense to send you the cassette itself, but I don't know if you have ready access to a cassette recorder, since the Sony may not be reliable. If you do have access to some other cassette machine that you could play back these tapes on (or if the Sony is behaving itself) it might be easier for me just to send you a tape, and then you could have my mellifluous voice to go along with it.

[. . .]

Had some speaking engagements a couple of weeks ago around San Francisco, and took the occasion to visit Jerry Friedman and also see my parents. Jerry is now one of the planning commissioners for Marin County, and as such works in the Marin County Civic Center, which was designed by Frank Lloyd Wright. I'd seen that building in pictures, and later as I drove by along the road, but had never been in it. It is beautiful and graceful beyond belief. It makes me realize again what an extraordinary genius he was, and how sad that we built so few of his buildings and tore down so much of what we did build. It is a joy just to be in this building; it delights one at every turn. [. . .]

Stayed with Jerry at his beautiful little house in Inverness, on the edge of a steep wooded hillside which looks across a little valley to wooded hills on the other side. The woods, trees, are right around the house on all sides—it almost looks like a tree house. Doves come and perch on the railing and feed, and there's 20 or 30 California quail who know him so well that when he makes a certain kind of noise they all come clucking, walking out of the woods, looking for some food. And the place is alive with chipmunks, which are tame enough so they will come and eat out of his hand. Really very lovely. He sold his Volvo and has a new car, one of the Japanese Mazda jobs with those rotary engines in it. He's been wildly enthusiastic about it in his letters, and when he let me drive it myself I must say I found it the best car that I've ever driven, better than, say the small BMW's that I've driven. I don't need a car any more than I ever did and am not the least bit tempted to drive one, but if somebody pointed a gun at my head and said I had to have one I can't think of any car that it would be more fun to drive—incredibly responsive, quick, sure on the road, and because of the engine, quiet—even at very high speeds all you can hear is wind noise, indeed you can hardly tell that the engine is running. So he's very happy with that, as he has to do a lot of driving around the country.

1964–1976

From there I went to San Diego and La Jolla to see my parents. That was a strange experience, certainly not what one would call a happy one. There seems to be every indication that my mother has some sort of small tumor somewhere in the brain, probably an aftermath of her previous cancer. It's hard for anybody to know, as she doesn't like to see anybody or have anybody see her when she's sick, and doesn't say much of anything to the doctor. I think this is a mixture of stoicism, shame, and perhaps fear that if she lets the doctors have their way they will wire and pipe her up and keep her living in bed for god knows how long, which I don't think she wants to do. When she is well she is very much her old self, but she has changed in her general movements enormously in the past year, she's quite feeble almost, walks rather slowly and sometimes quite unsteadily. Her friends at the old folks' hotel say that she practically never makes a public appearance until afternoon, usually shows up for some sort of activity, has a drink with friends, eats dinner, may go to a concert, but most of the rest of the time she is alone in her room, as if she could only budget so many public hours per day. I found myself thinking for the first time that there's a very real possibility that my father may outlive her. He has been moved, by her, to a convalescent (so-called) home not very far away, a quite pleasant place from which most inmates never depart—it is the last station on the line. I think he knows this, though he did not speak of it. Not that he was that active in Ellingson Court, but there was always some kind of a mythical notion that he was part of the real world, whereas this is quite frankly a place where most people are waiting to die. He is very comfortable, has three private nurses, which insures that all his needs are taken care of. Most of the people there are not that well off. The place itself is quite comfortable, and I'm sure vastly more expensive than most places, but there are not enough regular nurses to look after everybody all the time, and such nurses as I could see seemed rather casual. It is a sad scene. The hallways and a couple of the public rooms are full of these very old people, most of them moving hardly at all, some of them making various compulsive and repetitive motions—there is one lady who at intervals starts a rhythmic slapping of one thigh, so that one can hear this slap-slap-slap going on. Still another one every so often, for reasons perhaps real perhaps imagined, but which in any case the permanent staff have decided to ignore, begins to shout at the top of her lungs, "Help! Help! Help me! Help me! . . . !" She has a good powerful voice and lots of endurance and this is liable to go on for some time. This is a little unnerving. Dad's nurses usually try to get him in and out of the place, when he does go out, by an outside route, without going through these corridors, so that he doesn't have to see these people, but he does see them now and then and know they're there, and I think, though he does not talk about such things, that he lives in real terror that his brain may go altogether before his body does. He's very conscious of losing more and more of his memory, though on the whole he is sharp of wit and even occasionally quite funny, in a sardonic way, rather more than I remember him being. But he finds it harder and harder to remember more and more things, and this really terrifies him. This, and perhaps also the thought that he may outlive my mother. I think he had it sort of fixed in his mind that she would take care of him until he died, and the possibility that this may not be the case must be alarming. I now suspect that one of the reasons she sent him off to the nursing home was not so much that she did not want his ailments and his three nurses in their room, as that she did not want him and the nurses around when *she* was being sick. When she feels bad she is like an old wolf, wants to crawl into a den and simply hide out and feel better—or something, as the old story goes.

I arrived in La Jolla on a Friday afternoon. Mum and I had made a plan by mail to go together to the San Diego Symphony that night. It was really quite an occasion. It is one of the few things we share, this love for music, and to whatever extent gifts or inclinations are inherited I probably got my love of music and whatever talent I have for it from her. I have been pleased that she was in a place where she could hear quite a lot of music. I checked into a hotel, saw her, and then went over for a short visit with Dad. I hadn't been there very long when he said to me, "What do you think of these attacks on our President?" I thought to myself, oh god, one of these times. But I went into a routine which I have learned over the years, talked round and about the subject and got the water so thoroughly muddied up that not only did my father not know exactly what I was saying and where I stood, but the whole thing got to be too much trouble to follow and [we] let it drop. Or perhaps I don't give him enough credit for shrewdness, perhaps he simply saw that I took the other side of the matter and that I didn't feel like arguing with him. For whatever reason, this subject did not come up again, and just as well. Now and then I wonder whether in steering away from such arguments I am doing the right thing. A case might be made that in these late moments of his life I owe it to him to discuss such things candidly. But really, when we get right down to it he doesn't know enough to make it worthwhile or interesting to talk to him about politics, and in plain fact I guess I really don't like him enough, in a sense, to want to get into that sort of an argument. It is possible to argue fairly heatedly with people you're fond of, because there is always that tie that binds you together. But it just isn't any fun for me to argue with Dad, I would much rather keep whatever conversation there is on a pleasant if superficial level, and that's what we did. It's not easy, of course, even to find things to talk about. I came back again to the hospital on Sat. and spent about six hours there, talking with him and to some degree with his nurses. This helps to pass the time and to make a social occasion—he hears these conversations and feels he is taking part in them, though in fact he doesn't say very much. As time went on and I got perhaps more comfortable at being there and he at having me there, we found it less and less necessary to talk, and could sit quite easily watching *scores* of mourning doves feeding on bread crumbs on the grass.

Dad shares his room with a most extraordinary old codger, a Mr. B., who lived in Iowa for many years, in a town named after his grandfather, I believe, and later moved to Los Angeles, and finally to this place. Mr. B. is 95 years old and spry as can be. He is a funny looking man, almost like an Arthur Rackham version of an elf or troll, great big jug ears, large rather awkwardly shaped features, but a very pleasant and eager expression. His wits could not be more sharp. He has for some time been interested in history, and arranges through friends [to] borrow all kinds of books on American history, which he reads, and then digests into small essays or lectures which he gives to some of the other people at the Home. I think he puts on one of these performances every week, so this means that he has quite a lot of stuff to do that he calls work and that indeed is real work, as he is not just doing it for himself, not that I want to make some kind of definition of work out of that. I mean only that he is not just reading history to interest him, he is actually contributing something to the lives of some of the other people and it gives a kind of point, shape and purpose to his life that is altogether missing from my father's. Mr. B. is apparently very fond of Dad, and looks after him—he is much the more energetic of the two. He likes to talk, and at the drop of a hat will do a great deal of it—I suppose at that age I might be equally garrulous. (Some might say, why "at that age"!) But I certainly found myself thinking as I left this quiet and on the whole sad place that when we are young we had better get our heads full of good and interesting stuff, because when we are old that is all we are going to have. I think with awe and not a little envy of Leopold Stokowski, 90 years old, so feeble he practically has to be carried onto the podium, but still conducting, and exceedingly capably, symphony orchestras. And Pablo Casals was an active musician until a very few weeks before his death. This might be one good reason for music if there were no others.

[. . .]

I guess through the papers and an occasional *Herald Tribune* you get enough of the political picture here so I don't need to send you much of that kind of news, particularly with your mother running her clipping service. [. . .] Nixon is doing quite a lot of traveling in the South, and is now giving us a big show of the energetic President, talking about the energy crisis and "tough measures." I went into the drugstore the other day and heard some person saying that we should forget about Watergate and concentrate on the energy crisis which was much more important, a very sinister point of view which I suspect many other people share. I'm afraid that unless really terrible things are turned up, and they are apparently there waiting to be turned up if he cannot prevent it, he will weather the storm, and will then decide that he does in fact have the power he said he had, and can in fact do with impunity the things which he has done. In that case, we can expect him to do more. If he is still in office a year from now, I think we can certainly expect him to be waging a kind of war against his "enemies" which will go well beyond anything that has happened so far. I may be wrong about this, and I suppose my spirits will go up and down as they do. But when I think of this possibility I think once again quite seriously that I might in the not terribly distant future have to leave this country. I was not on his original list of enemies, but my name is in enough files, and I have written enough angry letters about him, including many to him, so that I would stand a good chance of being on some list of people he could do without. Partly because of my increased interest in music, and my connection with the young musicians at Apple Hill,[1] I was really fully resigned to living in this country and doing my work

---

1. Apple Hill, in Keene, New Hampshire, is a chamber music center for musicians of all ages and levels of skill.

here, if only it could manage not to get much worse than it already is. But now in darker moments I fear that it may get a great deal worse and very quickly, and in such moods I think again about where else I might go. If this ever got to be fairly serious I think I would want to go someplace where there was a really active musical life. From this point of view Toronto or Montreal might be possibilities, and perhaps even Stockholm. But these are not things for the immediate future—this is the next year or two. I have this next book to write, and the responses I've been getting from lectures make me think it will do well, and more cello playing to do as well. Write when you can, we are hungry for news. Love to John, and all my other friends.

Peace,
John

[TO EDGAR FRIEDENBERG]

January 10, 1974

Dear Edgar,

Thought of you a few minutes ago, in circumstances I will describe, and was reminded once again, as many times before, of the day in which, perhaps without meaning to, and certainly without my knowing that you were doing it, you helped me to solve a tiny moral dilemma.

The circumstances was or were that someone on the street asked me if I could spare some change, at which point I gave him a quarter.

The occasion was that summer at Harvard years ago, when I went over to your seminar. I brought up with you a conversation I had had with my sister, who was outraged at the hippies being on welfare and taking money which really poor people, people with no alternatives, really needed. What you said, drawing on your experience growing up in Shreveport, had to do with the folly or futility of making judgments about people's need. If they say they need it, why not assume they need it? What better evidence have we to go on?

This turned around in my head for a while, and somewhere along the line I made a little decision, which has made my life much simpler—to wit, anyone, of whatever age, shape, size, or appearance, who asks me for money on the street, gets a quarter. Standard price for all. I don't even think about what they might be doing or what they might be using the money for, and I am a little embarrassed when they start to tell me a story or give me a reason, and feel like saying (though I never do), "You don't have to give me a reason."

I figure, asking people for money on the streets must be a damn hard way to make money or keep oneself alive, and anyone who feels he has to do it or has the nerve to do it will get a quarter from me. Maybe if I weren't a tightwad I would give more. Perhaps sometime I will though I don't feel that looming up.

I don't know why I thought that might interest you, but anyway I felt like telling you, so there it is. Hope you are well. I await bound galleys of *Escape from Childhood* any day now; Dutton plans a pub date of April 30. The book should make me lots of new enemies, including most of the professional defenders of children. I have already started to work on a book called something like *Doing, Not "Education,"* which should make many enemies of a great many people in the "free school movement," a thing which I now claim does not exist. I say all this half tongue-in-cheek, half seriously. These books seem very important, and as you will see, and as I say, they draw in part on insights and writings of yours. I think they take me well beyond where I was before, and should start some interesting talk.

Ms. magazine is going to run a big hunk of *Escape* in their April issue. A wonderful break; I couldn't ask for a better outlet. Hope you are well. The big long-range project of my life, at which I am now hard at work, is to become a highly skilled cellist. Will explain later how this connects with and follows from my other concerns. Happy 74.

[John]

Holt spent two weeks as a visiting faculty member
during the summer session of Mercer University
in Georgia. Before making the arrangements
for this visit final, he corresponded with Terry
Todd, the professor who had invited him to Mercer, about what the subject of his talks would be.

[TO TERRY TODD]

3/23/74

Dear Terry,

Here I am, on a very pleasant spring day or near-spring day, thinking a bit about the months ahead, and in particular about my visit to
Mercer. I had a sort of flash or vision which I want to take up with
you.

The vision is of me coming to Mercer with a list of things I want to
talk about, and the students saying, "We don't want to talk about
those things, we are committed to working as teachers in public
schools, we want to talk about how to do that, how to change the
system, how to reform the system, etc." This is not altogether conjec-
tural; this has happened to me more than once, at conferences or
meetings of one kind or another.

Now the fact is that I don't want to come to Mercer to talk about
such things. If the students are interested in that, well and good,
but then let them find people to talk about it with who want to talk
about it.

Is there any way I can make it explicit beforehand that I do not
want to talk about such things and am not going to talk about them?
Is there any way we can find out beforehand whether there are in
fact enough people who want to talk about what I want to talk about
to make it worth your while to get me down there?

I enclose a copy of a letter I wrote—I may already have sent you
one of these—when another group asked me to come to a conference. In reply to my letter—the one enclosed—they wrote back that
Yes, they were very interested in talking about these things. They did
not convince me, and I did not go; a friend of mine who did said that
the conference turned out exactly as I had feared, and was a total
waste of time. I want for my sake and your sake to avoid that. I am

basically an obliging sort of guy, and really don't like standing in front of a group of people who want to talk about A saying that I don't want to talk about A, I want to talk about B. But the idea of spending even as much as ten days sitting (standing, lying, etc.) around with a group of people talking about the reform of the schools makes my heart sink. As the old saying goes, I haven't got the stomach for it. We've got a society rapidly going down the drain, and in times like these to talk about how we are going to change schoolrooms seems to me so wide off the target.

I suppose, reading this letter, you may be thinking, "This guy is asking me for some sort of guarantee that I can't give him—how do I know what people are going to want to talk about when he gets here? and how can I tell people, in the space of a brief announcement about a summer program, that one of the visiting speakers doesn't want to talk about this, that, or the other?" Fair enough. And I guess there is no way for you to find out how many people would want to talk about what I want to talk about. Or is there?

But unless something like this is done in advance, sure as God made little green apples I am going to be spending ten days talking about "educational reform," and it is now a cardinal rule of my life not even to spend one day talking about it. I just don't go to these conferences any more.

By the way—only it's not by the way, but central to the point—it would be a very good idea if people involved in this summer seminar, and certainly my part in it, would read, in addition to the things already mentioned, Studs Terkel's book *Working*, Richard Goodwin's *The American Condition*, Miriam Wasserman's *Demystifying School*, which begins to point out what the true social functions of school are.

But Studs' is the most important. How do we "educate" people for a world in which 90% of the work that people have to do, if they get any work to do, is crap, moron-work. How do you *prepare* people for lives not worth living? And above all, if the task of school is to prepare people to live and accept such lives, how does it make any sense to talk about humanizing, etc., that process?

The argument has come to seem to me absurd.

Well, let me know your thoughts on this.

Best,

1964–1976

Sir Richard Acland, of St. Luke's College in
England, visited Holt in Boston in January 1974,
and soon afterward arranged for him to spend
part of his upcoming trip to England speaking to
students at St. Luke's and at the University of
Exeter. He also proposed to show Holt various
schools in the area, a proposal to which he responded in the following letter.

[TO RICHARD ACLAND]

March 23, 1974

Dear Richard,

Nice soft Sunday evening—we have had moderately cold weather,
but not much snow. On the whole a fairly easy winter, and just as
well, too, with the fuel shortage and all.

Thanks for your good letter. I would love to spend more than a
day with you, but am not yet sure how many more would be possible.
I'm not quite certain when I will arrive in England. I am in the midst
of putting together a schedule, and so much depends on who will be
where at what time. I will probably need a day or so in London, just
to do some errands and look in on my publishers there. For the time
being it looks as if I will have the 18th with you, and another day,
perhaps two.

Now, about visiting schools. The truth of the matter is that while I
am with you I would rather spend my time seeing the country, which
is lovely at that time of year, and which I don't know well enough,
and also talking with you, and other friends of your choosing, perhaps. I am not very keen on visiting schools, even the very best. I do
a lot of this, and it troubles me. My hosts, who are very proud of
what they are doing, take me around, waiting for the magic words to
fall from my mouth, "It Is Good." What I am usually thinking is,
"What is all this in aid of, anyway? What does what is happening
here have to do with the future lives of these children or young
people, or the society in which they must live?" And I reflect, if the
children are older than about 10, that in a properly ordered society
they would not, most of the time, be in a school at all—there would
be more interesting, real, and useful things for them to do.

It is a little as if someone asked me to visit a very humanely run prison. Now I know that it is more or less possible to run fairly humane prisons—the Dutch seem to be able to do it—even in Britain or the U.S. But the fact that there may be such a prison here or there says nothing about the deeper issues about penology, crime, punishment. The British and American publics may tolerate a few humane prisons, as long as they are small, don't make too much noise, and don't have any trouble—i.e. no prisoners escape, or anything like that. But by and large citizens of our country want prisoners to be given a hard time, and as long as that is what they want, that is the kind of prisons we will have.

I suspect we are likely to tolerate a slightly higher index of humaneness in our schools than our prisons, and, at least in elementary schools, rather higher with you than with us. But still—only so much. Most people, in this country at least, ask the schools to do one of two things for their children. They say, (1) If you can, make my kid a winner (2) If you can't, teach him to be a quiet loser, not to make trouble. In the process, do to him whatever you think will get the job done.

I don't want to visit any more good schools. The implication—no, let me start again. What seems to hover in the air is the thought, "See, this is what all schools could be like, if we teachers and teachers of teachers just do our job right." No. Not so. I insist that the institution is by and large not humane because its functions are not humane. Its function is to prepare the great majority of people in modern society to do work not worth doing and on the whole live lives not very much worth living, and to believe that this is the best of all possible worlds, and that they deserve what they get.

Shaw once wrote, "Be sure to get what you like, or else you will have to like what you get!" The business of schools is to prepare a few people to get what they like, and most of them to like what they get. As long as they seem to be doing this satisfactorily the society will tolerate a certain amount of open classroom etc. sort of experiment. But a system of schools that challenges in any important way the going assumptions and values of society is a contradiction in terms.

So—no, I really don't want to visit a school, unless your heart is really set on showing me one. I guess a good host always wants to show his guest the very best thing he can possibly show him, and if this is the one thing in the Southwest of England that you would rather have me see than anything else at all, well, then perhaps that is what we should do. But it will have to have something to do with the matters that you and I are writing about.

[. . .]

Best,

[John]

[TO RICHARD ACLAND]

April 27, 1974

Dear Richard,

Thanks for most recent letter. We seem to cross in the mail.

If you don't mind, I would rather you not convey to the students the message in your letter.[1] It does describe quite accurately a part of what is in my mind these days. But the thing I would like the students to infer is a good deal more radical even than that—to infer from my talk and our discussion, that is. What I want them to infer, to begin to see, is that *no matter what they may be saying and doing in their classrooms,* as long as they are teaching in schools which have their present social functions, i.e. (1) indoctrination (2) jail (3) establishing a social pecking order, they are doing the work of the establishment whether they approve of it or not.

I have come to feel—but I want this to come out during our talk, not before it begins—that to speak of a non-conformist or radical teacher is a bit like talking about a pacifist soldier. "I hate war!" BANG! "I hate the Army!" BANG! "I don't believe in war!" BANG! "I think it is wrong to kill other people!" BANG! "People should live at peace together!" BANG!

The Army doesn't care what you think, as long as you keep on firing that gun and killing "the enemy." When you are in the Army you do the Army's work. When you can no longer do it, you get out. Same for the schools. When you work for the state's schools you do the state's work, whether you like it or not, whether that is what you think you are doing or not. Refuse to be a jailer—i.e. refuse to keep attendance records; refuse to be a labeler—i.e. refuse to give grades,

1. Acland had planned to distribute to his students a statement which read in part, "John Holt . . . will ask you to seriously consider your relationship, as a teacher, with the existing order of society. I think he will tell you that you have broadly two alternatives: you can either help your pupils to be conformists, or you can help them to be constructive rebels against the existing order."

or give everyone good grades—and you will be fired, for those are the things that are important.

What I would like the students to see before I arrive is copies of my article for the [*Christian Science*] *Monitor*.[2] We have sent a bunch of them on to you, and one is enclosed herewith. That will give us a good jumping off place.

Best,

[TO ELIZABETH JANEWAY]

June 20, 1974

Dear Ms. Janeway,

I have just encountered, and read, in the December 1973 *Atlantic*, your article on men's fear about women's liberation. I find your points very well taken. Indeed, in talking as I am about the granting of similar rights to what we call children, I encounter very much the same sort of reactions, from both men and women, that you have encountered from men—and I think for the same reason, that people with very little power over their own lives, whose only power consists in being able to order around people with even less power than themselves, are very reluctant to give up that last shred of power, and cling tenaciously and ferociously to whatever notions may justify it. I've been struck by this not very remarkable fact, that the attitudes of most "enlightened" people toward children, not the people who quite avowedly hate children, but those who most sincerely claim to love them and want to protect their interests, are almost exactly like those of Victorian (and many current) men toward women—attitudes very well expressed in Ibsen's *A Doll's House*. I think your point about the women's movement being part of an even larger movement of the powerless against the powerful is very well taken, and I would urge what may be unnecessary to urge, that women come to see children as members of that same powerless and victimized class, and as much in need of the same sort of liberation.

I suspect none of us will make much headway in working on these things until we begin to come to grips with those aspects of modern society which make almost all people, men, women, or children, feel powerless, not just powerless to shape events but powerless to

2. "Imagining the Future: The Learning Society," in the Apr. 8, 1974, issue.

exercise any important control over their own lives. As long as a large majority of the human race feels this way, they are likely to find what scapegoats and victims they can, whether these be minority groups, women, or children—or any other class that they may single out as being in need of "protection," "care," or "treatment." Thank you again for your interesting article.

Sincerely,

Holt first wrote to Ken Macrorie after reading his book *Uptaught* in 1970. *Uptaught* and *A Vulnerable Teacher* (the "new book" of the following letter) were about Macrorie's efforts to wean students from writing impersonal, academic prose—"Engfish," as he called it—and about the university experience in general.

[TO KEN MACRORIE]

August 7, 1974

Dear Ken,

Thanks for your good letters and for the new book. As you probably judged from Margot, I've had and am having a rather frantic summer and have only been in Boston about six days since early May, and won't really come to roost here again until some time late in September. I have been reading *A Vulnerable Teacher,* and like it very much. Later in this letter I will write a sort of statement that the publishers may be able to use. For the time being, I will comment more informally.

First of all, I was distressed to see that the publishers did not, in one of the front pages, list your other books. This is always something worth following up.

I like the book *very* much. It is extraordinarily candid and revealing. As always, your selections of student writing are very interesting.

I really don't know of any books, with the possible exception of my own *How Children Fail* and maybe Jim Herndon's *The Way It Spozed to Be,* in which a teacher has so openly discussed his own problems and failures. I particularly like those sections in which you say that, following a good idea or a good paper, you felt sure that the class was on its way, only to find out that it was not. I know how discouraging that can be.

Some of your stories remind me of my winter quarter in Berkeley. I taught the same course to four different sections, and they were as different as night from day. One was absolutely splendid—I didn't even have to push the conversational ball to make it roll. I simply came to the, as it happens, apartment where we used to meet (there was a big "student strike" at the time), would find people there talking, and would simply go ahead with whatever was being talked about. In [two of the other] sections I generally had to do a little more pushing and prodding to get the conversation going, though once it was moving it moved of its own volition. But the fourth section was a total disaster. I don't know even to this day how it got off on such a wrong foot, but not only did the students not want to talk, but they got into their heads the idea that I didn't want them to talk. And they didn't tell me that either; I found out because one of my students in one of the other sections knew one of the students in this section. I was about ready to give up in despair, and perhaps blow my top at the students and say I was sick [of] staring at their surly faces, when a couple of my students from one of the other sections came in, because they had missed their regular class, and coming in as strangers got some lively arguments going, which seemed to get us off dead center. In this case Fate saved me, nothing I did myself. So by the end it wasn't bad at all. But it was, as you say, an agonizing experience.

There's only one thing in the book about which I would want to argue, and will argue, and that is the chapter about the "free class." In the first place, I think it is inaccurate to call that class "free." It would be more to the point to call it empty. Your idea, like many of the bright ideas I've brought into my own class, seemed good enough beforehand; it just did not happen to fit any of the interests or even abilities of the students. Indeed, even without your sad experience, I think I would have been inclined to doubt that such an idea, however ingenious, would have been able to sustain a seminar through an entire semester, or whatever. But what troubles me more is that in these days, with some sort of domestic Fascism seeming to loom up a little larger on the horizon every day, so many people, when things go wrong, should make something called "freedom" the excuse. Your class wasn't bad because it was free, but because you were basically asking the students to do something they didn't know how to do and didn't particularly want to do, and neither you nor they could figure out how to get out of this box once you had all put yourselves in it.

I think we should recognize, too, that to speak of a "free" class within the context of a school or university is to abuse language. As long as we teachers are at least in part in the business of selling grades and credits, our classes cannot in any important sense be free. We must throw away the carrot and the stick, which is, for me, a good enough reason for not working any more in a conventional school situation. I sometimes say that I teach no more draftees, only volunteers. The last time I was asked to do a course or seminar in a university I said that I would do so on the condition that there were no grades and no credits. This ended the project, as I suspected it would. But I didn't want students in my room for any reason except one—that they wanted to hear what I had to say or get into some sort of discussion with me.

The best discussion in print that I know of this really inherent and impossible contradiction in the notion of "free" classes within a conventional school, is the book *The Teacher Was the Sea*, by Michael Kaye, published by something called Links Press. This describes the attempts of teachers in a genuinely free secondary school to run classes which they hoped would attract and interest the students. In time they saw that this was impossible, that the whole class format is so foreign to our natural ways of doing things that nobody except under some sort of duress will for long put himself into one.

I'm reminded of something that came up at Mercer University, when I was down there this summer for a couple of weeks during the summer session. A number of other interesting people were there, and it was our custom from time to time to get together in the student union cafeteria and just shoot the breeze. I remember one afternoon when three or four of us were sitting around the table having a very interesting conversation. As more people came in we added chairs and enlarged the circle and the talk went on. But there was a point at which the conversation simply could not hold together any longer as a single unit, and broke off into smaller conversations. Some sort of critical mass. I don't remember exactly when it was, but it was about when something like ten people joined the group. It was no longer possible to continue comfortably with the feeling that we were one group of people all talking about the same thing, and the group began to break up into two or three sub-groups. I have observed the same thing at dinner parties. A dinner party of six or even eight can be a single conversational group. Put ten or twelve people there and for some reason that ends. I don't altogether understand the dynamics of this. Now the very idea of a "true" discussion in a class of anything more than six or eight people is for that reason artificial. It isn't really a discussion or conversation, but a series of more or less connected short speeches. I think it would help us to be aware and candid about this with students, and at the beginning of a class in which we were obliged to deal with more than six or eight students, to admit that there was something necessarily and unavoidably artificial in this format, and that the discussions would not and could not be like the conversations which people have in their ordinary lives.

But at any rate, in these troubled times, I am alarmed and annoyed when I see freedom made the scapegoat for all sorts of things.

This is about the only negative note I can strike about your book. I will say for publication that I hope every teacher of English, at the high school and particularly at the college and university level, or everyone studying to be such a teacher, will read your book. Between you and me, I will say that I wish I could think of a way to make this happen, but doubt it will happen. At any rate, I think it will be an extraordinarily helpful book for those who have the good fortune and good sense to read it. Perhaps there's another sentence you can make use of.

Another memory. I went to secondary school at Exeter Academy in New Hampshire. This was at the very pinnacle of the private schools. They had received a lot of money from Harkness to make it possible to organize almost all of their classes as "discussions." Except in a few semi-lecture or demonstration classes, as in the sciences, almost all the classes at Exeter met around large oval tables in a classroom, perhaps a dozen students and a teacher, and the idea was that the work was to go on by means of some sort of discussion. Being a talkative kid I rather enjoyed the discussions, and could play this part of the school game very well. I never got less than an "A" in English, and, with the exception of *Vanity Fair,* and perhaps one or two others, enjoyed or thought I enjoyed most of the books I was assigned. On the whole, as I remember, we had quite a number of lively discussions in class. But I do not remember that any of these discussions, however lively, continued once we stepped out of the classroom. However animated may have been our discussion about Shakespeare, Shaw, Ibsen, or whatever, when we stepped out of that classroom door the discussion stopped, and we did not take it up until we were back in class again. In our private lives as students, in our bedrooms and common rooms or walking about the campus, we *never* talked about such things. I remember no exceptions whatever. That kind of talk was for classrooms. If it went well, so much the better. But it had nothing to do with our own real lives. Of course, I cannot be sure that this is the case with college students, and more particularly your college students, and it may very well not be the case at all. But unless you have very solid information to the contrary, I would think it might be prudent to keep that possibility in mind. And it might be something that you would want to discuss with your students in some of your lively and more successful classes. Though I can see a danger there, too. Perhaps if students were made too keenly aware of, or were made to confess, that their classroom discussions did not continue outside of the classroom, it might kill what had been going on in the class, which was better than nothing.

My cynical and perhaps demoralizing point is that I suspect that even in our best school classes we are doing much less than we think to make great literature a live or relevant or important continuing part of the students' lives. If I had to bet, I would bet that very few of the students, even in your best Shakespeare classes, read or will read any more Shakespeare after they [leave] school. Maybe not. This might be something worth enquiring about. I've said many times that I doubt very much whether Shakespeare will survive another generation of English teachers, and I think this would be almost equally true if all the teachers were as good as you are—and I really think you are most of the time damn good.

So how do you like them apples.

None of this takes anything away from what I've said about the worth of your book or the pleasure I'm getting reading it. I do hope it will be a great success. At least it might help to bring many teachers to the point to which I think I've finally brought myself, at which I could honestly say that for most of my students I think I was finally doing no more harm than good. It would be a great thing if we could bring any substantial part of our educational establishment to that point. But I have no hopes of it happening. But your book, if read and pondered by enough people, might move a lot of them in that direction.

And I would add, and this is something that may be useful for publication, that if English teachers would read and heed your book they would find their own work a good deal more interesting and exciting, which is no small thing in itself.

Very sorry to hear about your heart attack. I imagine that this is a very scary experience. When the heart goes along as it should we take it very much for granted. When it ceases to do so I should think it would be a strangely alienating experience, as if you had some slightly unreliable or even treacherous stranger inside your ribcage, who might at any moment decide to do you in. I don't know whether this is what you feel. Perhaps by the time you [read] this whatever the problem is may have been cleared up. They do seem to believe that a proper regime of diet and exercise can do wonders for ailing hearts, and I hope this will be the case with you. Do let me know more about how you are.

I am as busy as the proverbial one-armed paper hanger. I'm very pleased with the reception that *Escape from Childhood* has seemed to have so far. At last I got a decent review in the Sunday *Times* Book Section—the first time in six books that this has happened. And *Psychology Today* will publish a very good excerpt (written by me) of the book in their October issue, which should be a very good boost as they have a big and serious readership. Do you know the magazine? It is well worth getting to know. It may be one of the best vehicles for the sort of thinking that people like you and me are doing. They're not primarily concerned with classroom education, but they are interested in it, and much of what you have to say is relevant to their concerns. It's worth checking out.

Time to bring this to a halt. Thanks for a wonderful book. I do hope it goes well. If a good supporting statement can be pieced together out of the things I've said in this letter, fine; if not, don't hesitate to ask me for something more. Good luck to you.

Peace,

1964–1976

Michael Arlen wrote a piece in *The New Yorker*
about children's television programs and quoted
Holt's article about "Sesame Street," which had
been published in the May 1971 *Atlantic* as "Big
Bird, Meet Dick and Jane."

[TO MICHAEL ARLEN]

November 22, 1974

Dear Mr. Arlen,

I very much enjoyed your recent article about "Kidvid." I was
pleased to see your mention of my article about Sesame Street; I
wasn't sure that anyone had paid any attention to it. The Sesame St.
people, though they made nice noises about it, certainly didn't pay
any attention to it.

I would like to take the liberty of underscoring once again a point
I made in that article, and that seems not to have been clearly understood. Sesame St. does *not* teach reading. All it teaches is the alphabet. But there is no connection—literally, *no connection*—between
knowing the alphabet in a language, being able to say the names of
the letters in the proper order, and being able to read in that language, convert written words into spoken ones. I can read in three
languages in which I do not know the alphabet at all.

The only connection one might find between knowing the alphabet and reading is a very roundabout one, to wit, that most first
grade teachers will not try to help a child learn to read, or even let
him, unless they are satisfied that he already knows the alphabet.
They think of this as a required first step, and insist that it be done
before anything else can be done. To this extent, it may be true that
knowing the alphabet may help a child read, or at least that not
knowing it may be an obstacle between him and reading. But my
goodness, what an enormous elephant labors to bring forth this alphabet mouse.

Aside from that, though here you may have more information
than I do, I have not yet seen or heard of any statistics which would
indicate that the school reading scores of low income or inner city or
nonwhite children have in fact been improved by watching Sesame
St. For the reason I gave, I would be most surprised if they had. But

as far as I know, they have not. If you have information to the contrary, I would like very much to have it.

Indeed, I would welcome any indication that, even if it did nothing noticeable for children's reading or reading scores, Sesame St. in other ways made the world a more interesting or accessible or pleasant place for them. I guess it would be hard to find out the degree to which this was or was not true. Such things are not easily testable. But I don't get any very strong indication, from what I hear about poor and nonwhite kids in cities, that this has in fact happened.

This is not just nitpicking. What troubles me is that I think that for a very small fraction of the amount of money that has been spent and will be spent on things like Sesame St., programs could have been started and resources provided which would in fact have done a great deal for the reading of poor and nonwhite kids.

Anyway, thanks for a most interesting article.

Sincerely,

Bill Whitehead took over as Holt's editor at Dutton after Hal Scharlatt's death in February 1974.

[TO BILL WHITEHEAD]

December 2, 1974

_____

Dear Bill,

I am actually dictating this in an airplane, just taking off from Kennedy on its way to Boston. I left Los Angeles on this same plane after doing a taping with Dinah Shore. She is a very pleasant woman and was very nice to me, but in general the experience was a bummer, and I'm sorry we did it. I doubt very much whether, as a result of that program, we will sell enough books even to pay the cost of my airfare. The whole context is wrong for any kind of serious ideas. The show is about show biz, and really I am only on there as another kind of popular entertainer—somebody whose thing is not singing or dancing or playing the guitar, but making wild statements about children—which, I will add, at some point the audience found quite funny, something I haven't run into before.

As I sat out in front and watched them set up the stage, always an interesting sight, and all the preparations and rehearsals, I kept thinking, "What am I, a man of letters, a writer, somebody whose living depends on the printed word, doing working free for these people who are my competitors and enemies?" I address this question in a larger sense to you and to all publishers. Somewhere we got the idea in our head that these people are interested in pushing our books. They're not. If they thought the advertising they were giving us was worth much of anything, they wouldn't give it for nothing. We are a source of free entertainment of a rather exotic sort. I think we are fooling ourselves badly about who is using whom.

Beyond that, I have other strong reservations about shows of this nature. Dinah Shore is, as I say, a very pleasant lady. But none of these big-shot TV people have time to read any of the stuff that's sent them. You must know how the operation works. What they have is a "researcher" somewhere, who reads the book, makes a whole lot of comments, spends a lot of time talking to me on the telephone, and out of all this prepares a short script, which the star reads, and a few questions, which the star asks. But all of this comes out of a background of incomprehension, and the result is that the discussion stays on a most shallow and trivial sort of level. Even when the star is not trying to be critical or sarcastic, it makes the ideas look and sound silly.

I think I would say categorically that there is no use in my doing a talk show unless as a very minimum the following conditions can be met. The interviewer must really have read the whole book. If someone isn't willing to say to us in advance that he/she will in fact read the whole book before interviewing me, there's really no point in going any further with it. It's only out of such a reading that there can be any sort of intelligent conversation, intelligent enough to make somebody think that the book might be worth reading. And I would [ask] that when the interviewer has in fact not read the book, they don't say anything about it being a good book or an interesting book. They just say that there is such a book.

I really think we really have to be a whole lot more selective about these kinds of radio and TV spots. When I say "we," I mean first of all me personally, secondly Dutton as a publishing house, and thirdly, the publishing business as a whole. In all of the very extensive publicity work I have done for *Escape from Childhood,* I can count on the fingers of one hand those interviews which were extended enough and intelligent enough to have any chance of being really helpful in terms of sales or even in making the book better understood.

[. . .]

Have written some more good stuff for *Doing, Not "Education"* which will be on its way to you very shortly. Have no doubts about my ability to get a completed draft manuscript in your hands by the middle of December. I think it's good, but then, I like the stuff I write. Hope you are well.

Best,

[TO BILL WHITEHEAD]

Dec. 9, 74

Dear Bill,

Chapters 16 and 17 will soon be on their way to you.

A brief word about my ways of working. The material I have sent you is not a final draft, not my last word, but a working draft. I expect to be revising, rearranging, adding to and taking away from that material during the next month or two. Indeed, I am always fussing with a ms. right up until the time the ms. is closed and sent to the printer. You will have to snatch it out of my hands.

But as I do this revising I need to have your thoughts and editorial comments to work with, and the sooner I can have them, the better it is for me. So please send me these comments as you have them, and I will take account of them, discuss them with you, and incorporate many or all of them into my revisions.

As I say, I am always open to comments and suggestions—Margot here in the office has made many that are helpful. I won't say I will agree with every suggestion or comment, but I will think about them and they will affect what I do. So please don't hold back, or think, "I will wait until the book is finished." I need your help to finish it, if you see what I mean.

best,

1964–1976

Holt corresponded frequently with W. H. (Ping)
Ferry about peace and related issues. Ferry was
active in the peace movement, and had been
a fellow at the Center for the Study of Democratic
Institutions and the Research Institute for the
Study of Man.

[TO W. H. FERRY]

January 29, 1975

Dear Ping,

[. . .]

I feel more strongly all the time that a healthy and humane society
would put much less of a premium on abstruse and abstract knowledge than we do. In a decent world, we could learn about it by living
and working in it, and by freely sharing our ideas and enthusiasms
with other people who were sharing theirs. Sometimes I ask myself
an uncomfortable question. Would there be room in such a world
for my beloved Boston Symphony? I'm not sure. If the price of living
in a world without classes, without higher and lower, without officers
and enlisted men, would be doing away with Beethoven, Brahms,
Mahler, Sibelius, etc. I'd be willing to pay that price. To which some
might ask me, then why don't you pay it now? To which I reply, I'm
not so sure how my not hearing great classical music would help to
bring about a classless society, and in any case I'm not yet convinced
that is part of the price.

Have to start some serious rewriting on *Doing, Not "Education."* I
still think it's a good book with an important message, but for the
first time in my career as a writer, I find myself thinking now and
then, "Will anybody read this book? Will anybody understand or pay
attention to what I'm saying?" This is not a doubt I have had before.
It makes it somewhat harder to work. But my energy and confidence
go together, and as I am just recovering from a cold and am a little
low on energy, I am likewise a little low on confidence, and both
should increase before long. Don't give up hope of my coming to
Scarsdale. Last spring and summer somehow got away from me, and
from late April until the end of September I was almost continuously
on the road, far more than I intended. I won't let that happen again.
Anyway, keep in touch.

Peace,

Tony Hille had started an alternative school, and
was also interested in taking his children out of
school altogether.

[TO TONY HILLE]

March 11, 1975

Dear Tony,

Thanks so much for your wonderful letter of 2/25. I suspect that
my letter may have conveyed a feeling of doom that I don't feel. Actually, there is a very important political component in my cello, and
if I hadn't seen it or invented it, I would probably not be able to
justify spending the four to six hours a day I am now putting in on
it. My point is that modern society makes people feel powerless. I
keep thinking of the distinction that Erich Fromm made between
potency and dominance. People seek dominance over other people,
or identify themselves with dominators, because they don't feel po-
tent, capable of doing things, changing things. I would like to dem-
onstrate that it is possible for somebody of 50 years of age to do
something that *all* the experts say is flatly impossible, which is to become a really highly skilled musician. If I can do so, I think the point
could be extended to a great many fields other than music.

I'm not really downhearted at all. In fact, in my whole life I've
never enjoyed life so much so much of the time. Considering the
amount of suffering there is in the world, I have to defend myself
against a frequently self-directed charge of callousness. But my suffering would not help these other people. Indeed, the only way in
which I possibly could help them is through my wits, and they work
better when I'm feeling good.

You're almost certainly right that the new book will do even less
well than *Escape from Childhood*. At this point in your letter I ran into
the thing from Melvin Tumin—No Good Deed Will Go Unpun-
ished. I read that just before walking up to Symphony Hall to a re-
hearsal of the Boston Symphony, and thinking about it I laughed all
the way. No saying has so brightened up my life in a long time.

Partly because I am feeling good, my fertile brain continues to un-
reel projects for new books. I can think of two or three, right at the
moment, that may have exciting possibilities. One is going to be
about the whole myth of perceptual handicaps. I think I can dem-
onstrate quite conclusively that the observable phenomenon of kids

writing certain letters backwards *cannot* be explained by the hypothesis that they perceive those letters backwards. I will develop this in a number of different directions, and put forward a more parsimonious and plausible explanation.[1] My rough guess is that this book will catch a certain amount of attention. So my feeling is that if you can't hit them from one angle, come in and hit them from another.

Oddly enough, I've been doing a certain amount of lecturing on the subject covered by the new book, taking a very tough position about what the schools are really for and what they really do, and I'm astonished by the responses of these admittedly pre-selected audiences. I think a lot of them, teachers, educators, student-teachers, would like to reject what I'm saying, but they simply can't find a way of doing it. Well, we'll see. [. . .]

George Dennison and I, a few years back, were talking about our futures, and he said an interesting thing to me. He said, "There's one very important difference between you and me, John, and that is that you're a teacher and I'm not." I think he's probably right. There are really three things that I guess I "am"—a philosopher and man of letters, a teacher, and a musician. I can no more help trying to share my ideas and pleasures than I can help breathing. My point is that people who want to teach, in that sense, who have ideas and insights and skills and pleasures to share, have got to find ways of doing it *outside* the Schools—through books, or lectures, or films, or other sorts of resources. For that minority, probably not more than about 5%, who really dislike the Schools and what they are doing, I think the problem must become, not how do we change or reform the schools, which can't be done, but how do we enable our children to escape from them as much as possible, cope with them where escape is not possible, and perhaps more important, how do we provide sufficient richness of other resources so that what happens in school will not be very important. I think this is the way we have to go. [. . .]

You say, "the drawback is that the [school] game takes a toughness that young children don't yet have . . ." I think we can hardly overestimate and almost certainly underestimate the toughness and flexibility that all young children have. Otherwise, how could they live through what they have to live through? Besides, I know children who really find out quite early in life how to get the better of school,

1. He never did write this book, but did present his challenge to the accepted idea of perceptual handicaps in *Growing Without Schooling*, no. 5, and later in the book *Teach Your Own*.

though they may not put it quite that way inside their own minds. Let's just say, school is the army for kids, we happen to be living in a period in history when everybody thinks all kids should be in the army, we probably can't change that for a while, but just like people going into the other army, let's figure out how to make that experience as little painful as possible, and get what we can out of it.

[. . .] Keep in touch.

Peace,

[TO RICHARD ACLAND]

March 21, 1975

Dear Richard,

I was going over in the last couple of days some of the diary tapes that I made on my trip to Europe a year ago. It brought back memories very vividly. I made one of the tapes on the train going down from London to Exeter, and I thought again of what a lovely visit I had with you and Anne.[1]

I don't plan to make a trip this year, for three reasons. In the first place, the publishing business is not in very good shape and *Escape from Childhood* has not sold nearly as well as we had hoped. It hasn't been a failure exactly, but it has sold many fewer copies than any of my earlier books. There seems no possibility that it will, as they say, earn its advance, which means that I cannot expect to receive any more income from it. Indeed, the same is true of *Freedom and Beyond.*

Also, I have a feeling that with the permanent energy shortage upon us, I really don't have a right to fly all over the place in jet airplanes just for the pleasure of seeing dear friends. I have not yet reached the point where I am ready to say that I won't ever fly in one again, but I feel a kind of moral duty to restrict as far as possible my use of this kind of transportation.

Finally, I have come to realize that if I am going to make the serious effort that I want to make to become a really skillful musician, I have to make some rather merciless choices about priority. I really have to cut out of my life a lot of activities and pleasures in order to make room for the one I now know is most important. Perhaps by five years from now I will have discovered that the experts are right

1. Acland's wife.

and that a person of my age cannot become a really highly skilled musician. If so, I will make some new priorities, and perhaps resume a life more like the old one. But at the moment I feel I have to make an all-out effort. This means leaving Boston as little as possible, and only in the name of important business.

Am in the middle of revising the ms of *Doing, Not "Education."* I have hung back from it for a couple of months, almost afraid to look at it or think about how it needed to be changed, but now I've put enough distance between myself and the work so that I know what needs to be done and am eager to do it. I think the final version, which I should have ready in a month or so, will be a great improvement, and a good book. On the other hand, I suspect that it will be a hard message for most people to hear, and that it will not sell very well either. I now realize with some sorrow that one of the reasons that *How Children Fail* and *How Children Learn* have been so popular is that it is possible for people with rather sentimental notions about children to read them, find in them confirmation of these notions, and go on living and working very much as they have done. The later books make rather more of a demand on people, and are therefore more uncomfortable. I might add that they are not assigned reading in schools of education. The new book should make a good many friends of mine in the school reform business unhappy. I am saying that as long as the schools have their present social tasks, they cannot be reformed, and indeed, that those who make a work and a career out of trying to reform them may in the long run only be legitimizing an inherently bad and incurable institution. As perhaps I've said, it seems to me that the very notion of education, of some people deciding that other people ought to be made to learn things which will be good for them, is wrong. Needless to say, a very radical view, and one that not very many people can be expected to agree with. We will see. I will try to send you a copy of the ms or proofs as soon as we have enough of these available, but I'm not sure when that may be.

[. . .]

Give my very best to Anne and other friends around there.

Peace,

Holt met Nelson (Bud) Talbott when, as a United
World Federalists field representative in 1946,
he went to Dayton, Ohio, where Talbott was also
involved with the UWF. Holt remained friends
with the Talbotts (including *Time* correspondent
Strobe Talbott)—often joining them on the
camping trips that soon became central to the
friendship—for the rest of his life.

[TO NELSON TALBOTT]

8/3/75

Dear Bud,

So nice to talk to you, and so glad we could work out something. It
will be great to have a good visit with you all.

Temp got up to 104 that afternoon. Didn't break the official record, because they now record it out at the airport, which is cooler
than downtown. But it was probably the hottest day Boston has ever
had. Now some cool air has come in and we are livable again. But
it makes me think about the many parts of the world where 100 +
temperatures are common and air conditioning and even fans unheard of.

Energy. You're right, we can't go on using more and more. But at
what point do we level off. Right now, the average American uses on
the order of 25 or more times as much energy as the average Asian
or South American or African. Clearly these countries will not agree
to level off as long as there is this imbalance. They are going to demand a fair share. Yet even if we could level off right where we are
now, and there is not the slightest likelihood that we are ready to do
that—even then, there is no possibility that the poor ⅔ of the world
could attain that level of energy consumption.

If we are talking about a leveling off of the world consumption of
energy, we must at the same time talk about a reduction of energy
consumption in the advanced countries.

In this connection I think of Mr. Sailer[1] and his pamphlets about
atomic energy and hydrogen as fuel, and his talk about available
technology. He drives me crazy. Right now, you can go out and buy
yourself an electric car or truck, a windmill generator for your

---

1. Probably Vance L. Sailor, a physicist at Brookhaven National Laboratory.

house, solar heat collectors, even solar cells to turn sunlight directly into electricity. All this stuff is on the market. Much of it has been on the market for years—electric vehicles are a generation or two old. People all over the country are building energy self-sufficient houses. They exist! But no one can go out and buy, or even see, a hydrogen powered car, or furnace, or water heater, or generator.

Why this extraordinary bias against what already exists, in favor of stuff that is in many cases not even on the drawing boards? I offer an explanation. Most of these scientists work for an organization which I will call Big ScienceBusinessGovernment. SGB. All one thing, not three separate groups, and least of all three competing groups. All of these people, whether corporate executives or Physics professors or Washington bureaucrats, want to see SGB, or SBG, get even bigger and stronger. This is why they don't like forms of energy that lend themselves to individual, or small-scale, or community action. With the sun and the wind, people, groups, small businesses, small communities, can make their own energy, decide how to use it. With atomic and hydrogen power they have to be dependent on SBG—those technologies can't be applied on a small scale.

One of the reasons I am so strongly in favor of energy forms that can be used on a small scale is that they will tend to make people *responsible*. If someone has a house powered by electricity and solar power, and a car run by that electricity, he will be careful about how he uses electricity. Like me on a submarine (and ever since) he will turn out the lights when he leaves a room, will not drive when he does not have to, and when he does drive will not accelerate wildly from red light to red light, but accelerate very gently, and coast to a stop wherever possible, as I do when I drive in traffic. I would undertake to bet that, driving an American car in traffic, I could get twice the gas mileage of most drivers.

When people are close to their sources of supply, it makes them prudent. People who get their water from a well pay attention to the water level. When it begins to get low, or when they run into a dry stretch, they say, "We'd better be careful of water, use less water for washing, recycle the dish water on the lawn." Whereas, when New York City had a very serious water shortage back in the forties, and the city was asking people to cut down on their baths and showers, etc., my rich aunt and uncle said angrily, "*We're* not going to cut down on showers, why should we, it wouldn't make any difference if we did, other people aren't cutting down, why should we be the fall guys, and anyway, it's the city's fault, they should have seen the emergency coming and done something about it, and anyway, they aren't going to let the city run out of water no matter what happens, they can always tank it in if they have to, they are just trying to make us responsible for their failures, etc. etc." By luck, heavy rains saved the city from a really serious crisis. But that's the way they talked.

When people are what Illich calls "institutionally dependent," when all the things they need and use come from huge organizations hundreds or thousands of miles away, they become irresponsible, careless, greedy, selfish. That's why, even if atomic power and hydrogen as fuel were in fact what they are not, i.e. safe and technologically available, they would not be as good as sun and wind and perhaps waves and tide, from the point of view of energy consumption and energy responsibility. And that is why I don't like these SBG type solutions. Even if they worked as well as their advocates claim, and they never do, they would make people feel that there was no real problem, that we could always count on THEM to come up with something.

If the world is to be saved, it will only be when very large numbers of people think, "How *I* live, in my personal life, can make a difference," and begin to act accordingly, that is, to cut down, steadily, year after year, our personal consumption of energy and resources, in every way we can find to do it. Without that sort of personal commitment, nothing else will work. For me, that's the bottom line—all serious thought, talk and work on conservation has to begin there.

[. . .] So much for my reasons for thinking that questions of scale are even more important than questions of technical feasibility and safety. Other things being anywhere near equal, small is much better than large—the smaller the better, the larger the worse.

All for now,

Holt wrote to Alison Stallibrass after reading her book, *The Self-Respecting Child.*

[TO ALISON STALLIBRASS]

Aug. 13, 1975

Dear Alison Stallibrass,
Have finished your book. It is wonderful and badly needed. It is astonishing—and yet not astonishing, for children are children, to

be seen by whoever will take the trouble to look at them—how much we are saying the same things about children. Parallel thinking. You may have much the same feeling if and when you read *How Children Learn,* though I think your book is even more valuable because it deals, at least in part, with still younger children. The youngest child I write of in *How Children Learn* was about eighteen months.

[…]

There are probably some minor points on which we do not fully agree. I have observed by now a good many family quarrels about bedtime, and 99% of them seem to me unnecessary and harmful. Those few people I know of who have not made sleep an occasion for banishment and isolation, but have instead made it possible for the young child to go to sleep where the rest of the family was sitting, later moving him to his own bed, or who have all moved into the child's bedroom for a friendly going to bed scene and ceremony, have had no problems with bedtime, or children resisting sleep. What they resist is being sent away from everyone else.

Also, I have become totally and intransigently opposed to compulsory schooling, or indeed any and all forms of learning based on coercion, bribe, and threat. To take away from someone their control of their own learning, their exploration of the world, now seems to me a terrible crime against the human mind and spirit. I suspect you may not want to go so far, though I find in your book very powerful arguments and evidence in favor of my position.

[…] best wishes,

[TO GEORGE DENNISON]

3.8.76

Dear George,

So good to hear from you, and about Susie's[1] exciting adventure. What a wonderful thing for a ten-year-old to be able to do. At the end of my new book I advise people who really dislike the schools to take their children out altogether, which more and more seem to be doing. One of the books that seems to be looming up on my horizon might be called *Growing Up Smart—Without School.* But Susie's work with the [Bread & Puppet] Theater is certainly a case in point.

1. Dennison's oldest daughter.

I will look for your story in the *American Review,* which I'm sorry to say I don't see very often.

I am torn between thinking I don't spend enough time on political obligations, and that I spend too much. There is a continued, sure to continue, and I suppose healthy if frustrating tension in me between the private man, who really wants to be a serious musician, and the citizen–philosopher–man of letters. I have at least a thousand times by now washed my hands of this crazy, sick, self-destructive society, and just as many times turned back to it in fascination and exasperation with the thought, well, maybe something can be done here, or here, or here. This will probably go on.

January was cold here, though Feb. nice. I guess deep winter is pretty miserable in Temple.[2]

[. . .]

The new book should be out soon and I'll lean hard on Dutton to send you a copy. I think it is very good, and most of all by this criterion, that if people come out of the book agreeing with me in any large part, they have some really concrete and workable ideas about what to do about it next. I guess it has always been a part of my self-imposed task as a writer to give real ammunition to the people who agree with me, and I think I have done it here. This is what so irritates me about [Jonathan] Kozol's writing, both in *Free Schools* and his newest[3]—the things he tells you to do, if you agree with him, are absurd and don't get to the heart of the problem. Thus, to suppose that someone who is really concerned about poverty and injustice in this country can best oppose it by talking against them in public schools seems to me so nonsensical that I can hardly think about it.

For anyone who knows the score, and does not tell himself lies about what is going on, and what is likely to happen next, these are very tough times to live in, let alone keep one's energy, sanity, and enthusiasm. If you are doing all this, as I feel sure you are, that is no small feat. I think I am; despite my strong conviction that things are very bad [and] certain to get a lot worse, I really enjoy life immensely and only need about 48 more hours in the day to do all the things I'd like to do. One of which is, when the weather gets nicer, to pay you folks a visit. Maybe in May or June. 'Til then, stay well.

Best,

[John]

2. Maine, where the Dennison family lived.
3. *The Night Is Dark and I Am Far from Home.*

1964–1976

Gerald Walker of *The New York Times* asked Holt
to write a piece about abolishing compulsory
school attendance, and he responded with the
following letter.

[TO GERALD WALKER]

4.16.76

Dear Gerald Walker,

Please forgive my slowness in getting this letter to you. In the last couple of weeks I have been doing a great deal of traveling and lecturing, which has deflected me from thinking about your request.

In a very small nutshell, the proposal you asked me to consider and perhaps to write about was this: if, by abolishing compulsory school attendance laws, we make schools voluntary, then we can kick out the troublemakers and leave the schools and teachers free to work with those students who really want to learn.

In an equally small nutshell, my response would be that it would be a very good idea to make schools truly voluntary, something I have been urging for some time now, and that this would indeed solve most of all of our problems of discipline and disruption. But we cannot make our schools non-compulsory merely by abolishing compulsory attendance laws. What makes schools compulsory, far more than these laws, is the fact that they have a virtual monopoly on the various kinds of grades, credits, transcripts, diplomas, and credentials which people must have to do almost all kinds of work in society, above all most interesting, respected and well-paid work.

It is tempting to think of the schools offering to young people this choice—either come here [and] do what we tell you, or if you don't want to do that, stay away. But this choice is no choice at all if the consequence of staying away is a life of exclusion, exploitation, idleness, and poverty. It is no more a true choice than that offered by the robber who sticks a gun in your back and says, "Your money or your life!"

Indeed, I think one of the important causes of the extraordinary hatred that many poor young people, white and non-white, feel toward schools, is that they understand that their lives and futures are so controlled and determined by this institution that from the day they entered made clear that it disliked, feared, and despised them.

196

To make schools truly non-compulsory, and to give young people a true choice of whether to attend them or not, we must do much more than abolish compulsory attendance laws. We must take from the schools altogether the power they now have to grade, rank, and label their students, to make judgments about them which will follow them throughout their lives and to a very large degree determine what they can do and become. Where society demands that people show competence before being allowed to do something, as in driving a car, we must test that competence directly, i.e., we must not require that people speak Standard English or be able to pass exams about Shakespeare as a condition of being allowed to practice, or even to study, medicine or law. And we must separate very sharply the teaching of skills from the testing and certifying of them, i.e., we must not let driving schools be the only source of drivers' licenses.

Beyond this, though it may not be relevant to the purposes of this article, I must argue very strongly that the difference between obedient and disruptive children in school is not that the former "want to learn" and that the latter do not. The testimony of a great many teachers as well as students over the past ten years or so has made it clear that with few exceptions the schools do not give a damn whether their poor and minority group students learn anything or not. Not only do they make relatively little effort to teach them, but what they do teach has at best little or no connection with the needs, experience, or curiosity of these children, and is at worst biased against them or downright false. The schools, in short, teach poor children almost nothing that would help them understand the causes of their poverty or ways in which they might end it.

Rich kids understand as early as poor that school is a waste of time and that hardly anything they are told there is interesting, important or true. But they play the game anyway.

They are trained to want and need the carrots that the school hands out to them. For poor kids, and from the very beginning, there are no carrots, only stick, and they soon get used to the stick. It becomes one of the lesser hazards of a life which is already sufficiently bleak, grim, dangerous, and hopeless. We may be very sure that the child who first hits a teacher has been many times hit, and many more times than that insulted.

Beyond that, tests and experience have shown over and over again that there is almost no correlation whatever between what people are taught or even learn in school and what they do in society. The schools rarely teach the competence they claim to teach, (see Ivar Berg's *Education and Jobs: The Great Training Robbery*) and where they do, they usually teach it far less economically and effectively than more direct methods, i.e. traditional apprenticeships. Still less do they teach ethics, as a casual glance at the current performance of our learned professions clearly shows.

The most important reason for making schools truly voluntary is that they would have to begin to learn to do what they have never done, help people to learn what they truly wanted to learn, and make available to people ideas and skills that were truly useful and important in society, and all this efficiently and at a reasonable cost.

This may give an indication of my thoughts on this subject. Let me know if you want to pursue further the idea of my writing a piece for you on this.

Sincerely,

John Holt

CHAPTER 3

1977-1985

PREFACE

Holt wrote in *Instead of Education,* about his belief that schools have basically bad purposes and cannot be made into good places for children as long as they have those purposes, "There may be no one who feels this way except me. If there are others who do, I hope through this book to find out who some of them are." By the time the book was published in 1976, he had indeed found people who agreed with him and were interested in thinking seriously about learning and teaching outside of school.

Always the pragmatist, Holt was particularly interested in those parents who had actually found ways to take their children out of school and allow them to learn at home and in the surrounding community. After talking and writing for so many years about what life without schools might be like, he needed to see families who were actually living this life, and to learn from them what was possible.

In June of 1977 he wrote to a mother who would soon become one of the early homeschooling pioneers:

> I find myself writing letters, more or less about the same thing, to a number of people, a growing number, many of whom are now beginning to write letters to each other, and it seemed to me that a newsletter would be a way in which we could all exchange our ideas and experiences. I'm quite excited about this, have lots of ideas for things to put in it, think it could be very useful to many people.

Thus *Growing Without Schooling,* the project that would dominate the final years of his life, was born. In the first issue he wrote, "In starting this newsletter, we are putting into practice a nickel and dime theory of social change, which is that important and lasting social change always comes slowly, and only when people change their lives, not just their political beliefs or parties." In *GWS* Holt combined his desire to help, in an immediate, practical way, children who were suffering in school, with his long-term goals for a society in which schools would play a much less active part. The newsletter was (and is) as much about what to do Monday as about lasting social change.

Along with *Growing Without Schooling* he began running John Holt's Book and Music Store, a mail-order catalogue through which he sold his own books and other books he wanted to promote. He had grown frustrated with some of the limitations of the publishing and bookselling business—his own books were often difficult to find, for example, and books he loved were constantly going out of print—and founding the Book and Music Store was a response to this frustration. He wrote to Henry Geiger:

> . . . I am going to try to do something about [the unavailability of my books], following Ivan Illich's maxim that if an institution stops working for you, you not waste much time trying to make it into something very different, but think about doing without it. . . . I have decided to try to sell my own books—and, along with them, the books of a few other people . . . all books that I feel strongly about, and that do not seem to me to be getting enough exposure.

In addition to the ongoing correspondences that had begun in the early seventies, many of Holt's letters during this period were to parents about the specifics of taking and keeping children out of school, and about what to do afterwards. Through *GWS* he became good friends with many homeschooling families, and spending time with their children allowed him to write more of the close studies of children's learning that had characterized the book *How Children Learn.*

Working on *GWS* took a great deal of time, and kept Holt more closely bound to the office in Boston than he had been in earlier years. He wrote to Ping Ferry in 1980, "I don't know what to do about the time problem—I get further behind all the time, and I can't see any light at the end of the tunnel—can't even see the tunnel." The tension between his interest in *GWS* and the homeschooling movement and his increasing desire to spend several hours a day on music was constant in these years, and never fully resolved. But *Growing Without Schooling* allowed him to turn his frustration at the failure of school reform into what he felt was constructive activity, and to surround himself, during the final years of his life, with loving parents and children.

[TO JUDSON JEROME]

May 2, 1977

Dear Jud,

Tx fr yr nice ltr. Quick response. I have learned by experience that merely saying that a conference will be about alternatives to schooling does not in the least guarantee that it *will* be about that. I have by now talked to a good many groups of people on the topic *Instead of Education* or some variant, and invariably I find myself hashing over old and to me thoroughly tiresome arguments about we will always have schools, it is a cop-out not to try to reform the schools, deschooling is for rich kids only, etc. etc. etc. Unless the conference is advertised as being quite specifically about alternatives to schooling itself, about taking kids out of school, any school, free, alternative, or otherwise.

One of the things I feel more strongly every day is that life is short. When I think of the things I want to do, many of them in music, I am oppressed by the thought of how little time there is, time left in my life, time in a day. Going to conferences, even alternative school conferences, is not my idea of a high priority activity. It might be, but only if we were discussing very specifically (1) Ways to get children out of school altogether, and what to do then (2) Ways to make certain kinds of knowledge and skill widely or more widely available, without the use of schools. If the advertising, publicity, etc. can state clearly enough that the conference is about this and not about school reform, then I will go along. But I would put up a little side bet that *even* in this case we will find ourselves spending more time than I want to spend talking about school reform.

I don't believe in schools. It's not just that I don't believe they are reformable. I don't believe they are needed. I don't believe they were a good invention in the first place. I think the very idea that what we learn outside of regular life is better and more important than what we learn [in it] is mistaken, harmful, discriminatory, class-prejudiced, etc. I don't believe that most learning is, or must be, or need be, or even *can* be the result of teaching. I am ready to talk to people who say, "If we accept that idea as true or largely true, how do we act on it?" But I don't want to spend much time arguing about that idea with people who don't believe in it. I think it's fruitless.

I am not closing the subject with this letter, but trying to make myself clear.

Best,

[John]

[TO JAMES HERNDON]

6/11/77

Dear Jim,

I'm doing a gig at Sonoma State College on June 23–24. Are you and Arpine[1] going to be around that time—I'd like to see you while I'm out there, which doesn't happen too often any more. [. . .]

We've just found a publisher for my newest book,[2] about 85% finished, about how I got so interested in music so late in life, and what it feels like to start on something like the cello when one is fifty or so. This is a piece of good news, as the lecture business is way down—at least for people who go around saying wild things, like me. Looks like the word has finally got out to all the teachers' associations that J. Holt is the enemy, and trying to put them out of work (all true!), so I don't get many calls from them. And the college students are mostly interested in Watergate types and stars of stage and screen (as we used to say).

Still, am enjoying my life and music very much, trying to think up new ways to scuffle up a buck or two and keep things moving along. [. . .]

Just read *How to Survive [in Your Native Land]* again the other night. Enjoyed it as much as or more than ever. Found many things in it that I had more or less skimmed over or not noticed the first time,

1. Herndon's wife.
2. *Never Too Late*. The publisher was Delacorte Press.

perhaps because I was looking for or thinking about other things. I've been going around recently saying that the whole idea behind "education" is that what everyone knows, as a result of living and working in the world, is much less important than the things that people can learn only in school. Didn't realize that you had made exactly that point about the corn and the flax.

Well, let me know whether you'll be around, and whether a visit from me would be agreeable/convenient/possible, so we can make some plans. It will be nice to see you.

Best,

[John]

[P.S.] Started to look up something in *Survive* today, and before I knew it had read half the book again. Always a pleasure. There are things in there that will make me laugh if I read them 100 times. But coming back to the book after an absence makes me realize perhaps more than I did what a serious and sad book it is. It is indeed hard lines that them instruments of death aren't going to be changed into anything different. Talking at the alternative schools conference in Chicago, which turned out not to be bad at all, I said that with respect to all the things I consider important, I now understand that I am a member of a minority. Some of these minorities, say the one concerned about energy and the environment, might be as big as 5 or 10%. Most of them are smaller than that; with respect to the way I feel about children and how they should be treated, I am in a minority of about 1/100th of a %. And those minorities are going to remain minorities for the rest of my natural life. I am not going to see the U.S. that I would like to live in. What I hope for, and work for, is that these minorities shall grow—and as a matter of fact, I think that most of them are growing, even if very slowly. I get some comfort and pleasure from that. Most, I get, though, from little details of ordinary life. At age 54 I don't feel old, but I sure do feel life is short and not to be wasted.

But reading your book makes me realize how much I am looking forward to talking with you and Arpine, and who knows, maybe even drinking a beer or two. I'll whip this along in the mail, maybe even call you up in a few days. [. . .]

I guess I can go on reading and enjoying *Spozed* and *Survive* all the rest of my life, but being greedy, I hope you'll give us another one of these days.

Visited a kindergarten the other day, 5 and 6 yr olds, taught by an old friend of mine. One of the 6 year olds befriended me; we spent a lot of time talking very seriously about this and that. It made the teacher, really quite a nice and bright woman, very nervous; she kept pulling the kid away to work on little Montessori Egypt projects.[3] And this was on the next to last day of school! I was disrupting the class routine she had spent all year establishing. And *she* is in trouble in the school, on the ragged edge of being fired for being a bit unconventional. Has praised *How Children Fail* for 10–15 years now, and still does half of the things I talked about. The Dumb Class indeed![4] Something about the environment kills the brains of the adults as much as the kids. Have to be awfully smart and awfully mature/stubborn not to be done in by it. And I realize that one of the reasons, perhaps the main reason, I got fired from two of the three schools that fired me, is just this—that a lot of the children thought of me as a friend, not a Teacher but just a person, reasonably interesting and easy to get along with, who took them seriously. That was an intolerable threat to the others, perhaps all the more so because they might not have been able to say what was so threatening.

Well, I'm looking forward to seeing you.

Fell to thinking last night about *why* educators are the Dumb Class, maybe the dumbest of all the dumb classes we have in our society (which is plenty). One reason is that a lot of them have been in the dumb class for a long time; they're not very bright anywhere. In *Survive* you talk about all those things that teachers do outside of school. Maybe that's true of teachers in desirable suburbs or desirable cities like S.F. and Boston. Chances are it's true of damn few teachers in Hammond, Ind., or McCook, Nebraska, or even the city of Boston. Such big surveys of teachers as I have heard of suggest that most of them, in their private lives, are very average and typical Americans, which is to say that they mostly watch TV, have no active hobbies or recreations, and if they read, read mainly mysteries and the *Reader's Digest*.

But the other part of my answer, and the more important one, is that because of the universal rule, that when learning happens the

3. Herndon used the term "Egypt" to refer to schoolwork that had little or no connection to the real lives of the students.
4. Herndon argued that teachers were "The Dumb Class," just as incapable of learning anything new, or changing their views about themselves and the world, as children labeled dumb.

schools and teachers get the credit, and when it doesn't, the students get the blame, education is an activity which never gets any feedback. As you say, all we know is that it's better than going to jail—and somewhere I have a news clip about a couple of boys in South Carolina, bless their hearts, who, given a choice by a judge of going to school or jail, chose jail. Unsung heroes! And by definition, an organism without feedback can't learn anything, just stumbles around in erratic patterns, like a drunk.

A fantasy. Suppose we imagine a country, in most respects like ours, cars all over the place, etc. In this country there are auto mechanics, to which people take their cars when they break down. But for some strange reason, the rule in this country is that, when a mechanic works on a car, and later it doesn't run, *it is never the mechanic's fault.* Everyone agrees on this; it is like part of a religion. Mechanics work on cars, everyone hopes they can fix them, the mechanics even hope they can fix them, say they want to fix them. But they are not obliged to fix them, are not held responsible when they don't. They just say, and everyone agrees, "We can't fix your car because it is a lousy car." Everyone else shakes their head in sympathy—"Too bad you got stuck with such a lousy car."

In such a country, what kind of people would tend to become mechanics? What kind of people would, after a while, fill up the auto mechanic business, and the auto mechanic training business? How much would they learn about fixing autos, or even, about how to learn about how to fix autos? They wouldn't learn anything. The business, though it might attract, for a while, a few people who really liked fixing cars, were good at it, wanted to do it, would for the most part attract and be filled up with natural incompetents looking for a refuge. Since the good mechanics would make them all look bad, they would mostly try to squeeze them out.

An absolutely sure-fire, 100% guaranteed recipe for making an institutional Dumb Class is to set up an institution which is not held responsible for the quality of its product, or work. Education is the #1 example. The Armed Forces are another; wars are usually won by the armies which can most get rid of their peacetime incompetents and find out who really knows how to do it. World War II is full of such examples. Every so often, wars come along and shake some of the deadwood out of the Armed Forces, so that at least for a while they have some people in them who really know how to do their work. But this never happens with schools. On top of everything else, we have tenure, which really locks in the incompetent. I forgot to say, in our mythical country, if you have been an auto mechanic for five years without actually blowing up a car and killing everyone in it, then you can't be fired, you can be an auto mechanic all the rest of your life.

Of course, this example breaks down when we ask the question, "How would people keep their cars running?" The answer is that they'd learn to fix them themselves, or else they'd take them to a lot of people who didn't *call* themselves auto mechanics—since, officially, only licensed auto mechanics could work on cars. A whole bunch of places called maybe Wrench Parlors would spring up. People would go by with their cars and just happen to mention that the car wasn't working right and someone would say, "Well, it might be the ——, let's take a look," and after a while the car would be fixed. You can carry on the fantasy from there, if you want.

We need an equivalent of Wrench Parlors, for kids and adults to hang out in, where they can do stuff and in the process show each other how to do it. The most important part of *Instead of Education,* which the publishers wouldn't let me put in the body of the text, with the probable result that most people won't read it, is the section about the Peckham Health Center. Doing places, that's what we need more of.

I imagine a Music Center—100 individual practice rooms, 25 or 35 chamber group rooms, 10 orchestra/band practice rooms, a few rooms for groups to give performances in—but not a school, not a conservatory, no teachers or courses, just a resource for musical people to use. A musical clubhouse.

Well, that's enough of this for now.

John McDermott arranged a lecture for Holt at
Moravian University in Bethlehem, Pennsylvania.

[TO JOHN MCDERMOTT]

11.21.77

Dear John,
Back home in Boston on a gray Monday. Typed the final pages of my new book last night, and feel good about it.

Wanted very much to say to you and Jack[1] how much I enjoyed my short visit to Moravian. On the whole, I enjoy my work as a lecturer, in spite of reservations I will talk about, but I don't remember many visits that have been as interesting and pleasant as this one to you.

Many of the things I ask teachers to do, or propose that they do, are so small, and so simple, and so easy, and so cheap, and so nearly certain to bring improved results in their classes, that I never quite get over being surprised and depressed by how few of them ever try them out. I have been giving enthusiastic speeches to teachers now for about 13 years, and at all these meetings, which by now must include something like 100,000 teachers, there are always quite a few who look as if they're interested in what I am saying, ask questions, etc. But from all the indications I have, not one in a hundred, no not one in a thousand, ever tries out even the simplest things I have suggested. Whatever textbooks and workbooks are handed down by their superiors, they use, and figure out one way or another to blame the faults on the children. A minority of them do think about how to make their classrooms nicer or happier places, but even among that minority hardly any put any hard thought into the question of how to become more competent.

I wish you would share this next thought with Jack. I always say that people have to work in ways they believe in. If you folks think that by getting students in your class to read certain kinds of books, and by having them hear people like myself, you can help make them into the kind of teachers who will later do things differently, that is fine. But I feel some sort of burden of proof is on you to find out whether this in fact happens, whether your ex-students, when they get out in the schools, do in fact teach differently from other teachers. I find myself wondering whether you try, and with what results, to keep in contact with some of your ex-students, and what they say about their work, and the influence (if any) of your teaching on that work.

What I suspect, and fear, is that for all of their reading of Dennison, Herndon, Holt, etc., your ex-students are teaching in just about the same way as all the other teachers. If you have reasonably hard evidence to the contrary, I would really be interested in hearing it. If you have no evidence, I think it might be a good idea to start collecting some.

1. Jack Dilendik, another professor in the education department.

I used to think, when I ran around giving inspirational speeches to teachers, that I was helping to change teaching and education. I believe I understand much more clearly [now] what my function is as a lecturer to educational conferences—that is, the reasons for which these people hire me. I have spoken of the primary and secondary purposes of schools. Secondary purposes are all those things about democratic values, cultural tradition, communication skills, critical thought, best that man has thought and done, etc. The primary purposes are (1) to keep kids out of the adults' hair, (2) to grade, rank, and label them, (3) to prepare them for life as mass producers and consumers. Most teachers don't even like to think about those primary purposes. Some teachers understand that they exist, but think that they can carry out the secondary purposes anyway. The hard fact is that the primary and secondary purposes cannot be carried out in the same institution, they are altogether incompatible. This is an extremely unpleasant truth, which most teachers shy away from, and one of the functions of uplifting educational meetings, etc. is to disguise it, to make teachers think that their secondary purposes are in fact primary. Teachers used to come up after my talks and say how wonderful it was to hear what I said and how much they wished they could do it in their classes, and most of them felt just as good for wishing as if they had actually done it. Well, even as an entertainer I say what I think, and can't help getting carried away with it. But I only really do it for money, and would do much less of it if I didn't need the money. I don't like wasting words, and least of all when they come as much from the heart as my own do.

[. . .] But I want to end where I started, by saying that my visit with you was really very pleasant and interesting from start to finish. Thanks so much. Give my best to your daughter. Tell her if she wants to write a letter to me, I'll be glad to get it, and will answer.

Best,

[John]

[. . .]

Holt first wrote to Daniel Fader in 1971 when the publishers sent Fader's new book *The Naked Children* and asked for Holt's opinion. To the publishers he wrote, "[Fader's] descriptions of life with his five black students are as moving, as beautiful, and as charged with meaning as anything that has been written anywhere. There are lessons in this book which, if we will only hear them and heed them, will go a long way toward solving the problems in our decaying city schools."

[TO DANIEL FADER]

3.11.78

Dear Dan,

What an extraordinary and unexpected surprise to see you at that conference. [. . .] You may know of the French expression "Esprit d'escalier"—all the things you think of on the way home that you wish you had said. The thing is, I always find a way to say those things later. I learn an immense amount from my second thoughts after a meeting. Indeed, by the time you receive this I'll have spoken at another meeting where I will have said all the things I wish I had said in Montreal. So, nothing is lost.

[. . .]

Since almost everything I say at meetings finds its way into print sooner or later, I can't help hoping that a lot of what I heard you say might find its way into the pages of another book. Any chance of this?

I'm reminded once again, as I was when I spoke to the same meeting in Illinois, that though I think I am a pretty damn good public speaker, one of the very best, there are some people who do that better than I do, and you are one of them. Your talk to those people in Montreal was extraordinary—extraordinary to me at least, perhaps not extraordinary for you, though it may have been an exceptionally good day even for you. I am a little reticent about saying this. Words are in my mind like "the greatest performance I have ever heard," but of course the whole point is that it wasn't a performance, you are speaking out of your heart and your life. I thought as you spoke that if you wanted to be a stand-up comic, you could be one of the best in the business, and if you wanted to run for office you could probably do that too. But even that may not necessarily be true; what gives your words their coherence and power is that they are hooked up with a purpose. Or, to put it a little differently, one of the reasons you are so funny is that (like my friend Jim Herndon) you are serious.

I often think in my own speaking that I wish there were more humor in it. Occasionally, especially with an audience that really likes what I am saying, and with whom I feel completely at home, I can be quite funny, though perhaps in a somewhat different style than you. But I have also learned that humor must be effortless, and that to "try to be funny" would be a fatal mistake for me.

Talking to those folks after your meeting, I remember that you said something about making people feel good about your work. I felt a pang of conscience about this, because I certainly hadn't made much of an effort to do that in my talks at the meeting. But then later I thought, suppose you think that the people are doing real harm, which is what I think. In fact, this makes it very difficult for me to know how to speak to meetings of teachers. I've come to believe, strongly, although possibly wrongly, that the experience of school, from first grade on, is *deeply* harmful to almost all children, that most teachers, most of the time, do real harm. Furthermore, I am no longer able to believe, as I once did, that huge numbers of them would do very differently and much better if, as I once said, "they only knew how or dared." I have seen what is for me sufficient evidence that this is not the case. One of those pieces of evidence is this, that teachers who try to be what you and I have tried to be with our students (which got me fired from three schools in spite of the fact that test scores were higher), meet *first of all* the hostility, resentment, contempt of their colleagues. Even before they get in trouble with the principal or the parents, they are in trouble with their fellow teachers. I have been told this over and over again by educational innovators in many parts of the country, and I believe it to be so.

If we list the harmful practices of schools, among them tracking, which I was certainly glad to see you come down hard on, I cannot think of a single one which teachers have opposed in any organized way. The one possible exception might be class size, but I don't think teachers oppose that for the right reasons. Every other one of the destructive practices of schools, which teachers could do a lot to change if they wanted to—certainly in places where the Union is strong, as in New York—has been, if anything, supported by organized teachers' groups. Not only, then, do I believe that most teachers are doing great harm to their students, but I no longer believe that there is among them any great wish or will to do anything very different. I think of Charles Silberman's statement about the "appalling incivility" with which almost all adults in schools treat almost all students.[1] My own experience conforms to it.

[. . .]

I am quite often asked to sympathize with teachers, and it reminds me of times when supporters of our war in Vietnam would say to opponents of that war, "Why don't you show a little sympathy for American soldiers?" I used to think that I was ready to show them all the sympathy of the world, once they stopped doing harm. In like manner, I want to say to teachers, "I'd be glad to be on your side, if you will just stop hurting the kids." I suppose charity, Christian or otherwise, ought to go further than this. I remember A. J. Muste's famous (and horrendously difficult) words, "If I can't love Hitler, I can't love anybody." I know what he means, but I haven't got to that point yet, and don't know if I ever will. I have come to feel for schools, as much for their stupidity as for their cruelty and inhumanity, a dislike so strong that it comes very close to what I might call hatred. I am not comfortable with this, don't like feeling this way, keep looking for reasons—they have to be real reasons—for feeling some other way, and so far I have not found them. The schools seem to me to get steadily worse, and worse in ways they would never have dreamed of a century ago.

For such reasons I have decided, when I talk to groups of teachers, not to talk very much about schools in any large sense, or try to make them into something different, but something much more modest— how to become competent at one's daily work, how to teach the three R's skillfully and well, as in the meeting at Montreal. But very often I find that teachers are not interested in that. Large numbers of them seem perfectly content to accept whatever the administration hands down in the way of texts, workbooks, teachers' manuals, and to say that children who don't learn by these methods have something wrong inside their heads, must be some kind of mental

1. In Silberman's book, *Crisis in the Classroom*.

cripples. I talk to teachers about taking responsibility for the results of their own work, and not accepting excuses in place of performance. Most of them don't want to hear such talk.

So, I know I ought to be more charitable than I am, but I don't really know how to go about it. I have become an adversary of the schools. I mean to do all I can to make them noncompulsory, to find ways to help more and more people and/or their children escape from them, and to take from them by law their power to make definitive and lasting judgments about people, i.e. their power to grade and label. Anyone who wants to join me in that work, teacher, administrator, or whatever, I will welcome as an ally. Other people, I'm afraid, are adversaries. A professor of Education at B.U. just wrote me a letter, and signed it "Your would-be ally." I thought, you ain't no ally of mine, not unless you will join me at striking at what I think is the heart of the evil. Which he does not. He talks a good deal, not very eloquently or persuasively, about humanistic education, but I don't know of a single bad school practice which he has publicly opposed.

This letter has turned out to be a good deal longer than I thought it would be when I started, but that's what happens to men of letters. I can't say what a pleasure it was to see you again, and I certainly am not going to let that many years go by before we meet again, especially as you come by this way. Let's really make strong plans to get together when you are on the Cape or on your way there. I like riding the bus down to the Cape; I consider that part of my native land, and my strictures against travel don't apply to it. Even New York City has become foreign territory, though I have almost always enjoyed myself there; I don't think I've been down there in close to two years now.

Say hello to my friend Elliot Berg there in Ann Arbor. I know people say things like that to people all the time, but he is really a very refreshing and jovial person, and an original, independent, unstuffy thinker. I think you might hit it off extremely well. In any case, say hello to him for me. Great to see you again. Keep in touch.

Best,

[. . .]

[TO IVAN ILLICH]

5.24.78

___

Dear Ivan,

Your manuscript about language arrived in this morning's mail, and I instantly read it.[1] I can't tell you how excited I am by it. It digs very deep, it is a kind of foundation for all the other things that you, and I in my own way, have been talking about.

I hate to think how few of your hearers at U. Mass. may have understood you. But for those that did, it will make a great deal of difference.

The whole piece connects itself with a deep anger that I have felt for a great many years now, but not really been able to understand or express, when people talked about "literacy." I don't mean literacy in the narrow sense of being able to read and write, but in some larger sense of being able to "talk good English," or whatever language is intended.

Even in some of my earliest books I argued fiercely that children from our poorest communities, whom the schools were constantly labeling as "inarticulate," could in fact and did in fact talk to each other in their play and when outside of school, with the greatest expressiveness and fluency.

I think of the insufferable Basil Bernstein's[2] doctrine, very popular in Great Britain, about the language of poor people being a "restricted code." Have you been familiar with that particular remark? School people in Great Britain, and I guess here too, like your friends in the South Bronx, have long felt it was part of their mission to save children from the language of their parents.

I find myself remembering something you said to me quite a number of years ago, that has always stuck in my mind. We were talking about writing, and you were saying that you envied me my ease in English. You went on to remark that you had never had a "mother tongue." Those were your words. You went on to say that you spoke a great many languages, but all as learned languages. I don't think

1. Published in the fall of 1979 as "Vernacular Values and Education," in *Teachers College Record*, vol. 81, no. 1. The book *Shadow Work* is a fuller treatment of the same subject.
2. Basil Bernstein is a British sociolinguist and author of the book *Class, Codes and Control*.

the distinction between learned speech and the vernacular was as clear for you then as it has become. But I must assume it was thoughts like that that led you to the thinking and reading and writing that produced this article. I remember you saying that when you were sorting out your own thoughts, it was often most comfortable for you to do it in Latin.

There was a time, not very many years ago, when I was seriously thinking of emigrating from the United States to another country. I was afraid that under Nixon and Agnew we would have some kind of Fascism in which I would hardly be safe, and in any case which I would find so disagreeable that I would not want to be around it. I can just barely manage to live in the USA as it is, but that would have been too much. I had thought of emigrating to one of the Scandinavian countries, either Denmark or Norway, both of which I love though in rather different ways. A number of things held me back, but perhaps the strongest, or one of the strongest, was that I would have to give up the use of English. I realized that I loved the language I speak and write, and feel it so much as a part and extension of me that giving up using it would be like amputating a leg. I knew that, since I am good at learning languages, I could learn to speak Danish or Norwegian fluently, as fluently as I wanted to. But they would never be an organic part of me in the way that English was, and I knew that I would miss this very much.

I remember something else, too. When I went to France in 1952, having had some school French as a kid, I really could not speak a word of it. I began to learn the language, a little bit by study, but mostly by reading it and hearing what people were saying around me. Later I went on a long bicycle trip through France and down into Italy, in the course of which I became quite good at speaking French and could even speak a little Italian. In those days there were very few Americans traveling in Europe, even in the big cities, and very few people spoke English. I, being quite shy then, was very pleased to find out how warmly people responded to my efforts to speak their language, and I think one of the reasons for this was that I tried to speak it the way they spoke it. I learned later that there were Americans in Paris who spoke a French that was much more fluent and "correct" than mine. But this French annoyed—might not annoy any longer—a great many of the French people with whom they came into contact, precisely because the American was using French *only* as a tool, to get *from* French people whatever he wanted. He was not interested in trying to become part of a community of French-speaking people. But I was, and it made a great difference to my hearers. I can remember, when I was still speaking really very little Italian, some Italians complimenting me on my Italian. I protested that I knew very few words. They said that wasn't what they meant at all, that I spoke such Italian as if I *were* Italian. I think this must be very close to the point you are making.

You are certainly right about academic speech. One of my vivid memories of early days in Boston was of meeting Jerome Bruner, whom I had earlier met in Colorado, after a football game. He invited me to come with him to a small gathering at his house, at which some friends would come in for drinks and talk. There were perhaps a dozen or so people there, including Bruner and Albert Guerard, a noted scholar and expert on, among other things, Joseph Conrad. I was then in no way an educational radical. I was perfectly prepared to have the highest regard for Harvard and similar universities. I liked Jerry Bruner, as little as I had seen of him, and was greatly flattered at having been invited to his house. But a strange thing happened. He and Albert Guerard got into some kind of a conversation/argument about some literary or philosophical point. They talked with great brilliance, and I only slowly became aware with growing surprise and quite literally *horror* that they did not give a damn about anything they were saying. They were talking as an exercise in talk, and to impress their hearers. My reaction to this was a naive one, and so I think entirely trustworthy. I was absolutely appalled by this performance, and I don't think I ever went to Bruner's house again, though I would see him once or twice in the course of my work.

One of the reasons, as a matter of fact, that I like professional musicians is that they are very no-bullshit people. By this I mean, of course, performing musicians, not critics, scholars, etc. Music, their instruments, their voices, are the tools with which they work, so they don't think of language as a tool, and express themselves, on the whole, with a lot of the simplicity and directness of peasants. Not as much, of course, since simply by virtue of living in this corrupt society they have been corrupted. But they don't talk to impress people.

In another way we have come independently to the same conclusion. I find myself thinking, saying, and writing more and more in recent months that the very idea of a full-time teacher is deeply mistaken, that whatever teaching we do we ought to do as an incidental part of the rest of our life. I hardly think any more that it's possible to be a full-time teacher, I don't care [in] what kind of school or institutional setting, without somehow corrupting the relationships between oneself and other people, and I guess that is exactly the point you are making.

I really respond very strongly to this splendid piece of yours, because I have felt, in ways these anecdotes illustrate, a growing horror and anger at the corruption of speech in human life. There is a sense in which almost everything we hear these days is a lie, even if technically it is not untrue.

One of the greatest compliments that people have ever paid me about my books has been to say, after they have heard me speak, whether to a meeting or to them personally, that I write just the way I talk. I always say that I *think* of my writing as talking.

Actually, if this letter sounds a little bit stilted, it is because I am dictating it, not writing it out on a typewriter, and oddly enough this is a little more artificial.

In the last year or two I have found myself really *hating* schools with an intensity that seemed to me almost irrational, and that I could hardly explain even to people who agree with me a lot. I told a group of people who call themselves "Humanistic Educators" or "Wholistic Educators," full of talk about "helping children to become human," and similar nonsense, that if I really had a choice of having to send a child I cared about either to one of their schools or some grim, old-fashioned school where they hit them with sticks, I would pick the old-fashioned school. I think very few of them had the faintest idea what I was talking about. At least the teachers in the rather old-fashioned schools I went to did not pretend to be, or try to convince me that they were, my friends, or think that they were "helping" me. It wasn't much, but it was something.

So, thanks once again for writing this wonderful piece, and for sending it to me. I feel very excited and much fortified after having read it. I hope it will soon find expression in another book.

I'm very well here. I feel always under great pressure of time. Editing *Growing Without Schooling,* and the wonderful letters people write me, and other things as well all fill up my mind with thoughts that I want to write down, but could hardly write even if there were 72 hours in a day. This is frustrating, and all the more so because it makes a kind of pressure to drive music out of my life, and I am unwilling to give that up. But I am generally in good health and spirits, as I hope you are. Give my very best to whatever friends of mine may come through Cuernavaca.

Peace,

[John]

P.S. [. . .] Funny, one last memory. *Years* ago, even before I started working as a teacher, I remember meeting some parents who had effectively turned their own home into a school, who were, like your friends, nothing but teachers to their own children, and I was simply horrified by this, for reasons I could not understand at all.

[. . .] I quote all the time to other people the remark you once made to me about the belief of modern man in the infinite power of process to create value. I really did not understand that when you first said it to me, but I have come to understand it very well. The only difficulty is that once we begin to look at modern society through that particular pair of spectacles, it becomes even more horrifying than it would be anyway.

Don't know whether I told you, but the book I have written about my experience as a late starter in music, *Never Too Late,* will appear in October. There is a little mention of CIDOC and these ideas in it. When I get corrected bound galleys I will be sure to send you a copy.

[John]

P.P.S. Further thoughts on your piece. It just occurred to me that in another way my thinking has been running somewhat parallel to yours. For a couple of years now, in various speeches, I have been making the point that what you very aptly call "vernacular" knowledge has been downgraded by society in favor of "taught" knowledge. I have been talking to people about a "hierarchy of knowledge," according to which the things which are much more abstract and remote are valued much more highly, carry more credit with them, than things which people can learn from everyday life. I say this is a highly political decision and has highly political consequences. It diminishes the power, capacity, and self-respect of ordinary people.

One example I gave is that the international academic world would turn upside down with excitement if we were to unearth somewhere the day to day memoirs of an ordinary Egyptian workman. Whoever found and decoded these memoirs would get all kinds of honors, lectures, grants, etc. But if an ordinary working man or woman of today were to write down his or her thoughts, who would pay any attention—except as a kind of freak curiosity, perhaps. But deciding what somebody thought 2,500 years ago is more important than what somebody thinks today is, as I say, a perfectly arbitrary decision.

Needless to say it is a decision that always and everywhere works in favor of those who are already privileged. It is precisely the people who have the most power and leisure who can afford to spend a lot of time learning what is not immediately useful in their lives. I have no objection to people learning what is not immediately useful, but I don't see why they should be treated as more worthy or honorable or deserving of power and privilege than the people who concentrate on what is closer to hand.

Indeed, I think the remoteness and abstractedness of the thinking of most of our academically trained experts is one of the truly serious social diseases of our time. They make a mess of almost everything they lay their hand to, precisely because they have lost the ability to think about daily events, or even to believe that daily events have any value, that anything can be learned from them.

Mabel Dennison, one of the founders of the First Street School of George Dennison's *The Lives of Children*, was now teaching at the Sandy River Free School in Maine.

[TO MABEL DENNISON]

7.19.78

Dear Mabel,

Thanks for yours of 6/22, and good news about the garden. Every so often I think about that marvelous kale you cooked in the wok. I don't know that I ever ate any vegetable as good as that.

Thanks for kind words about my book.[1] As it happens, I reread *The Lives of Children* for the I don't know how many-th time. As always, I was moved by the familiar passages in it, and as always found a couple of things in it that I was reading as if for the first time. I must have read them before, of course, but for some reason they

1. Dennison had written about reading Holt's books, but did not specify which ones.

never made quite the impression on me as now. But when I came to the end of the book I had a to me quite astonishing reaction. I have always been so moved by a number of passages, particularly about José and his reading problem, that I have never been able to read them aloud to other people without choking up. But this time, when I reached the end of the book, I did something I haven't done since my Uncle died, and that was the only time in my life that I did it— rather odd circumstances, which I may tell you about some day. What I did was to burst into sobs. I suspect they are the kind generally called "racking." Even as I was swept by this storm some other part of my mind was astonished by it, and some other part of my mind astonished by the way it sounded. It sounded almost like a kind of harsh, dry laughter. But it wasn't that at all. I'm not altogether sure what it was. Must be partly this, that I manage to live and actually stay very happy and busy in this society only by agreeing to forget or ignore a large part of what I really know about it, and beyond that, agreeing with myself to accept as more or less natural and unchangeable a whole lot of things that I once could never have accepted. But this seems to me to be the price of living here without going crazy. But there was more to my grief than that. There was something awful about the fact that, having been shown the way, and a way that we could so easily have taken without a great deal of trouble, we took another way. And I suppose I was feeling too, what I once felt quite strongly in Denmark, a kind of lost patriotism, a feeling that one lives in an essentially sensible and decent society which is on the whole getting better. As I say, I am mostly adjusted to living without this feeling—what Edmond Taylor years ago called one of the most important spiritual vitamins. But now and then I am painfully reminded of the enormous differences between what we might have been, ought to have been, had every chance to be, and what we in fact are.

Anyway, this particular storm didn't last very long, but it surely surprised me when it was going on.

I'm probably repeating something I've said many times, but I think that a considerable part of what children need is to be left alone, not only left alone by adults, but left alone by other kids, except perhaps for a special chosen friend or two. Another important part of what they need is the opportunity to associate, as freely as they wish, and more or less as equals, with a range of adults who are busy with serious work—work other than looking after kids. The more I think of the idea of making a life's work of looking after children or doing nice things for children, the more terrible, empty, manipulative, corrupting, etc., it seems to me, no matter how nice the people may be who are doing it. I feel that the world is full of interesting, important, and indeed urgent things to do, and that we ought to be busy doing them—catching the few pleasures, like my music, and welcoming children to do them with us so far as they wish and in whatever ways they can. [. . .]

I agree that children have enormous valuable resources, which we lose at our great loss. But I don't think they *think* of themselves as having them. Children take their health, energy, enthusiasm, spontaneity, etc., for granted, and indeed, it is probably only adults in a rather decadent civilization, who have lost so much of these qualities, who would even bother to notice them in children. In a proper society, grownups should have even more of these qualities than children since they would have had more time to develop them. It is no doubt true, in a civilization such as the one we live in, that many adults are mostly failed and spoiled remnants of children, but I don't think there's any special biological reason why that should be so.

I envy you eating trout! My goodness . . . !

[. . .]

To return to children and adults, I think children need adults quite frequently at certain moments, and at these moments want the adults to be available without question or condition. Much of the rest of the time, the children don't need adults at all, are happy floating around on the fringes of the adult world, as when eavesdropping on big adult parties, but above all, they don't like to feel that they are needed *by* adults.

The music book is really nice, I've enjoyed writing it, I think people will love reading it, and if it should prove to be a big success, I think it will certainly solve a lot of [financial] problems for us here. But we won't find out about that for about six months.

So, keep in touch and I will do the same. Love to all of you.

Peace,

[John]

Jon Daitch, who had been active in the free school
movement, wrote accusing Holt of being apoliti-
cal and individualist, and Holt replied with the
following letter.

[TO JON DAITCH]

10.10.78

Dear Jon,

Thanks for your good letter of 9/7, and kind words about my
books.

I don't say this with any sense of reproach, but I think if you had
read *all* my books you would understand that I am not on some "individualist" side as opposed to "community development" side. Such
differences as I might have with Jonathan Kozol do not revolve
around the issue of whether community development or political ac-
tions are important, but about what *kinds* of community development or political action are likely to produce useful and lasting
results. I think—for example—that to hold Cuba (or China, etc.) up
to people as some sort of model of what ought to be done in the
United States is just pure moonshine.

Freedom and Beyond is an intensively political book. I tried to make
clear in the latter half of it why schooling, and things done in
schools, could *not* alleviate or change, much less do away with, poverty, and indeed only reinforced poverty and inequality in a country.
I haven't budged an inch from that position. I enclose a couple of
issues of our magazine, *Growing Without Schooling*. The story "Politics
of Schools" in #4, and the story "And Real Ones" in #6, make this
same point. From the point of view of the holders of wealth and
power in this country, it was a stroke of absolute genius to get blacks
(and other non-white minorities) to dissipate their political strength
and political capital over a period of 25 years in a peripheral issue
like "integrating schools," rather than talk about the redistribution
of income and wealth. A perfect strategy! Just get poor sections of
society, white and non-white, quarreling with each other over a
scarce supply of diplomas, and you can keep both groups in their
place for generations. Which is what has happened.

[. . .]

I'm not going to take a lot of time to say why I think the move
toward greater personal, neighborhood, local, and regional

self-sufficiency is *in fact* the most revolutionary development in modern politics (in the U.S. or anywhere else).

But let me tell a story, which I'm going to get in print one of these days. I went to a meeting, in Boston, and after the meeting was greeted in the halls by a man whom in fact I do not know very well. He is one of the most well-known and highly respected men of the Left in the United States. If you heard his name, you would know it, and you would think of him as one of the Best of the Good Guys. And he really is, too—he has been a tireless and courageous worker on behalf of peace, poor people, etc. He asked me what I had been doing, and I told him about something which I had just seen which had excited me enormously then and excites me enormously now. I said I had visited an outfit called the New Alchemists in Woods Hole, Mass., and there had seen the most astonishing development. These people have found that in a double-walled plastic tank, standing about 5' high and only a couple of feet in diameter, they can raise a tropical vegetarian fish called Tilapia. What happens is that the sun shining into the water in the tank grows algae, and the fish eat the algae. There is no other input of either energy or food into the tank. Yet one of these small tanks, just sitting there, can in a year produce as much as 100 or 200 lbs. of high quality fish. What this has to say about poverty, poverty of people all over the world, and also about the poverty of people in our cities, and about the possibility of people even in cities raising enormous quantities of their own food and improving their own diet is quite obviously immense. *Truly* revolutionary. I told this nice man about this development, and he looked at me with a perfectly blank face. After a moment or so he said, in complete bewilderment, "But I don't understand what I'm supposed to make of that."

This is the trouble with the political Left, why it doesn't get anywhere—and I think you would have to agree that in the U.S. at the moment it isn't getting anywhere. It thinks that carrying a sign in a picket line is political action, is revolutionary political action, but that raising one's own food is not. This, interestingly enough, was the case in the Adams-Morgan community development experiment in Washington, D.C. This was a very low-income, racially mixed neighborhood. Some people began to start a project in which people were recycling their own wastes, getting their own energy, and raising a lot of their own food, on rooftop gardens, in fish tanks, raising sprouts, etc. It turned out, in this particular community, that the non-whites were perfectly willing to join in protest meetings, marches, etc. But none of them were willing to take part in food-raising or self-sufficiency activities.

To return to the New Alchemists, I don't read *every* issue of *every* publication of the Left, but I read a lot of them, and to this date I have never seen the New Alchemists mentioned once.

[. . .]

But you get the general drifts of my thoughts. I refuse to stand still while any "non-political" label is put on me. I don't ask you to agree with my ideas about what constitutes effective political action, or action for social change, but I do want you to understand that I am not indifferent to such matters.

Hope this doesn't all sound too argumentative. I think after reading the first six issues of *GWS,* which you should have by now, you will see a little more clearly my own thoughts and how they are running. Thanks again for writing, and good luck to you.

Best,

John Holt

[TO MABEL DENNISON]

8.8.79

Dear Mabel,

Thanks for your nice letter and drawing.

Yes, I guess I really do love children, or at any rate most children, certainly most young children—as they get older, if enough bad things are done to them, they can get pretty ugly pretty soon and I see some really ugly ones around the streets of this town. But when they're little and new in the world they mostly tend to be very nice folks.

But even as I say this I can hear the angry voices of about 100,000,000 mothers saying "It's easy for Holt to say he likes kids. He doesn't have to take care of them, cook three meals a day for them, clean up their mess, listen to their fights, take them here, there, everywhere else, etc., etc., etc . . ." Of course, they're perfectly right. I think if I had become a father, say, anytime in the last ten years or so, I might have been a pretty good one, but who knows?

Somebody once asked me if I ever thought of adopting a child. I hadn't really, but when I think of it, the answer is instantly No—until *GWS* gets established, which may be some years in the future, I haven't got more than enough money to support myself, and no time at all. To which some people could reply that it's easy to think children are great if they don't interfere with your life.

Well, all that said, I still think I like children better than most people [do], understand them better than most. I don't take this as a sign of any special virtue on my part, just different kinds of good luck. I certainly think that, since the world is full of them, it's a hell of a lot more fun to like them than not to like them, just as, if you live in a place full of all kinds of birds, it's probably more fun to know something about birds.

Working away at the ms. of a book on home schooling. Super-busy, enjoying life, hope you are the same.

Best,

[John]

Of Jean Liedloff's *The Continuum Concept,* a book about how the Yequana Indians raise their infants with almost constant physical contact, Holt later wrote, "If the world could be saved by a book, this just might be the book."

[TO JEAN LIEDLOFF]

12/22/79

Dear Ms. Liedloff,

I have to write to thank you for *The Continuum Concept,* which (after intending to for some time) I have just got round to reading. I have read a lot of books about children and childrearing, and I do think that yours is the most fundamental and important that I have ever read.

I think it is one of those books that, if enough people could read it and act on it, would change the world. I certainly will do all I can to bring it to the attention of people, including the readers of our magazine (title above).

I faintly wish you had given it a different title. There's nothing in the title that would tell people what it was about, if they didn't know, or even to suggest that the book is about children at all. It sounds like a Physics textbook. I fear this may have thrown off a certain number of people who might otherwise have read it. Hope not.

I also wish a little that you had put very early in the book what you wrote on p. 211 (Warner edition): "There is reason to believe that the missing experiences can be supplied to children and adults at any stage." This is very important. I can imagine that some mothers, reading your horrifying comparison of the early life of a continuum baby and the early life of a typical American child (or modern child in almost any developed society), would be nearly overcome by grief and guilt. Indeed, I know one, at least, who to some degree cannot stop mourning over what she failed to give her children in the earliest years—even though she is now doing her best (very good, too) to make up those missing experiences.

How has the book sold? What is more to the point, have many of the people who read it written to you? In the book you suggested some very sensible research that might be done. Do you know of anyone who might be doing some of it (other than Doman-Delacato) and with what results? Are there more or less organized efforts to spread this understanding of child rearing among a wider number of people? I know of *Mothering* magazine—are there any others like that?

It would be wonderful if there were ways to bring the book to the attention of pregnant mothers. I wonder whether some of those classes that women (and often their husbands) go to, are using the book, and whether the Lamaze, Leboyer, La Leche[1] and home birthing organizations are pushing it. (They certainly should!)

Suddenly thought of *Babies in Loving Arms* as a possible title.

[. . .] I could go on and on about the parts of the book that I particularly loved and that were important to me. Instead, I will only say once again that it is very important for me to learn about any groups there may be who are trying to put the lessons of this book into effect, and that I will be grateful to you for anything you can tell me about them—as I am grateful for the book itself.

1. Lamaze and Leboyer are methods of childbirth without unnecessary medical intervention, and La Leche League is the international breastfeeding advocacy and support organization.

I hope the book is doing well, and that you may write another, someday, answering on a much wider scale some of the questions I have raised in this letter. Good luck to you.

Best wishes,

John Holt

Ping Ferry put Holt in touch with Grace and James Boggs, authors of *Revolution and Evolution in the Twentieth Century*. They corresponded several times about revolution and blacks in American society.

[TO GRACE AND JAMES BOGGS]

3/25/80

Dear Grace and James Boggs,

[. . .] Some thoughts on revolution. A real rev has to stand with one leg on philosophy, ideas, ideology, call it what you will. The other leg has to stand on economics, and I don't mean economic theory but economic action. No movement for social change will get very far in the U.S. in the 80s unless it has a firm economic base. It is impossible to imagine that people could make a revolution or even work effectively in that direction as long as they are wholly dependent for all [their] material needs on the present economic and political system.

I'll refer again to what I said in the first issue of *GWS*, that true social change begins when people change their lives, not just their political ideas or parties.

I offer what I might call Holt's First Law of personal economics. Nobody who makes a low wage, or no wage, can afford to pay someone else a high wage to do for him anything he could learn to do for himself. But our poor communities, black and otherwise, must be full of people doing just this.

Roughly what does a city black family with children pay for food a year. Of course, it varies from family to family, depending on the number of children they have and other things. Would an average figure be $1,500 a year? Let's say so for the sake of argument. I have seen figures to show that urban whites who are members of food buying cooperatives can save as much as 40% of their food bill in a year. Take ⅓ for a rough figure. That means that simply by buying food cooperatively at wholesale rather than retail prices, 1,000 urban black families could save half a million dollars every year.

These figures could probably be greatly increased if these families raised and made some of their own food—which is perfectly possible. If, for example, they bought wheat, ground their own flour, baked their own bread, learned to make tofu [. . .], had garden[s] in vacant lots and on rooftops, raised some sprouts, etc. etc. (I'll be sending more information about all those things fairly soon), we could easily imagine that our 1,000 families could save a million dollars a year.

Now obviously if they just turned around and spent it on new cars or tape recorders or bigger TV sets [and] other unnecessary consumer goods, nothing would be accomplished. But suppose they thought of this money as wealth-producing capital. 10,000 families in ten years could accumulate $100,000,000. That is quite an economic base. And long before this figure was reached, the community in which those people lived would have been radically changed, physically, morally, politically.

It has become the fashion to say that when earlier immigrants came to this country there were plenty of jobs waiting for them. This is only half-true. In many cases they created the jobs. There was no garment industry in New York to speak of until Jewish immigrants created it. They created it by making their own clothes, saving up enough money to buy sewing machines, with which they made clothes for other people, and so on. In many big cities the food retailing business is largely controlled by Italians. They created that business, starting with buying food at wholesale markets and taking it back in pushcarts to their own slum neighborhoods, where there were no stores.

One thing blacks certainly can't afford to do is pay teachers $10 per hour to tell them things they could find out for themselves. They couldn't afford it even if the teachers were any good, which most of them aren't. I keep hearing that the black community needs doctors. What it needs much more than that is *knowledge about medicine*—about diet, health, common drugs and remedies, first aid. But this stuff is lying around in books. When I was on a submarine, 90% of the ailments for which most urban people now see a doctor were treated by a Pharmacist's Mate, a young guy of about 21 with a high school diploma and perhaps another year of training. Poor communities need pharmacist's mates more than doctors.

Another way of saying what I am saying is that poor communities (cities, regions, nations) are poor for among other reasons this one, that as fast as money comes into the community, in whatever way, it goes right out again. The trick is, once money gets into the community, keep it in the community. Italians in the fairly low-income North End community in Boston can probably go through the best part of an entire year without ever having to buy anything from a non-Italian. Food, clothing, shoes, drugs, repairs—they get them all from people who live close to them.

[. . .]

I'll bring this to a close, but will be writing and sending more stuff along these lines.

best,

John Holt

[TO HARTMUT VON HENTIG]

8/25/80

Dear Hartmut,

How nice to hear from you again! Please, not to worry (as the British say) about not answering that other letter. Time flies so fast for me that it seems no time at all since I wrote it. This is perhaps only partly true; it is truer to say that I have lost all sense of time in a conventional sense. I experience at one and the same instant the feeling that something happened yesterday and also that it happened a very long time ago.

At any rate, I have not been thinking, "Why doesn't Hartmut answer my letter?" In fact, till your letter came, I had forgotten that I had written you that long letter. Perhaps before I write some more I should go and find it (or try to), so as to avoid repeating myself. Miracle! I found it!

As before, I'm going to write ideas as they come into my head, in no order of importance. I re-read my remarks about Berkeley, that up until third grade children seemed to mingle across racial barriers but that after that they tended to split apart. Since I last wrote a man in Boston called me up. I have known him slightly before, well enough to know that he is a man of the Left, who in principle approves of school integration. What he had to say was that one of his boys was in the second grade at [a] school in Roxbury, which is known for being one of the best elementary schools in the city, and that there was so much racially organized group violence in the second grade, which in practice meant gangs of black kids beating up on white (in other places it is surely the other way round), that his son couldn't think about anything but whether he would be beaten up that day. Finally the father decided that he had no choice but to take him out of school.

This may not be a bad place to say that, from the reports I get, which means hundreds of letters from all parts of the country, children in schools are noticeably more violent, among each other, than they were ten or fifteen years ago. This is equally true in small towns and big cities, and in all parts of the country, and among all income classes. I can think of a number of reasons why this might be true. Some of them are the schools' fault, many or perhaps most are not, but the schools make the problem worse.

To return a second to more personal matters, I am sorry that you are feeling short of energy, tho considering what you have been through I can understand it. But the answer may not be to slow down; it may be to speed up. I have never in my life been busier or felt more oppressed by the lack of time to do the things I wanted or even needed to do. My office and desk are a shambles and my apartment worse; I would be ashamed to let you in, it would take three solid days of cleaning up and cleaning before I would do that. (In my mind's eye I see your lovely house—and by the way, I haven't been across the water since then, and am not sure when I will be able to go, I lack both the time and money for those kinds of voyages, which I enjoyed immensely.)

Where was I? Oh yes, energy. But I have never felt healthier or more energetic, or, in spite of my deep worries about the state of the world and this country (which is in an ugly temper these days, really quite terrifying), I have never been happier. From repeated experience I have learned that no matter how busy I get I must not neglect to get regular hard exercise (in my case, exercising with weights and barbells, and occasionally running and swimming when the opportunity comes up). And I must not let the pressure of work drive the cello to the wall. Come what may, I keep an hour or an hour and a half a day for playing. I need it for my sanity. In times like these we must not neglect our pleasures. If you love music, an hour a week is not enough to listen to it. But I have found that making music is even more satisfying than listening, especially as I am beginning to get to the point where my own playing is a pleasure to me.

I'm not sure what were the last issues of our little magazine that I sent, but I'll send along the most recent six, just to give an idea of how things are moving along. As you can see, the magazine has grown larger, changed its format, and broadened the range of its interests. My deep and long-range concern is not just to get children out of schools but to help knock down all the barriers we have put up between children and the world of serious adults, and as time goes on we will have more and more to say about this theme.

Putting out the magazine is an immense labor, far more than I thought it would be, and also an immense source of joy and satisfaction. We get so many wonderful letters from parents, so many that we are only able to print a small part of them. If on the one hand the work we are doing does not reach more than a small number of people, it is true on the other hand that to these it makes an immense difference.

[. . .]

I see that in my previous letter I referred to the many letters I get about the brutal treatment of children in our elementary schools. These letters continue. I don't print them in *GWS*, for many reasons: we don't have enough space, most of our readers already know that schools are bad, we are more interested in how to get out and what to do instead. But these letters, about stupid, brutal, and cruel treatment of even very young children in schools, continue to come in, from all parts of the country.

Haven't much to add to what I wrote in that earlier letter. It seems more true than ever. A couple of points, though. One of the ways in which schools have changed in the last ten years is that they have lost their sense of mission, both the sense of having a noble task to do and the sense of being able to do it. Even ten or fifteen years ago, when I talked to school people about letting children learn about the world in the way they wanted, they would spend quite a while talking about the knowledge needed to live in a technological society, or the great traditions of Western culture, or the best that man has thought and done, or democratic values, or whatever it might be. There was always the idea that the schools were teaching really valuable and important things. If we talked long enough, the deep motive usually came out in the end, that we had to get children ready for real life, which was bad. But now this comes out in the first minute of talk. School people hardly even pretend to be doing anything else. It is the Army for kids, a bad place where they get ready for the bad world outside. It is *astonishing* how quickly, freely, and unashamedly they admit and even insist on this. To parents who want to teach their children, the schools *only* say things like, "How will he fit in?" or "You can't shelter him from the world forever, what are you going to do when he has to go out into it?"

[. . .]

One of the things I have discovered during recent years, but even more sharply during the last year or two, is that it is increasingly difficult to talk to school people about any changes in school without making them angry. Five or more years ago I decided that it was pointless to talk to teachers about making the schools into very different places—none of them thought they had the power to do that, so why frustrate them talking about it. I decided instead to talk about changes that they could make, and could make without getting themselves into trouble—small changes in the way they taught reading, arithmetic, etc. When I speak to teachers I still feel a strong desire to give them some ideas that, if they want to, they can *use*. But I find to my utter astonishment that even to talk about a slightly different way of teaching reading or addition makes most of them angry. They see this as "criticism," and demand to know why I am criticizing their schools, or say, "How do you know what we are doing in our schools?" Sometimes an educator will claim that they are already doing what I am suggesting, a claim which, if pursued very far, turns out to be a simple untruth. It is *extremely* difficult to talk to people in education—and most difficult of all at the college or university level—without getting into an unpleasant kind of verbal battle. And I really make an effort to do it, try to stay out of useless arguments and stick to possibilities of fruitful action. At almost every meeting someone will ask me, in a voice already challenging and angry, "Just what do you think is wrong with the schools?" I never answer the question, say instead that I think this would lead us into fruitless argument.

What I mostly say to school people these days is that it would be in their best interests to cooperate with homeschooling families rather than oppose them. I try to keep the discussion to this subject. But people keep trying to turn it into an argument about what's wrong with their schools.

Occasionally at meetings of teachers I have heard other people, from here or there within the educational establishment, give the kind of speech that teachers like to hear, and to which they give frequent and enthusiastic applause. These speeches say, one way or another (1) Teachers are doing a wonderful job (2) They are the most unappreciated group in the country (3) No one else could do what they do (4) American schools are the best in the world (5) If the schools have problems, the causes are *all* outside—bad children, bad families, television, not enough money, too much interference by "non-professionals" (how they cling to that term!), etc. The schools have made themselves immune to experience by creating this ideology—which has always existed to a degree—that when things go well the schools deserve the credit, and when they go wrong others deserve the blame. You can not say to school people that the results of their work show that a different method is called for.

[. . .] Whew! What a diatribe! Of course, there are exceptions, at all levels. Every so often I meet one, and I am always happy to do so. But they aren't many, and they usually don't stay long. I receive hundreds of letters from former teachers and sometimes administrators, saying that they had hoped to make schools better but eventually got fed up and got out. I think of the people entering teaching in any given year, perhaps 5% might be people of real ability and idealism. Many of them don't even make it through ed school, and of those that enter schools, most don't stay long.

[. . .] What keeps me sane (tho some might disagree), busy, and mostly happy in spite of all this is that I never did and do not now define myself exclusively or primarily as an "educator." I am interested in human growth and learning, but only as part of a larger interest in society. Perhaps my deepest interest could be described as "How can we adults work to create a more decent, humane, conserving, peaceful, just, etc. community, nation, world, and how can we make it possible for children to join us in this work, how can we take down the many barriers we have put up between the young and their elders?" Except insofar as we find answers to *those* questions, there is very little we can do under the name of "education" to help young people grow up into whole, intelligent, sensitive, resourceful, competent, etc. human beings. This is not the old argument that we must reform society before we can do anything about education. It is to say that the only way young people can grow up well is by having constant and free access to adults who *are* working to make a decent society. Unless we have a sense of mission, the children will not have one—but our mission can't be simply "children."

At least, mine can't. To spend all of one's time and energy thinking about how best to deal with children does not seem to me like serious work for a grown-up.

Which is to say that the presence of an army of child specialists would probably be bad for children, no matter what this particular army believed.

I think that children need to live a considerable part of their lives free of the influence of adults, and out from under their eyes, and that in another large part of their lives they should have as much access as they want to adults who are busy about their adult affairs. I have seen over and over again how children love to hang about at the edges of serious adult talk, perhaps only understanding a little of it, but intuiting that it is serious and stands for the world that they themselves are entering into.

They get none of this in school, and almost by definition, they can't. A school is a place that exists only to take care of kids, and *as such* is more likely than not to be more bad than good for kids, no matter who is running it, and even if you and/or I were running it.

This thread, of helping young people find work worth doing in the world, and helping them to find and join with adults who are doing that sort of work, is something that will run more and more through *GWS* as time goes on.

I was enormously encouraged to read in the *New York Times* only a few days ago that in the last year or two the number of small farms in New England, which had been declining for years, had risen sharply. We are learning once again to produce our own food, and this can only be a good sign. And many of these small farms would and do welcome young people as workers and apprentices.

The big picture in the U.S. is discouraging. There are large and visible signs everywhere of a society in a state of collapse. For thirty years or so, ever since I first understood more or less what Fascism was about, I have felt that we were ready for it, that it would only take the right combination of circumstances and leadership to tip us in that direction. This seems to be truer now than ever.

At the same time, there are hundreds of very encouraging small pictures. On a small and local scale Americans are doing a great many interesting, constructive, significant things—building a new and very different society under the shadow of the old. It is with this work and these people that I identify myself. Do we have time? Useless to ask the question. All we can do is work, hope for the best, and take care not to neglect our pleasures and joys—in my case, mostly music.

[...]

One of the very hopeful signs in this country is a growing movement which I find hard to name. De-centralist. Counter-economy. De-institutional. It includes people going back to the land, running small farms, or even raising more of their own food while doing other work; people setting up very small businesses or crafts; mothers having their children at home under the care of a midwife; mothers breastfeeding their children—latest reports are that more than half the mothers in the U.S. and Canada (mothers of infants) are nursing their children. I find this a truly revolutionary statistic. And people are taking care of their health instead of rushing to the doctor. There is a growing and I think healthy distrust of the institutionalized experts who have controlled more and more of our lives, and a determination to take back some of that control.

And if it is true, as I'm afraid it is, that on the whole Americans dislike and distrust children more than ever, it is also true that a growing minority of young parents are *deciding* to have children in a way that few people ever did before, not because it is what everyone does—for a great many now do not—and not because they don't know how not to have them, but because, knowing how hard it is to rear children in these times, what a responsibility and burden it is, they really want to do it anyway. We could speak of conscientious parents as we have talked of conscientious objectors. These people are, I think, still a minority. Our poor and minority groups are continuing to have a lot of children and are, on the whole, very bad parents to them—much worse than their grandparents were. During all the years of slavery and oppression there grew and flourished in the black community a tradition of loving and nurturing child care, which was a source of the strength that enabled them to survive. From all I hear, at least in the cities, this tradition has disappeared—young black parents are more likely than not inclined to be (for perhaps understandable reasons) harsh, peremptory, and brutal to their children.

But even in our inner cities there are signs of a new kind of leadership—not the Jesse Jacksons or any others of the people who get their names in the paper, but people who are saying, in effect, if our communities are going to be decent places to live, we are going to have to make them that way, no one else is going to do it for us.

We are beginning to give up here, at some cost and with some pain, the destructive notion that the federal government, if we just passed the right laws and spent enough money, would solve all our problems for us. I wish there could be political expression of this idea under a more humane man than Reagan, who also expresses and perhaps mainly expresses nothing more than callous greed. But some people here are trying to shape a new politics, and I feel myself involved somewhat in this work.

In this the political labels and remedies of the past are meaningless—conservative, liberal, socialist, Marxist, etc. To what seem to me the chief issues of our time, at least here, these labels and ideas are mostly irrelevant.

So much for the news from here. I have to confess that I am not going to do anything quickly about your manuscript. I am hard at work finishing my own book, about home education,[1] starting work on some others, and doing all the work connected with GWS. And I think my editor is no less busy.

As I say, I don't know when I will cross the water again. Too busy and too broke even to think of it—if I leave the office for a week I come back to a nightmarish stack of paper. So I think we are more likely to meet here than there.

Good luck in your struggles with the bureaucrats, a race apart, and everywhere alike, no matter what country they live in or what political label their government may wear. I once met a Swedish educational bureaucrat at a conference, and for all my feeling that Sweden is a fairly humane little country, this man was one of the most terrifying human beings I have ever seen in my life, in his certainty of his own rightness, his arrogance and ruthlessness. I thought, given the right combination of circumstances, this man could run a concentration camp.

Hope to see you here before too long. Don't neglect those pleasures!

best,

[John]

1. *Teach Your Own.*

1977–1985

Swedish teacher Åke Bystrom worked to spread
Holt's ideas in Sweden, and arranged a lecture
tour there for him in the spring of 1982.

[TO ÅKE BYSTROM]

Feb. 6, 81

Dear Åke,

Good to get your letter.

You ask if I am arguing for a utopia. Well, I certainly am arguing
for a society which is quite different from the one we have, and I
wouldn't be arguing for it if I didn't think it would be better, so to
that extent I suppose you could use the word utopia. To the extent
that Utopia means some kind of ideal society fashioned according to
a Master Plan, that is exactly the opposite of what I am arguing for.
There is already far too much Master Planning done in my country
and yours. Your master planners have had somewhat better success
than ours, perhaps because they are dealing with a much smaller
and (so far) more homogeneous country, without a lot of the stresses
and strains that plague us.

But Sweden as much as the U.S. is living at the end of an era and
the beginning of a new one. For 150 years we have all been consum-
ing non-renewable resources at a gluttonous rate, and the very rich
and wasteful societies we have built on these resources are beginning
to crack and fall apart. That process of collapse is more advanced
here than with you, and I daresay many Swedes think they can avoid
altogether the mistakes and problems we have here. I don't think
they will be able to; the super-industrial societies of our time are psychologically as well as politically and economically fragile.

[. . .] All for now. Best,

Jonathan Kozol, whose book *Death at an Early Age*
helped him become known as one of the school
reformers of the sixties and seventies, turned
his focus to illiteracy in the early eighties, and his
Illiterate America would be published in 1986.

[TO JONATHAN KOZOL]

4/6/81

Dear Jonathan,

By now you have that stuff about the Kurzweiler[1] reading machines. Obviously the technology is right at hand to make, and for not too much $$, the kind of reading machine I talked about in one of my earlier books, perhaps *Freedom and Beyond*. Voice simulators are not hard to make; they are putting them into little alarm clocks, children's Speak and Spell games, etc., stuff selling for under $100.

For under $5,000 and perhaps much less than that I'm sure they could design a Reading Machine more or less along the following lines. There would be keys for the 26 letters of the alphabet, in alphabetical order. There would be a small viewing screen, much smaller than on most word processors. The student would use the keys to spell out a word he wanted the machine to "read." As he hit each letter the letter would appear on the viewing screen. There would be a delete key and a back space key, so that he could erase errors or make changes. When he had on the screen the word he wanted, he would punch a little Speak key, and the voice simulator would "speak" the word. That is, if it was a word. If it wasn't a word, the voice would say, "It's not a word."

There's a question of whether we would want the machine to pronounce syllables if they were pronounceable. It would make the machine more complicated and expensive, but it would have its advantages. The voice could "say" the syllable, and then say, "It isn't a real word." If the syllable wasn't pronounceable at all, it would say, one way or another, "Can't pronounce that word."

For simplicity's sake it would probably be wise to limit the length of words to seven or eight letters, which are about the longest words of one syllable. To program the machine to take all words would

---

1. Actually called the Kurzweil Reading Machine, this was a machine for the blind that converted printed material into spoken English.

make it far too expensive. And there's no need; anyone who can read a thousand words or so has enough information to decode almost any words he is likely to meet. The rest is mostly practice i.e. real reading, with maybe a look at a dictionary now and then.

There might be a case to be made for putting a Rhyme key in the machine, so that when you had punched in a word and the machine had said it, it would then show on the display, and say all the words that rhymed with that word. On the other hand, if the student could change any letter in the word, he could do this for himself.

These are questions to talk about with technical people.

I think it's worth saying a word or two about why for many illiterates, particularly young teen-age males, machines might be far more effective instructors than people.

1. There is no shame in admitting ignorance to a machine, as there is in admitting it to a person. Many illiterate youths would not admit to anyone that they could not read, and indeed, would probably not even go to a reading center if the word "Literacy" were involved with it. For such people, we would have to call the machines Talking Machines, or something like that, so that illiterate youths could pretend (to friends, etc.) that they were interested in hearing the machines talk, not trying to learn how to read.

2. Machines can keep a secret; there's no danger that the machine will tell anyone *else* that you can't read.

3. Most of these young people like machines, are at home with them, spend all the time and money they can find on space war machines.

4. Most of these illiterates will have learned to believe that they can't learn from adult teachers. Here, as I said, the situation of the Cubans was *more* favorable. They were dealing with people who, not having ever been taught, had no reason to believe that they could not respond to teaching. The American illiterate will think, "People have been trying to teach me to read for years." He's not likely to think that a new person will do any better.

5. Conversely, these same kids think of machines as having superhuman and magical powers, and might be able to believe that the machine could do what no person could do i.e. teach them to read. They would give to the machine the kind of trust and confidence that they would never give to another human teacher or to themselves as learners.

6. The machines never get angry, lose patience, make sarcastic remarks, etc. In that sense, the students could trust them. Perhaps I am only repeating what I said in #1.

If vowel keys on such machines were marked in a different color, students would soon learn that the machine could not pronounce letter groups that did not have a vowel in them.

I suppose a machine could be built that, after saying a word, would, if the student asked, tell him what the word meant. But that would probably make the gadget terribly expensive. The point is to use the machine to get the student to the point where, *if he wants,* he can continue on his own. At this point in the reading program there would be more need and use for real reading materials, and also, live teachers. The machine would be to get students past the first hurdle of the basic skill of decoding words. I doubt very much whether anything else would do this as effectively. My guess would be that most students would crack the basic code/s of written English with only a few hours, ten or so, maybe much less, work with the machine.

I'll bet that some smart people in this field could throw together a pilot model of such a machine in a few months or less. It would be worth talking to them.

All for now. Best,

Holt had been interested in children's invented spelling for some time when he discovered Glenda Bissex's *GNYS AT WRK,* a book about how the author's son taught himself to read and write.

[TO GLENDA BISSEX]

6/21/81

Dear Glenda Bissex,

I have just been reading, with more pleasure than I can accurately describe, *GNYS AT WRK,* and even though I haven't finished the book, I have to begin a letter to say how much I am enjoying it, and how true, important, and altogether *enchanting* it is. Your delightful son Paul just leaps off the page. It is lovely to see him (as so many children) developing a sense of humor and irony at about the age of 9 or 10. What fun it must be to live with him and see him grow.

I am all the more glad to see the book because, of the books I have seen that make the point that children are independent, resourceful and powerful learners, this is the first that is both simple and interesting enough to read so that many teachers might read it, and that they would see as having come from *inside* the school establishment rather than outside.

What you are saying about the capacities of children I have been saying for many years, with little visible impact on the schools. At first my words were called "romantic criticism" and dismissed indulgently; now they tend to be taken as a pure attack on the schools and rejected with anger.

On just that matter of children being able to find and correct many of their own mistakes, if given enough time and not put under too great pressure to be "right," I have said this to many hundreds or perhaps thousands of teachers. Almost all respond with total skepticism and many with downright anger. By the same token, people who say to large meetings of teachers that children are generally lazy and worthless and will never do anything right unless made to, are greeted with loud spontaneous applause.

So I hope your book will do something to change these ideas. My, how they do need to be changed!

[. . .]

About children who teach themselves to read. I have been asking people, at meetings of teachers or reading teachers, whether any of them *knew of* (not had done) any research to find out roughly how many children teach themselves to read, i.e. learn without any formal instruction. I have written this question in two books and in our magazine, and asked it in face to face meetings with by now well over five thousand teachers, and so far not one person has said that she or he knew of any such research. If no one has indeed yet asked this question, it certainly is an odd oversight. From my own very informal samplings (letters, etc.) I would guess that in families in which adults read a good deal, and read aloud to children, some very substantial percentage of the children figure out how to read without formal instruction, perhaps as high as 25% or even more.

[. . .]

Thank you again for your lovely book, which I plan to add to the list of books we sell here (we run a small mail-order book business, since many of our readers live far from a good, or any, bookstore). I hope that a great many people read it, and will do what I can to make that happen. I also hope that Paul's love of writing and reading will survive the next few years of his schooling. Mine did not; though I never got anything but A in English, after the age of 14 or so I never read any books that were not assigned—at least, not until some years after I left college.

Sincerely and gratefully yours,
John Holt

[TO W. H. FERRY]

7/5/81

Dear Ping,

Despite rain, nice 4th July celeb. last night. Fireworks on the Charles. I am a sucker for fireworks. I love the big bangs. It occurred to me as I shouted and yelled in excitement and pleasure that people who had heard bombs go off near them might have a rather different feeling about loud noises. It might not seem like such fun to them. And I also thought about the really Big Loud Noise, the H-Bomb, the flash that would burn out our eyes even as we saw it, and then burn us up to a cinder, the bang that would blow down our buildings. I believe it as someone who has never seen an animal bigger than say, a cat, might believe a friend, known to be truthful, who told him about lions and tigers and giraffes and elephants. But it would be very different from seeing them.

It may be that most people will never believe in the H-bomb until the one that actually does them in. Now and then I try to think of one going off when I am in my apartment, the whole building collapsing on me in a heap of rubble, me lying there thinking, "Well, they finally did it." I can play those games of the imagination, but I can't scare myself with them.

Whereas, when at three AM some drunken revelers (I hope) began buzzing my apartment doorbell, I felt real fear, my heart pounded, the adrenaline flowed. Were these burglars who, hearing no reply to the doorbell, would then break into the building? As it happens, I had just that day read about some burglars who killed their victims. I was plenty scared. Odd, what will and will not scare us. I look out my office window at the Prudential tower, and imagine the blast that could blow it down as easily as we kick over a child's tower of blocks. I can indeed imagine it. But I can't (like the old fairy tale) make myself shudder.

[. . .]

Best,

Jonathan Croall, A. S. Neill's biographer, wrote to ask Holt several questions about Neill, among them how Neill had influenced his work, and whether Neill was easy to talk to. The biography was published in 1983 as *Neill of Summerhill.*

[TO JONATHAN CROALL]

10/22/81

Dear Jonathan,

Thanks for yrs of Oct. 10. Glad you are doing Neill's biography and wish I could help you more with it. [. . .] I only saw Neill on three occasions. First one was when I visited the school, on a rainy March weekend in 1965. Next was the meeting at Leila [Berg]'s house. But I was only there one evening; I had to go off the next day—to my great regret—to a not very interesting conference at Oxford. My most vivid impression of that evening was of Neill and Bob MacKenzie telling each other bawdy Scottish jokes. I had not seen that side of Neill on my first visit; we had spent a lot of time together talking about the school. The third time I saw Neill was when I visited him, at the school, for about three hours or so, on a lovely July day in the year of his death. I was on my way home from a trip to the Scandinavian countries. Thinking it might be the last time I would be able to see Neill, I had asked Ena if it was OK to come out and visit. She had said, yes, it was OK, but I might have the trip for nothing, because Neill tired very easily and might only be able to talk to me for a few minutes. As it was, except for a half hour when I ate lunch, we were together from about 11:30 AM or so till about 3 PM, when the taxi came to take me to the train back to London—I was leaving the country next day. Some of the time we talked quite a bit; at other times there might be long silences. After one of these, thinking that I might be tiring Neill beyond his strength, I made as if to go, but he pressed me to stay.

Of our conversation I remember only a few bits. He said that he was past the point of having any ambition, or of being disappointed because of not having achieved some ambition. He had no great hopes for British education, or education in general, or Britain in general, or for that matter the world in general. He thought that things were generally going to get worse. As for death, he had no fear of it. He did not believe in any afterlife, good or bad. Dying was like—and here he made an imitation of someone blowing out a candle. But he added, "The only trouble is that I can't stand not knowing how it's going to turn out." A feeling I understand; when my time and turn comes to die I suspect I'll feel much the same way.

My book *Escape from Childhood* had just appeared, and since it was a book that I thought Neill and I might disagree about, since I had said that children wanted not to be protected from the adult world but to get into it as soon and as far as they can, and that they liked working and feeling needed and useful, I thought we might have some interesting talk about it. But soon after I arrived he said, "I haven't read your book, John. I can't read more than a page or two any more, I can't concentrate, as soon as I've read a page I've forgotten what's in it." He did not ask me to tell him what the book was about. I don't remember even speculating about this at the time. Looking back from here, I'm not sure whether, knowing the title of the book, he wished to avoid an argument with a friend, or whether there were just other things he was more interested in talking about—being old, facing death, looking back on his life.

I can't say in words what made this last meeting a very close and intimate occasion. Some of the time, as I say, we would talk about something. Then there would be long silences. When these came, I did not attempt to stir up the conversation, just waited till he began to talk again. These silences were not awkward, certainly not to me.

I think some of the time he must have asked me about my own work and what sorts of things were happening in the States, but I don't remember this very clearly.

When the cab came, he walked with me to the door, and said good-bye to me, standing on the front steps.

The first time I came to Summerhill, I arrived on a cold rainy

March Saturday, having driven over from Leicester. Ena had explained to me, I think in a letter, that we could only visit the school on a weekend, could not eat any meals at the school, but could go to the Saturday night general meeting. Two other guests arrived at the same time, one a lady from Schenectady, NY, the other a young man who had hitchhiked all the way from India to England just to see the school and Neill. In my Summerhill Society piece (or somewhere) I think I may have said that I thought the school was unwise in treating this young man and myself as visitors "coming to look at the animals in the zoo." I felt then, and still do, that they could have made use of us, could have shared with us any children who might have been interested. Anyway, what happened is that the three of us spent quite a bit of time with Neill in his house. He was suffering from pain in his sciatic nerve, and could move very little. The young Indian had brought with him many photos of his home in India, and of places seen in his trip. Very interesting.

Some of the time we must have talked about the school. Of the book *Summerhill,* then just out in the U.S., I remember Neill saying, "What's in it, I haven't read it." I thought it was a cryptic joke; turns out that it wasn't, he really hadn't. It was a very considerably edited collection of excerpts from Neill's between the wars books. It gave a rather two or even one-dimensional picture of Neill.

Of the school, I remember Neill saying that it had changed, that it was full of Americans, some of them very disturbed; that parents and their doctors often lied to him about the children who were sent there; that it was hard to run the community when so few of the children there had grown up in the community. He also said that before, they had never had locks on their doors, since no one had anything worth stealing. But the Americans had a lot of valuable property, so doors had to be locked up.

For all Neill's skepticism and discouragement about the state of the school at that time, I was impressed (as I wrote) by the general meeting, and above all, by the liveliness and happiness of most of the little children that I saw there.

Here my chronology betrays me a little. At some time during the weekend I watched an important rugby game with Neill and his taciturn brother. I don't remember the other two visitors being there. Neill explained that he didn't understand rugby, and I certainly didn't. How I began slowly to get a feel for the patterns of the game, I described in *How Children Learn.* The brother said hardly a word.

Maybe by that time the visitors had gone back to the hotel. But I seem to remember going back together. At any rate, we had supper together, returning to the school for the very interesting general meeting and the party that followed it.

I do remember that next day—Sunday, I guess—I was at the school, walking around, looking at what there was to see, which wasn't very much, since the pottery/woodwork shop was locked. The weather being bad, the kids were in their rooms. Had it been a nice day, I would have had a much better sense of the real life of the school. As it was, except for the meeting, I really never did get to see the school in action.

But I started to say that while I was walking around a bell rang, and all the students came from this place and that to another general meeting, to which we were rather pointedly not invited. Later two or three of the little children were ejected from the meeting—I described this in the Summ. Society piece. They were not downcast a bit, but in high spirits, imitating in a very funny way the speech of whatever meeting chairman had thrown them out.

I did not conclude from this that the Saturday night meeting was a sham, a Potemkin village cooked up for the guests, since some important things were discussed. But I was curious about what was discussed at the Sunday meeting.

It may have been Sunday afternoon, after that meeting, that I saw the rugby game with Neill and his brother. The point of all this is that I did not have a great deal of time to talk to Neill that weekend, perhaps a few hours. All in all, in all three of my visits to him, I could hardly have spent much more than twelve hours, at the most, in his company. So I could not say that I knew him well.

It must have been at the first meeting that we talked about music, and that I found out that he liked opera, and Wagner in particular. And I think it was at that same meeting that he told me that he didn't read a great deal, that most of the books he saw bored him. Indeed, we must have had at least a couple of hours worth of talk on that first weekend, but I can't quite fit it all in. Perhaps he and I talked in the morning, and later on the other visitors arrived.

It now pops up in memory that I spent the night at the school, on a sofa or couch in some room. I ate meals at the hotel or pub in town but didn't sleep there.

I left the school on that first occasion glad to have had a chance to spend time with Neill, liking him very much, enjoying seeing and hearing the ideas made flesh, so to speak, but also a little disappointed at having seen so little of the life of the school. I think I said to friends, "I didn't see much of Summerhill but saw a lot of Neill." In the long run, perhaps that was better.

Of the meeting at Leila's, I think I remember that we stayed up fairly late, drinking whisky and enjoying Neill's and Bob's stories. I had to get up quite early the next day to go to the meeting at Oxford, and I think I may have left before the others woke up. At any rate, I didn't have much time to speak with them.

In answer to one specific question, I liked Neill, was comfortable with him and, I think, he with me. I found it easy to talk to him. But again, I have to say that when I first met him he was already very old, not in very good health, perhaps physically tired and certainly discouraged by what he felt was his failure to make any important impact on education, British or otherwise. I remember him saying in 1965 that there was only one other "pioneer school" (his phrase) that seemed to him authentically free, and that was Kilquanity, in Scotland.

I have a faint recollection of him saying—or perhaps he said it to someone else and I read it—that he was pleasantly surprised by some of the developments in the British state primary schools, when that so-called primary school revolution was at its height. If he said this, it would have been at the meeting at Leila's.

Neill had no influence on the development of my ideas. Those ideas were well formed, out of my own experience, before I met Neill or even heard of him. But I was glad to learn that someone had been putting into practice for years what I had just discovered for myself.

Summerhill was a very influential book here during the late 60's. But since it greatly oversimplified and sentimentalized Neill's thought and work, its influence was often short-lived. That is, people would read *Summerhill,* and rush out to start an alternative school, not understanding that human freedom is a more complicated and difficult matter than that book suggested. Still, it was one of those books that helps to shape an era, and if (like my own books) it didn't do much to change the schools, it changed the lives of quite a number of people, and is probably still doing so.

Neill was surprised by the popularity of *Summerhill* in the U.S. In '65 he told me that when Harold Hart phoned him to ask about using quotes from Neill's books to make the book *Summerhill,* Neill said, "OK, if you want to throw your money away."

[. . .]

I wrote Neill a number of letters, some fairly long, but then I like to write letters. He didn't; I only got perhaps two or three letters from him, handwritten, very short.

I think he was a great and important man. But I really did not know him at all well. Good luck with your book.

John Holt

Charles Terry of Exeter Academy sent Holt a
book he had just edited about moral education in
boarding schools, and asked Holt's opinion of it.

[TO CHARLES TERRY]

12/21/81

Dear Mr. Terry,

Thanks for *Knowledge Without Goodness Is Dangerous.* I have only browsed through it. Hope to read it more carefully when I finish my own book, the revised version of *How Children Learn.*

As I read, some thoughts and/or questions came to mind, which I'll set down in no order of importance.

1. I wrote in *Instead of Education,* re [Lawrence] Kohlberg, that learning morality through discussions was like learning poker by playing with matches. You only learn morality, like poker, *by making choices in which you have something to lose.*

2. Why do the top-ranked private schools take so few high-risk students, kids who have always done badly in school?

3. It was true not very long ago that one of the questions that selective colleges ask about applicants is their class rank. Does Exeter have a class rank, and does it give out such information? What is the morality of that?

4. In the 1972 elections, 86% of my class voted for Nixon. No doubt in more recent classes there was a more even split. I wonder how many voted for Reagan.

5. In my four years at Exeter I do not remember ever continuing

247

a classroom discussion outside of class, or hearing any other students doing so. It may have happened, but I never heard it.

6. Nor do I remember ever hearing any student say that in some personal moral crisis he was helped by a member of the faculty. It may have happened, etc.

7. Even though I earned very little money, I gave money to Exeter every year—until they built that gym. Then I thought, if you guys have enough money to spend X millions on that gym, you don't need money from me. Maybe by now the whole community makes use of it.

8. What would happen, at Exeter or any other top-rank school, if the percentage of graduates being admitted to top-ranked colleges were to decline significantly?

9. Does anything in fact happen to faculty who regularly cut down students?

10. I can remember very few faculty who were deeply admired when I was a student. Some were very much liked, some very much disliked; about most, we were neutral. But I can remember very few who could have been said to exert a moral influence on the students.

11. Certainly in matters sexual, and in most other matters, the moral tone of the school was set in the butt rooms, and it was generally low. We were mostly good boys, because we had learned that it paid to be. I think we may have been looking, more than we realized, for ideas to believe in and older people to admire. We were perhaps hungry for more than we were offered.

12. Is the Vietnam war much discussed at Exeter these days?

13. Same for morality of atomic weapons.

14. Same for World War III, possible consequences, how to prevent it. How many students think it can be prevented?

15. Same for conscientious objection, draft refusal, etc.

16. When a friend of mine, some years ago, was a senior at Harvard, I asked him if he and his fellows ever argued with their professors. He laughed and said the profs all *told* the students to argue. But none ever did; they knew that the only way, at least the surest way, to get A's was to say what the profs had said, with the words just touched up enough to sound like original thought. How would my question be answered at Exeter?

My questions and comments have an obvious drift. I think that Exeter and comparable schools are not particularly moral communities; that they would like to be; that they don't know how to be;

that they don't understand what might be the price of becoming so; that if they found out the price they would probably not be willing to pay it. But I have not been in close touch with the school and am ready to admit the possibility that I might be completely wrong. That's why I ask those questions.

Have to say in closing what a pleasure it was to read a book that looks and feels as nice as yours. How I wish my publishers would make my books look and feel like that. What I get is "perfect" bindings, surely one of the great misnomers of history. Who did in fact design and print the books?

How much do Exeter students know about how books get published, designed, printed, distributed, sold? Very little, I'll bet.

Thanks for the book, and good luck.

Sincerely,

John Holt

Joanna Picciotto, a high school student, wrote
frequently about her dissatisfaction with high
school, and her thoughts about possible future
work.

[TO JOANNA PICCIOTTO]

1/1/82

Dear Jo,

What a funny feeling to write that date on the letter. Where in the world did 1981 go? Time goes faster for me every year.

Nice to hear from you. You know, I hate to think of you starting letters and tearing them up, etc. Send whatever you write; what the hell, this isn't English class. Anyway, I'm glad Christmas was pleasant. I didn't have much fun growing up at home, but my folks really made a pretty good effort at Christmas. Kind of a truce, like the old medieval peace of God.

[. . .]

Want to ask a question I've never brought up. I may be asked to speak at some kind of anti-nuclear meeting in New York fairly soon, hence these questions. Do you personally think, or worry, or dream, much, or at all, about the possibility of an atomic war? Do your friends? Is it something you talk much about together? If so, what are your thoughts? Do you think there is likely to be a big nuclear war in the near future? Do you expect to survive it?

Intellectually, I've been aware of the danger of nuclear war ever since 1946, and spent six full-time years of my life working for world government trying to do something about it. But emotionally, I've never accepted the possibility as real. Never have had a dream about it.

I'll be grateful for anything you can tell me about this.

My blood runs *cold* at the thought of your being a teacher. Don't take your ideas of what teaching is like from *Up the Down Staircase*, which from word one was written with an eye to the movies. I can see how easy it would be to identify with the heroine, but teaching in real life isn't like that.

Most of the people in teaching, and I mean something like 90% or more, are incurious, unintelligent, mentally lazy people who distrust, dislike, fear, and even hate kids. There may be a few schools in which such people do not make up the overwhelming majority, but there are damn few. I did my teaching in elite private schools, and, liking children, I was in a small minority even in them.

And ask yourself, in your own school, how many teachers have you known that really interested you? How many that you really trusted? How many that have helped you with the problems of growing up? How many to whom you might go to for help if you were in any kind of serious trouble? How many have you thought enough of as friends to keep in touch with after you are no longer in their class? How many of them do you look forward to being friends with in years to come, and even as an adult. Six? Two? Any at all? And yet your school is a super-elite school, one in ten thousand.

You would not like most of the teachers in most schools, and you would not like the kids either. My guess is that the movie has given you some notion of being one of the teachers that the kids like and trust. In most schools the kids don't like or trust any adult. Their unspoken and perfectly justified question to you would be, "If you're such a good person, what are you doing in this stinking place?"

And even if you were going to go into teaching someday, I would implore you not to go right out of college, but to do some other things first, so that when you came into a classroom it would be as an adult woman with some knowledge, skill and experience behind her. I didn't start teaching till I was 30; if I had started at 21 it would have been a disaster.

[. . .]

Well, life these days is hard and confusing, for young and old alike. You don't say anything about dancing; I hope it doesn't mean you have given it up. Amidst the confusion of life, and of planning your own life, one good rule would be, *stick to what you do well.* Chances are that in the next few years a number of different kinds of jobs and work will appeal to you. You may make twenty different career decisions in the next few years. Meanwhile, unless you grow to really hate it, which I don't think you will, don't give up dancing. Stay with it, if only on the grounds that it *is* something you know you're good at. In a tough world, it makes a big difference to be able to say, "Well, this is one thing I'm good at, anyway."

The experience of doing a difficult (and in this case beautiful) thing well is an experience that most people never have in an entire lifetime. Don't give that up lightly. It's the one chance our dumb society is likely to give you for a long time to come to do serious, difficult, demanding work. If you let that go you've got nothing left but mostly dumb school assignments. Even if you could get an interesting, *real* job somewhere, which at your age is very unlikely, your folks would probably not let you work at it. So dance is your one chance, a chance you're very lucky to have, to do something real and serious. Until something else *more* real and serious comes along, I'd be more sorry than I can tell to hear of you giving it up. The fact that you may not want to be a professional dancer someday has very little to do with what I'm saying here. The point is to spend some of your time making an all-out effort at something which is demanding, serious, and which can be rewarding.

I wouldn't be mad at you if you gave up dancing so that you could spend more time listening to bands, or whatever. But I'd be sorry, sorry, sorry. I'd say, "Jo made a bad bargain, and the time is going to come when she is going to find it out for herself, and regret it very much."

But maybe all this is much ado about nothing, and you're not thinking about giving up dancing at all, in which case ignore this outburst.

The one serious thing I did at boarding school and college was play squash racquets, at which I became intercollegiate champion. It was the one Rock of Gibraltar of my life. If I hadn't had it, I might have become a drunk, or gone nuts, or something. High priced schooling turned me from an intense and curious little kid to a fairly skillful teen-aged goof-off. I did what I had to (was afraid not to), got fairly good marks, but there was nothing at all in college that I gave a damn about, except squash. I don't much care what you choose to throw yourself into, but I don't want you to become a teen-aged goof-off, of which our world is terribly full.

Tell me what you can about the nuclear thing. Don't rack your brains; if it's just something you and yr friends don't think or talk about, fine, tell me that. My hunch is that young people don't talk much about it these days, but I could be wrong.

If you're really dying to do some teaching, there are probably some organizations in D.C. with which or through which you could arrange to spend some time tutoring little kids. I'm almost certain such things exist; I know they did once. Or you might even find ways to do some tutoring with little kids in your own school. I'm not knocking dreams; much of my own life begins with dreams. The thing is to turn dreams into reality as much as you can.

Pouring rain here. Still struggling to finish the revised *How Children Learn,* which keeps growing on me. I keep finding new stuff that I want to put in it faster than I can get it in. Have to get busy and button it up.

Have a big 7 week lecture tour to Europe (where I haven't been in 8 yrs) coming up in the spring. Shd be interesting, though I shudder to think of the work I will have to do when I return. Other than that, life goes on here much as before. Did I tell you *People* magazine interviewed me—don't know when it will come out. Enclose an article about me in *Yankee* magazine.[1] The six year old in the picture is one of my special friends, and we were really playing, the picture wasn't faked. It was an improvised jam session. So, take care, good luck, keep in touch.

[TO JOANNA PICCIOTTO]

1/26/83

Dear Joanna,

What a nice surprise to get your letter. You sound in fine fettle. What worried me a little about your giving up dancing was that it might leave a kind of big vacuum in your life—but it doesn't seem to

1. The *People* magazine interview was never published. The *Yankee* magazine article was "The Education of John Holt," by Mel Allen, in the Dec. 1981 issue.

have done that, you seem to be busy with lots of good things, which is fine. These are tough times to be young, and one of the things that makes it hardest for so many young people, including probably many you know, is that there isn't anything that they care much about.

I wouldn't worry about it being "selfish" to have a career like a writer or journalist. By the way, these are both very difficult careers to start right now. Newspapers are dying every day; the number of graduates from journalism courses is about *40* times as great as the number of journalism jobs opening up; book publishers are all running scared and are very reluctant to publish anything but established authors and/or junk. Making a living as a writer is a tough row to hoe, and having any kind of college degree isn't going to make it *one bit* easier. When you submit an article or book for publication, the editor doesn't give a damn what college you went to or whether you went at all. The question will be, is the article any good, or is it what we want for our paper or magazine.

It's nice to know a person your age who doesn't just want a comfortable and secure job but wants to do some kind of serious and meaningful work in the world, and to some small degree make it a better place. I can't give much advice about how to do that—there are probably as many ways as there are people. But one piece of advice I can give—if you want to make a difference in the world, and not just enjoy the trappings of success and power, then you'd better learn not to pay much attention to what "everybody says." Everybody Says that you can't "make it" unless you go to a good college, and after you get through with that Everybody Will Say that you can't "make it" unless you go to work for some big organization or law firm or whatever it is, and soon you will be rolling right down the same groove that all the people are in who got the world in its present condition. At every step of the way Everybody Will Say, "Don't make waves, don't make trouble, and someday you will have power and influence and can make a big difference." For most people that someday never comes. Anyway, it's a long haul, at best, and even if there is anything in the idea of "I'll do what they tell me for a long time, and eventually I will get to the point where I can do what I want," I doubt that you have the temperament for it right now.

My inclination is to tell people, when they ask me for advice, and you haven't done exactly that, to move as quickly and directly as they can to whatever it is they want to do. If you want to write, write; if you want to do something about food production, get in touch *right now* with a lot of the people who are learning the most about efficient ways of raising food—and by the way, these are things I follow pretty closely and about which we have a lot of info here in the office— none of the big universities know anything about this whatever. They are all committed to what I will call the industrial model of agriculture, which is a spectacular failure in Russia and almost as great a failure here.

What you stand a good chance of learning at the high powered universities and grad schools is how to fit into the system as it exists. There are no guarantees even about that, since there are a lot more people trying to find comfy jobs within the system than there are jobs for them. Still, you have already proven that you are pretty good at that game, if that's the game you want to play. But I think you will continue to hate playing it—and you will have to go on playing it for many years even after you get your Ph.D.—and I don't think it will enable you to do the things you really want to do.

The advantage of that road, and the reason many young people take it, is that it is kind of like an Interstate Highway—large, clearly marked, just the thing for high speed driving. A lot of young people take that road because it is such a good road—never mind where it goes. Also, Mom and Pop, to continue the metaphor, will pay for the car, the gas, and the tolls, as long as you stick to that road. The other roads are not very big or smooth or clearly marked or easy to find, and there are many places where there are no roads at all and you're going to have to make your own trail. It's hard, risky, uncertain, and in your case, your parents will almost certainly not like it. (Perhaps I do them an injustice—I know *my* parents didn't like it.)

[. . .]

OK, that's all for now, take care. It might make school more bearable if you wrote a lot about it, what happens there, why you don't like it. In other words, make it the raw material for your writing.

[Love, John]

This is the next morning and it turns out I do have a couple of other things to say. [. . .] About "making it." A Prof. of Ed. at Columbia named Frank Jennings had something to do with *How Children Fail* finding a publisher. After it came out he said he was going to give me some advice that I would not like, but that he urged me to take. Get a Ph.D. he said—or no one in education will pay any attention, you won't have any influence. Well, I didn't do it. I don't know how much influence I've had on education, but for sure it's a hell of a lot more than Frank Jennings (a good and smart man, by the way) ever had.

[. . .]

What you may have to choose somewhere down the line is between the *appearance* of power (of which Washington is full) and the reality of it. There's a famous story about JFK, a man, by the way, whom I never liked, admired, or trusted. He was an assiduous seeker after power. The story is that not long before he was murdered he was sitting in the Oval Office talking to a friend, and said, "I'm just beginning to discover that all these buttons on my desk (he was speaking of metaphorical buttons, of course) *aren't wired up to anything!*" In other words, he was discovering that he had almost no power whatever over the U.S. government, that he could give orders and plan programs, but that he could not be sure that anyone would ever carry them out—and might often be sure that people would not carry them out.

My advice is, never pursue power. Do as much as you can, right now, of the work that seems most important to you. If you do that work well enough, power will come to you. If you can find a way, perhaps by writing about it as I have suggested, to make school an enriching (even if unpleasant) experience for you, something from which you gain something *right now*, then by all means go. Otherwise, have as little as possible to do with it. And that is all for this letter!

Merloyd Lawrence edited Holt's last four books
for Delacorte/Dell. At the time of this letter,
Lawrence had switched her affiliation to Addison-
Wesley.

[TO MERLOYD LAWRENCE]

6/13/83

Dear Merloyd,

Here is a list of books that I would like to write in the not too distant future. For some of the books, much of the material is already written; for others, ideas exist in my mind but little or no writing has been done.

1) A book about children learning in home situations and ways in which parents do or might help them. There is a great deal of material on this in *GWS*. Some of it we cut out of *T[each] Y[our] O[wn]* for lack of space; much has come in since that went to press. For titles I have thought of things like *"The Basics" at Home* (or *in the Home*) or *The Three R's at Home*.[1]

We have so much good material on this that if for whatever reason A[ddison] W[esley] was not interested in doing a book on this right now, I would seriously consider getting out some kind of 8½ × 11 book under our own label—*The GWS Book of Math* and/or *The GWS Book of Reading and Writing*. [. . .]

2) The book of book reviews that you and I have talked about doing. Some of the reviews in *GWS* I would expand; would probably write some that have not yet appeared in *GWS,* and would write some other material about the kinds of things that I like in the children's books I select.

3) A book about schools and how to make them better, the book I wrote about in that long brainstorming letter.

4) [. . .] There is a great deal of material that I am really very eager to get into print, and to bring up to date with further writing. I'm not sure whether by the time I get around to doing this I will want to use the Marva Collins[2] stuff or not. I would probably want to mention her, but I might not want to write a long chapter about her, as I previously had proposed. But I would like to write a long chapter about Herndon, and if Dennison's book goes out of print (which, things being what they are, it probably will) I will want to write a lot about it.

5) Another book about music, including lots more stuff about playing the cello. I have a lot of material for this right now. Not sure what to call it. Sometimes I think of *Adventures with a Cello*. There popped into my mind *Still Not Too Late* (since I will be writing about beginning the violin) or *The Later the Better*.

6) A short book about economics, for which I already have quite a lot of notes. This book will take off from the idea that orthodox eco-

1. This was the one book of the list for which Holt did sign a contract, but he was not able to complete the manuscript before he died. In 1989 Merloyd Lawrence brought out a collection of previously uncollected pieces, on the "basics at home" theme, titled *Learning All the Time.*

2. Marva Collins left the Chicago public schools to start her own private school in a poor, all-black Chicago neighborhood. Her book, *Marva Collins' Way,* is about the success of this experience.

nomics, of both the left and the right, has very little relation to reality because of a couple of deep, almost unconscious, certainly rarely articulated assumptions, which I claim are totally mistaken: (a) Anything we can't count, doesn't count (b) Anything we can count, we count as a plus.

7) A short book about economics, but more of the micro kind than the macro, for children. This has been floating around in my head for a couple of years now. For a title I think of *The Lemonade Stand: A Look at Economics, for Children.* I start with the example of a child or children selling lemonade from a stand, and from there go on to discuss the meaning of economic and accounting terms like capital, labor, depreciation, assets, liabilities, opportunity costs, and the nature of some economic decisions. Someday I'll do a brainstormer on this for you. I am very drawn to this book, even though it is still shadowy in my mind.

8) Someday, down the line, I still want to write about dreams.

This seems to be all for the moment. For the time being, I think I would give top priority to the books about 3 R's at home and the book review book, partly because we have so much material available already, and partly because they will reinforce our work here, and help get more customers for our book list and/or *GWS*.

Does this give us something to work on? Within the next month or two I would like to get a definite answer from Delta, and to begin talking to A.W. about a first book with them. I feel a certain sense of urgency, not just because I want to get a contract signed to get some money in here, but because I have so *many* books that I do want to write—or put together—that I want to get going.

Will stop to get this in the mail.

Gastronomic note. My old friend Ping Ferry was in town the other day, at a meeting in the Parker House. He took me to dinner in their restaurant afterwards, and it was one of the very best meals I have had in this (or any) city. Also, very quiet, not crowded or rushed. For dessert they have *souffles!*

I'll see you soon.

Best,

[John]

[TO MERLOYD LAWRENCE]

6/14/83

Dear Merloyd,

Sent that last ltr off to you last night; then woke up this morning realizing that I had left *off* the list two books we have talked a lot about and that I very much want to do, plus a third that I only thought about this morning, which is perhaps not ready for a book right now but may grow into one.

Since I listed eight books in the previous letter I'll just go on with that numbering.

9) Book about children and work. Prob not enough material for this right now, but by a year or two from now should be plenty.

10) Book about children and computers, poss. title *Children, Computers, and the Rest of Us*. Mostly a worried and skeptical look at the situation, but also material (from *GWS* and elsewhere) about children who are having a lot of fun with computers and are learning from them.

11) A book, title perhaps *Freedom and Discipline*, perhaps using material from the first half of *Freedom and Beyond*, but with much new material added.

Who knows, by five years from now I may have enough material to do a book about playing the violin, which would be #12. But we can hold that in reserve for a while.

[. . .]

It's kind of exciting to think of all these books waiting to be compiled and written—like airplanes lined up on a runway waiting to take off. I think of Gibbon's patron—"Scribble, scribble, scribble, eh, Mr. Gibbon?"

[. . .]

That's all for the moment from your prolific friend. [. . .]

Best,

258

Kathy Mingl, a *Growing Without Schooling* reader,
wrote asking for Holt's thoughts about dealing
with people in schools, and how to live with
disagreeing with so many of them.

[TO KATHY MINGL]

6/17/83

Dear Kathy,
    Thanks for your good and long letter, and for all the work you put
into writing it.
    [. . .]
    You have given me many things to think about. Let me begin with
your question, "What would be the result of trying to convince teachers and school authorities that they are wrong?" Since I have been
engaged in that task for about twenty-five years now, I think I can
give a pretty good answer: Nothing. Now let me qualify that. As far
as the large system goes, nothing. A certain very small percentage of
people within that system change their ideas, but then most of them
soon leave the system, or are thrown out of it. Here and there, there
can always be found little pockets of encouraging change within the
schools—but most of them don't last. The great majority of schools,
in terms of all the things I care about, are considerably worse than
they were 25 years ago when I and others started talking about . . .
what we talk about. They are for the most part more rigid, more
mechanical, more fragmented—and they have invented the Father
and Mother of all alibis—Learning Disabilities. And there is not the
slightest sign that they are likely to begin to get better—again, in
terms of what I believe in and care about in children.
    If I say that I don't think there is one chance in a million that the
schools, in any large sense, will change their ways in the next decade
or two, I say it in the spirit in which I would say that I don't think
there's a chance in a million that I will run a four minute mile or play
the Dvorak Concerto in Symphony Hall. If I had all day long to work
on it, and nothing else to do, I might manage the concerto, but almost certainly not the four minute mile—I am the wrong body type,
and no one of my general size and build has ever been a good miler.
There is nothing bitter in this remark, and no self-hatred—I like
myself just fine, and actually think I am going to continue to improve

259

on the cello. But the odds against that much improvement are so great that we can say it is about impossible.

I once believed, certainly hoped, that what brought people into teaching was above all else a love for children, a pleasure in their company, and a desire to see and help them grow. In the chapter "Schools Are Bad Places for Kids," in *The Underachieving School*, I say that most teachers would teach a lot better than they do if they knew how, or dared. This is not so. If I were to try to write down all the experiences, first, second, and third-handed, that have led me to this conclusion, it would take hundreds of pages, probably several books, and at the end you would not be convinced, so I'm not going to start piling case histories on top of your head. Most teachers teach the way they want to teach, and ignore or furiously resist the possibility of teaching in some other ways, even when those ways are opened to them. One of the things experience taught us about small alternative schools within public systems is that it is extremely hard to find teachers who will teach in such schools, and when they do, the teachers in the main system ostracize them.

I have by now seen this demonstrated many, many times—if you teach in unorthodox ways, and as a result get *better* results than most of the teachers in a school, those teachers will not admire you, ask you for advice, etc. They will be angry at you, and will do what they can to undermine your efforts and if they can, get rid of you. This is not theory, but experience. I did not want to believe it and indeed refused to believe it until a *lot* of public educators told it to me.

What brings 90% of people into teaching is what brings 90% of most people into the work they do—all things considered, it looks to them like the best job they can get. It has been true for 50 years, at least, that the overwhelming majority of teachers get the lowest scores on the college boards, go to the least selective and demanding colleges, and get the lowest marks there. (But schools are not very different even in countries like Sweden, where you have to get the best marks to get into a teachers college.) Very few people become teachers who *might* have become doctors, or lawyers, or scientists; they go into teaching because they have no other choice, or no other white-collar choice.

I don't think that the proportion of teachers who dislike or like children is very different from what it is among most people in this country, so the proportion of people who like children, in colleges of education, is about what it is elsewhere—maybe 10% at most. The trouble is that most of the people who really like and trust children, or even who find them interesting, do not stay long in schools—it is simply too painful to have to work, day after day, side by side with people who feel just the other way.

I *wrote How Children Fail,* and *How Children Learn,* and most of my other books, to show just what you said, that with the best will in the world, the things we normally did in classrooms hurt children more than they helped them. I assumed, not as now merely for the purposes of argument and public relations, but because I really believed it, that when teachers saw that, many of them would change their ways. Of the many tens of thousands who heard me lecture, and the perhaps million or more who read my books, perhaps a thousand or two did try to change. As I say, most of them are now out of schools, and many of them are homeschoolers. But the system as a whole remains where it was—only worse.

As far as helping teachers to trust themselves, I've been on public record for at least fifteen years now saying that teachers should be the bosses in their own classrooms, that they should be able to decide what they will teach, when, where, and how, and how they will look at the results. You can't offer teachers more in the way of trust than that.

I say that, by the way, not because I think all or even most teachers are good teachers—I think most of them are very poor teachers, as I was very poor when I started. I say it because it is only from one's own experience as a teacher that one can learn to teach better. Bad as most teachers are, the only possible way of having them get any better is to give them final authority and final responsibility in the classroom. No teachers' organization has ever made this, or anything close to it, a part of its platform. All of them grant without argument to higher educational authorities the right to tell teachers exactly what to do. And when you suggest to teachers themselves that they should have final authority and responsibility in their classrooms, most of them reject that idea. They don't want to have to decide what to do, and bear the responsibility if it doesn't work. They want someone else to tell them what to do, and to take the responsibility if it doesn't work.

Oh, they are indeed like children—but the kind of timid, frightened, neurotic children that you see now and then, but not very often. Since I myself was a fairly timid and mostly self-hating young person at age 20 or so, I know what kind of time and effort, and good luck, it takes to get out of that way of thinking about oneself. The chances of most teachers finding themselves in a life situation that might make such an effort possible are again about one in a million. There is no way, other than the way I proposed above, which most teachers would angrily reject and fight with all their strength, to make the average school into a place where that kind of thing could happen.

Nobody anywhere in education has worked longer or harder than I have to try to give teachers—by making them the bosses in their classrooms—the trust they need in themselves, or the chance to gain, as I did, that kind of trust from their own experiences. In fact, nobody else is saying this *at all*—not that I have heard. "Make teachers the bosses in their own classrooms" is as radical an idea as "Make children the bosses of their own learning." No one wants to hear it, *least of all teachers.*

As far as not losing tempers and calling them idiots is concerned, I agree. I think I have spoken to some two thousand or so meetings of teachers, and the kind of treatment and response I meet has made people afterwards say to me more times than I can count, "John, I don't know how you can be so patient with them." I can think of only three or four times when I have been goaded beyond endurance and have lashed out at someone—which I have always regretted later. But it hardly ever happens, and I know it didn't happen at the meeting at which you heard me speak, because I can remember thinking at the end of it that it was a very pleasant meeting.

In other words, I *always* do offer to teachers exactly what I offered to students when I was a classroom teacher, the chance for a fresh start. But they don't listen, or at any rate don't respond.

I will probably write another book somewhere in the next few years about how to improve the schools, in which I will say some of the things I say here. But I will also say, if we are going to improve the schools, we must not tell ourselves or the public that certain things are so when they are not so. It's a little like Alcoholics Anonymous—and I have known intimately some alcoholics who reformed, and others who didn't, and died of it, and someone I am very close to is right now at a kind of crossroads about this. One of the absolutely tried and tested principles of AA is that an alcoholic cannot be cured until she or he is willing to look in the mirror, or into the eyes of other people, and say, "I am an alcoholic." We will get nowhere with the schools by saying, as so many reformers have tried to, "You're doing a wonderful job, and here's a way in which you can do an even *more* wonderful job." We have to say, "Things are bad, and here's why they're bad."

Let me give an example. One of the fictions of schools is that the teachers like the kids. Most of them don't. Most adults don't like kids much, and they mostly like the ones who are good looking, docile, obedient, articulate, etc. Everyone talks to teachers about how important it is to like kids, how much the children have to have love, etc. I would say, "Most of you don't like kids, and there's nothing wrong with not liking them, and there's no reason why not liking them should make you into a bad teacher. You can't make yourself like kids by telling yourself that you ought to. What you *can* do and *must* do is be fair—treat them as nearly equally as you can; to be just—not make them pay for the fact that you don't like them, but treat them as well as you treat people you do like; and to be respectful and courteous—which is something that very few people do, even among those who like children." Forget big words like Love. Concentrate on little words like Please and Thank You. How many adults, above all in a school, ever say Please or Thank You to children?

Well, I can't quite be sure whether your letter to me was saying, in effect, "Go on doing what you're doing," or "Do something quite different from what you're doing." If the former, I say, "Thanks, I will." If the latter, then "I'm sorry, but I've been doing that." No one has worked harder to give the schools useful and *usable* advice.

I expect to keep offering it. But I would be crazy to think that very many people were likely to heed it.

Well, thanks once again for your good letter. It has been useful as well as fun for me to write this long reply, and I probably will be able to make further use of some of it, especially if and when I get around to writing a book about improving the schools. (I have a lot to say about that, that neither I nor anyone else has said.)

best,

[TO SUSANNAH SHEFFER]

12/29/83

Dear Susannah,

What a nice Christmas present your letter was! And *never* worry about making your letters too long. Letters with as much good stuff as you put in yours can't be too long—and anyway, I am a fast reader.

Fast typist, too—when I get warmed up I can almost type letters as fast as I could dictate them.

[. . .]

Very interested to hear of your plans re Swarthmore. I was very happy to hear from you earlier how much you liked the place, partly because as a friend I was happy that you were happy, and also able to use the institution for your own purposes, and also because I was glad to learn of an institution that *could* be used for humane purposes. (Which may still be true.) But I am ever more glad that, feeling that for the time being at least it is no longer serving your purposes, you have decided to take a leave from it. You had a good reason for going there, you have a good reason for leaving, and if and when you go back you will have a good reason for going back. You may find in time that there are in fact doors that you want to go through that can only be opened with that particular kind of key. But I am glad that you are looking at other possibilities.

This calls to mind one of my favorite of all answers to tough questions, one given by the Quaker George Fox to William Penn. Penn had been converted to Quakerism, including a belief in peace and non-violence, but at one point he asked Fox a very hard question: "What shall I do with my sword?" It is almost impossible in the year 1983 to understand emotionally what that sword meant to Penn—it was a symbol of his manhood, his courage, his allegiance to the King, his identity as officer and gentleman. A lifetime of experience was wrapped in it. And yet, insofar as it was a weapon designed to kill, he could no longer use it or believe in it. So, he said to his mentor Fox, what shall I do with it. And Fox gave him an answer so true, beautiful, humane, understanding, and *useful* that, when telling this story aloud, I can hardly repeat his words without choking up. "Why, wear it," he said, "as long as thou canst."

It puts tears in my eyes to write it.

Someone, hearing about my cello playing, once said to me, "I think I'll take up the piano someday." I said (all this in the context of a very friendly conversation), "Well, as a matter of fact, you won't. You will never take it up as long as you are only 'thinking about' taking it up. If you take it up, it will be because you can't stand not to."

And Swarthmore for you was like the sword—you wore it as long as you could.

Very int what you tell me about the students at Swarthmore. "No sense of work worth doing . . ." It's 30 years since Goodman wrote *Growing Up Absurd,* and it's no less true today than then, maybe more true.

Couldn't there be *someone* at an institution of higher learning whose main work would be to help students find work worth doing (as opposed to "good jobs"). Would it be possible to get students themselves discussing the difference(s) between "good jobs" and work worth doing. What might come out of such a conversation.

Actually, even in science, even in business, there is a lot of work worth doing in this country. The problem for young people is that they don't know where it is or how to find it or go about looking for it, or who they might ask for help in finding it. The problem, too, is that most work worth doing probably doesn't pay much money, though there might be some exceptions, and most students at places like Swarthmore (or maybe anywhere) do not want to come to grips with the question, "If I could find some work worth doing, how much would I be willing to give up in order to do it?"

[. . .]

One of my favorite proverbs—my favorite of all, come to think of it—is (supposedly) a translation of an old Spanish proverb: "Take what you want," says God, "and pay for it." The three great arts of life are (1) Finding out what you truly want (2) Finding out what it costs (for it always costs something), and how by thought and skillful bargaining you can reduce that cost to a minimum (3) When you have found the lowest possible cost, *paying it without complaining.* Very hard for people to do, and #3 hardest of all. Of those people who are smart enough to understand what they really want, most then think or hope that somehow they can get it without paying anything, like shoplifting.

As I write this I look out the door and see that my five-year-old friend Chris, having played most of the day with his many small cars and trucks, is now working the office vacuum cleaner. In his life in the office—he comes almost every day with his mother, who does a lot of work for us—work and play, fantasy and reality, are so closely intermingled that you can't tell one from the other. I suddenly see it for the first time—if children are not allowed to mix play with work, they soon forget both how to work and how to play.

Chris, with the help of his very nice older brother, is figuring out how the vacuum cleaner works.

[. . .]

The thought suddenly came to me that one of the great advantages of doing work worth doing, even if it doesn't pay very much money, is that you get so much smarter doing it. To be 100% involved in your life and your work is a "high" that most college students could hardly imagine, or could hardly imagine could be attained without the aid of drugs, etc.

[...] I see homeschooling as part of a larger cause, or a means to a larger end, the integration of children into adult society. And as I said in the very first issue of *GWS,* it is about how people can find life worth living and work worth doing without having to go through the medium of school. A life worth living and work worth doing—that is what I want for children (and all people), not just, or not even, something called "a better education." This was the central point, understood by almost no one, of the book *Instead of Education.*

[...]

Herndon is wonderful! And that book,[1] comic as it is, is one of the saddest books ever written—which *every reviewer* missed, including Nat Hentoff, who is smart enough to know better. They all talked about it as a message of hope. It was no such thing, but a message of defeat and despair. [...] In the early part of the book, when he wrote about why he went into teaching, he said that he saw it in part as a way of making America healthy again. If he could find out how to work in his class, he could spread that to the school, thence to more schools, perhaps all schools, thence to other parts of society. In the next to last chapter he says it can't be done. "I agree that it is hard lines."

It's enough to make you weep—in fact, it sometimes has.

The last chapter is only about what do you do, how do you live, how do you survive, when you find that your native land has gone *incurably* bad, that with all the skill and energy and dedication in the world, and with the example an unquestioned success, you can't even change one small school, let alone schools as a whole, let alone anything else. How do you live? The last sentence gives the answer—a good answer even for those who, like me, have not quite given up hope—[which] is by finding what pleasure you can (which is a lot) in the small daily events of life.

It's a valuable book, and might someday be much more so. It is a book about how to live without hope. How to live in Russia, or

1. *How to Survive in Your Native Land.*

Czechoslovakia, or Poland. Or the United States if and when we become some kind of dictatorship.

I saw Jim last a few years ago in San Francisco and we had a nice visit together, confessed that to our great surprise, in spite of having been disappointed in all our deepest hopes, we were on a day to day basis happier than we had ever been. [. . .]

Thanks once again for your fine and welcome letter. And a Happy and Interesting New Year to you.

love,

[John]

[TO STEVEN PEARLSTEIN, *BOSTON OBSERVER*]

3/6/84

Dear Steven,

I just turned up the 12/10/82 issue of the *Observer*, which contained a piece by Ted Sizer about the teaching of writing.[1] At the time I wrote him a letter about it—but decided not to mail it, thinking, "What would be the use of getting into this kind of a fruitless argument?"

Having read it again, I can't resist the temptation to point out to you that, like practically everything written about the schools in the last year or two, it has almost no connection with reality.

Sizer is talking about a hypothetical English teacher named Horace, "who believes in rigorous teaching of writing," but who does not have the time for "thoughtful critiquing, in red ballpoint pen in the margins and elsewhere" of his students' writing. Give him fewer students, says Sizer, and he can assign longer papers and fill up more of the margins with his red ballpoint, thereby supposedly making better writers.

All this is right out of Dreamland.

In the first place, schools like Andover, or the very similar school I went to, in which English teachers have the time to do what Sizer suggests, do not turn poor writers into good ones. None of the students I knew in four years at such a school improved their writing

1. Theodore Sizer's *Horace's Compromise: The Dilemma of the American High School* was published in 1984.

skill much as a result of being there. The hot shot prep schools do not assign a much higher percentage of A's to their seniors than they do to their entering classes. Those who come in good writers, probably leave good writers; those who come in (by Andover standards) relatively inept, leave relatively inept.

In the second place I knew as a student and later learned as a teacher that students, even at these hot shot schools, *do not read,* far less ponder, the little scribblings in red ballpoint pen. Students who get A's on their papers may enjoy reading any complimentary remarks a teacher may have put on them; having read these, they throw the paper away. Students who get C's and D's throw the paper away without looking. When, as an English teacher at hot shot Commonwealth School, I told my students that I was perfectly willing to edit their papers in as much detail as they wanted, if they were then willing to re-write them, not one student ever took me up on the offer.

In the third place, that's not how good writers are made, anyway. We learn to use language well under one condition and one only, when we use it to say or write things we want to say or write, to people we want to say and write them to. When schools like Andover produce, as now and then they do, some really good student writing, it is because the students have been given an opportunity to write on a subject of their choosing to an audience that they really want to reach. Little red marks have nothing to do with it. Behind all good writing is the thought, or the hope, that what one writes may make a difference, if only in giving some real pleasure to someone, perhaps to oneself. Few students of the Horaces of this world ever get a chance to do such writing. In six years of writing English papers in hot shot school and college, and I never got less than A in English, I wrote only one paper that I would now like to be able to lay my hands on.

In the fourth place, even if little red marks could produce better writing, or help to produce it, what students need more than anything else is practice. If the amount that students write is limited by what teachers think they can correct, or even just read, the students will not be writing enough. To young people I meet who tell me they are serious about writing and ask how to do it better, I say that as a bare minimum they ought to think of writing at least a thousand words a day and preferably more than that. It could be in the form of letters—a wonderful art form, by the way, and perhaps the incubator of most good writing—or in journals, or simply in free-flowing streams of consciousness. But the first requirement of a writer is that he be able to get the stuff out, and more than anything else, young people need practice in that. When I gave some English students, then seniors at Berkeley, and therefore the hottest of hot shot students, the assignment of writing stuff that no one else would see, writing for themselves alone, an experience they much enjoyed and found revealing and helpful in many ways, they told me that never in their entire careers as students had anyone ever asked or suggested that they do that.

The chances of persuading any English department faculty to take this approach to writing, above all in hot shot schools, is about the same as the chance of you or me jumping over the Prudential Building. So the Horaces will go on doodling their more often than not sarcastic little remarks in the margins of papers, and the students will go on ignoring them, and thinking that writing is something you do to get marks from an English teacher, and things will stay right where they are.

Yours for reality,
John Holt

Vivian Paley's books are about young children in
the classroom, particularly their fantasy games.

[TO VIVIAN PALEY]

9/10/84

Dear Mrs. Paley,

I have just read, with enormous interest and pleasure, your new book *Boys and Girls*.[1] I had previously read *Wally's Stories*, which I also enjoyed so much that I had intended to write you earlier, but somehow never got around to it. But your new book is so delightful and stirred up so many thoughts in my mind that I could not put it off any longer.

[. . .]

Part of our work here is to run a small mail-order bookstore,

---

1. The full title is *Boys and Girls: Superheroes in the Doll Corner.*

which started off as a way to make my own books available to people who had been unable to find them in bookstores, and gradually spread out to include many other books, and, in time, other kinds of materials. As we add new books to our list, I review them in our magazine *Growing Without Schooling,* of which I enclose a few copies for your interest—including the issue in which I reviewed *Wally's Stories.*

Something you said in *Boys and Girls* makes the point, but better than I made it, that I was trying to make about *Wally's Stories.* You said—I can't put my finger on the exact page—something to the effect that when little children are using art materials they are not making "something" but simply making. You are absolutely right. Little children painting, for the most part, do not have some kind of picture in their own mind which they are trying to reproduce on the paper. Nor are they even experimenting, in the sense of thinking to themselves, "I will just put this color here and this color here and see what happens." They are simply painting. Of course they are interested in what happens after they have painted, though probably less interested than most of the adults who look at the painting.

I suspect that the same thing is true of little children's talking. When they talk, I do not think that, at least much of the time, they have some part of a model of reality in their minds which they are trying to express in words and so convey to someone else. They are just making things out of words, for the sheer pleasure of doing it. Therefore I think it may be a mistake to inquire too deeply into the "meaning" of everything that they say. Or, at any rate, if just for the pleasure of the exercise we want to speculate about these meanings, we ought to be extremely skeptical about our own conclusions. And I feel that we ought not to coax the children into conversations about this or that so that we may better understand what goes on in their minds.

The distinction I am trying to make here is a rather subtle one, which applies equally well to conversations between adults. When I talk to my friends, I am of course interested in the meaning of what they say, and beyond that, what these meanings may tell me about their larger structures of thought. But I do not engage my good friends in conversation *so that* I may probe further into their minds. In other words, I do not carry on conversations as if they were some sort of psychological examination. The difference is between two (or more) people freely exchanging gifts of their own thoughts and

270

ideas, and one person, more or less in the position of the psychologist, probing into the mind of another.

I am personally *enormously* put off by people who I think are trying to analyze me. I am tempted to rephrase the old quotation, "Judge not, that ye be judged," into something like, "Analyze not, that ye be analyzed." It seems to me an impertinence, some kind of serious invasion of privacy or liberty, to inquire more deeply into the thoughts of another person—let me rephrase this—to try to learn more about the thoughts of another person than they want to reveal. This is perhaps a very old-fashioned view.

Actually, these thoughts arise in part out of a very serious concern. I don't think, of all the many harmful and destructive things that most schools do these days, anything is more harmful and destructive than the kind of pop psychology which they practice on their students. This would be bad even if they were competent at doing it, and they are a million miles from being so.

[. . .]

I also like very much what you say about being worried, not about control, but about the appearance of control. However, as a practical matter, the appearance of control is for most teachers critical. I was a rather unconventional teacher myself for a number of years at both the elementary and secondary level. I was fired from the two schools in which I taught fifth grade, for a number of reasons, one of which was that I did not seem to be exercising control in the way that the other teachers did. As a plain matter of fact, I had excellent control in my classrooms; I could, on the whole, prevent the children from doing those things which I really did not want them to do, and could generally get them to do most of the things which I did want them to do. I hardly ever had to shout or shush at the children, something which other teachers in the building, as I could hear through the walls, spent a great deal of their time doing. So, as was the case with my friend Jim Herndon in his book *The Way It Spozed to Be*, my methods of control brought results. But they did not look like other people's methods, and it did not look like I was bossing the children around and making them obey orders, and this got me into considerable trouble. Most working teachers know that nothing will more quickly bring down on their heads the disapproval of their colleagues, or indeed the real possibility of being fired, than the appearance of not having firm control of their classes. So this is not a minor concern. But I think you are absolutely right, the things we do to achieve and maintain the appearance of control are often destructive of any real discipline and authority.

I come out of *Boys and Girls* with a number of thoughts, questions, speculations, which I would like to share with you. I hope you will not feel that the length of this letter puts you under some kind of obligation to reply. I'm writing partly to tell you what is in my mind, but partly simply to get my own thoughts down on paper so that I may be able to consider them at greater length, and so that they will not be rattling around in my head as they are at the moment. I often find, when my mind is captured by certain kinds of thoughts, that if I get them down onto paper I am to some degree freed from them, able to think about other things, knowing that I can come back and look at these thoughts later, and so it is with this letter. I am not trying to prod or coax you into a discussion of these matters. On the other hand, if what I say in this letter stirs up some thoughts which you feel you would like to send me, I would be most delighted to hear them.

One thought which comes very much to mind as I read your books is something that Paul Goodman said back in the 60s, that most children in our society are *over-socialized,* that is they spend far too much of their time in the company of far too many other people. I get this impression very strongly from your description of your classes. But I have also felt this way about every one of the kindergartens and pre-kindergartens I have ever visited, which adds up to quite a few. I've always felt that there was too much going on, unless of course, by some stratagem, which often includes Montessori, the teacher makes sure that nothing is going on. The children have too much input. More stuff comes in than they are able to chew up and digest. I hear it very strongly in these conversations, which you so well reproduce, in which a bunch of children start saying, "Let's pretend." One child will say let's pretend this, another child will say let's pretend that, and still another child will say let's pretend something else. It seems that no child ever has time to take a thought and live with it for a while, try it out at leisure, work out its consequences. I happen to believe very strongly that fantasy is a kind of research tool for children, a way in which they attempt to understand better various parts of reality, and if their fantasy-experiments are continually being interrupted by somebody else or turned into some other experiment, this seems to be very unsettling.

[. . .]

There is a very important difference between the fantasy play of the girls and that of the boys [in the book], that the girls draw their fantasies, or many of them, out of their experience of real life, whereas the boys draw theirs off the TV screen. One of my objections to television—one of many—is that it does our fantasizing for us, provides us with ready-made daydreams. For the reason I have given, and others, I think fantasizing and daydreaming are extremely important, even for adults. But their usefulness disappears when we stop, so to speak, rolling our own.

[. . .]

I love the very ending of your wonderful book. Thanks so much for writing it, and forgive me for inflicting this interminable letter on you. I hope you may find some things of interest in it. Anyway, good luck to you in your work, and I hope you will write many more books. And do give my special love to Charlotte[2] next time you see her.

Sincerely yours,

John Holt

2. A girl in the book.

EPILOGUE

In 1982 Holt discovered a tumorous growth on the inside of his left thigh. He had accumulated a file of material on alternative cancer treatments over the years, as part of his general interest in self-reliance as opposed to institutional dependence. Already very skeptical of the conventional medical establishment, he was reluctant to go to a doctor or surgeon, and decided to treat the tumor with large doses of vitamin C. He continued to take vitamin C and to monitor the growth of the tumor for the next couple of years. By the spring of 1984, however, managing the tumor had become a daily burden, and he was ready to look for a surgeon he could trust. Friends recommended Dr. Bernie Siegel of Exceptional Cancer Patients (ECaP) in New Haven, Connecticut. Siegel, a supporter of unconventional therapies, has since become widely known for his book *Love, Medicine, and Miracles*. In September of 1984 Holt went to New Haven to have the tumor removed.

After recovering from the surgery in Boston, he wrote in *Growing Without Schooling*, no. 43:

> One of the thoughts that kept coming to my mind as I struggled with this cancer was, "Why me?" Travelling on planes in July and August, now and then I would look around and see people smoking, drinking their two cocktails before lunch, and generally eating and living unhealthily, and I would think, not so much in resentment as in simple curiosity, "How come I got this thing and they did not?" Like many, I had believed for some time that cancer is caused by, or at least made much more likely and destructive by tension, stress, unresolved conflicts. But at first this didn't seem to have much to do with me . . . It wasn't so much a matter of having a sudden revelation as of very slowly having faint hunches, which became clearer and more certain the more I thought about them and talked about them with others. By a week or two after surgery I felt that I knew what had

274

been the unresolved conflicts in my life, and how I would change my life to resolve them.

The first and most serious conflict that I found was between my work (with children, parents, and the homeschooling movement) and my growing love for music and need to make music. For years I had been saying, "*Someday*, when I get less busy, I want to really work hard on the cello and see how far I can go toward becoming a good player . . ." But I never did get less busy, and this "someday" kept disappearing into the future. I decided that this had gone on long enough, and that I had to start turning someday into today . . .

The second thing I found out about myself is that I am tired of talking to school people, educators, meetings of teachers, educational conferences, and all that, tired of talking to people who are not really looking for new ideas or ways to improve their work, and who do not take seriously what I say and never did . . . For some time, to people who have asked me, "Why have you given up on schools?" I have said that I haven't given up on them, that I was as interested as I ever was in making them better, if only I could see a way to do it. I learned from my cancer that even if this was true for a while it is not true any more. I have indeed given up on schools. According to Dr. John Goodlad, Dean of the School of Education at UCLA and author of the book *A Place Called School*, [schools] have not changed in any important respect in close to a hundred years. They certainly haven't changed in the forty years of my adult life . . . As I said in *Instead of Education*, they are bad because they start with an essentially bad idea, not just mistaken and impossible, but bad in the sense of morally wrong, that some people have or ought to have the right to determine what a lot of other people know and think. As long as they start from this bad idea they cannot become better, and I don't want to take part any longer in any public pretense that they can . . .

The third thing I found out about myself was something that I had perhaps known for some time but had tried to ignore, namely, that I need *space* in my life, and really dislike the feeling with which I have been living for many years now, that even with twice as many hours in the day I could never manage to do all that I have to do, but would just keep falling further and further behind . . . I learned that . . . I had to define my work in such a way that, without spending every evening and weekend in the office as I had been doing, I could actually get it done . . .

With these resolutions Holt did indeed begin to make actual changes in his life. He raised his lecture fee so sharply that he received fewer invitations, which is just what he had hoped would happen, and he began to spend more time on music. But by the spring of 1985 the cancer had returned, and this time he was unable to defeat it. He died at home on September 14, almost exactly a year after the original surgery.

Though he had sought effective alternative treatments after

discovering the tumor, a letter written in June of 1984 to Dr. George Wootan, another supporter of unconventional therapies, reveals that Holt had always suspected that he might not be able to cure himself. In the letter he had written:

[I]t is possible that none of these treatments may work—none of these people claim 100% success rates, tho their rates are high. In that case, I will die of cancer sometime in the next year or two.

I looked that fact squarely in the eye earlier today, and I found out a terrific secret about myself, the knowledge of which is one of the most exhilarating experiences I have ever known. I am not afraid of death. Lying in a hospital full of tubes and in worse and worse pain, yes. Death, no. I had hoped this might be so, and have tried to train myself to live in the knowledge of my own death. But it was mostly an unreal exercise; my real idea about myself was that I would live to be 90, or 100, being a healthy person from a long-lived family. But now I confront squarely the fact that I may die, not at 90, but at 62 or 61 (which is what I am now). And the thought that comes to me is, well, if that's the way it is, that's the way it is, all those big projects (learning the piano, etc.) are just going to have to be left undone. Too bad. What I have to do is get things in order here so that this operation [the office] can run without me, and I think within the next year we may be able to do that.

Was Holt ready to die, or would he have loved to be able to live several more years? George Dennison, who died of cancer himself two years after Holt did, wrote in a piece that was read at Holt's memorial service:

In the last weeks of his life John spent eight days with us at our home in Maine. Something happened one day that gave me a glimpse of the very heart of his life. He was so weak he could walk only a few steps at a time and with canes. It was beautiful weather. I took him driving to see the views from certain hills—long views of wooded slopes, fields, streams, our large river, and several ponds. Again and again he said, "How beautiful it is!" He was sitting beside me in the front seat. We drove on and he began to talk about his work. "It could be such a wonderful world," he said, "such a wonderful place." His body began to shake and he dropped his head, crying uncontrollably—but he kept talking through the sobs, his voice strained and thin. "It's not as if we don't know what to do," he said. "We know *exactly* what do to, and it would work, it would work. They're going to wreck it."

We do all have feelings of this kind, but not many people, at the end of life, would feel this heartbroken passion for the world itself. It seemed to me that the deepest and most sustaining things in John's character had been revealed in that moment. And like so much in his work they were rare and fine.

APPENDIX: BOOKS MENTIONED
IN THE TEXT

Berg, Ivar. *Education and Jobs: The Great Training Robbery.* Boston: Beacon Press, 1971.

Berg, Leila. *Look at Kids.* Penguin Books, 1972.

———. *Reading and Loving.* London: Routledge & Kegan Paul, 1977.

Bissex, Glenda. *GNYS AT WRK: A Child Learns to Write and Read.* Cambridge: Harvard University Press, 1980.

Bruner, Jerome. *Toward a Theory of Instruction.* Cambridge: Harvard University Press, 1966.

Cleaver, Eldridge. *Soul on Ice.* New York: McGraw-Hill, 1967.

Collins, Marva, and Tamarkin, Civia. *Marva Collins' Way.* Los Angeles: J. P. Tarcher, Inc., 1982.

Croall, Jonathan. *Neill of Summerhill: The Permanent Rebel.* New York: Pantheon Books, 1983.

Dennison, George. *The Lives of Children.* New York: Random House, 1969.

Dillon, Jim. *Personal Teaching.* Columbus, Ohio: Charles E. Merrill, 1971.

Fader, Daniel. *The Naked Children.* New York: Macmillan Co., 1971.

Forer, Lois G. *No One Will Lissen.* New York: John Day, 1970.

Friedenberg, Edgar. *The Vanishing Adolescent.* Boston: Beacon Press, 1964.

———. *The Coming of Age in America.* New York: Random House, 1965.

Fromm, Erich. *Escape from Freedom.* New York: Avon Books, 1941, 1969.

Goodman, Paul. *Growing Up Absurd.* New York: Vintage Books, 1956.

———. *New Reformation: Notes of a Neolithic Conservative.* New York: Random House, 1970.

Goodwin, Richard. *The American Condition.* Garden City, N.Y.: Doubleday, 1974.

Hentoff, Nat. *Our Children Are Dying.* New York: Viking Press, 1966.

Herndon, James. *The Way It Spozed to Be.* New York: Simon & Schuster, 1968.

———. *How to Survive in Your Native Land.* New York: Simon & Schuster, 1970.

Holt, John. *How Children Fail.* New York: Pitman Publishing Company, 1964; rev. ed., New York: Delacorte Press/Seymour Lawrence, 1982.

APPENDIX

――――. *How Children Learn.* New York: Pitman Publishing Company, 1967; rev. ed., New York: Delacorte Press/Seymour Lawrence, 1983.

――――. *The Underachieving School.* New York: Pitman Publishing Co., 1969.

――――. *What Do I Do Monday?* New York: E. P. Dutton Co., 1970.

――――. *Freedom and Beyond.* New York: E. P. Dutton Co., 1972.

――――. *Escape from Childhood.* New York: E. P. Dutton Co., 1974.

――――. *Instead of Education.* New York: E. P. Dutton Co., 1976.

――――. *Never Too Late: My Musical Life Story.* New York: Delacorte Press/Seymour Lawrence, 1978.

――――. *Teach Your Own.* New York: Delacorte Press/Seymour Lawrence, 1981.

――――. *Learning All the Time.* Reading, Mass.: Addison-Wesley/Merloyd Lawrence Books, 1989.

Illich, Ivan. *Celebration of Awareness.* New York: Doubleday, 1970.

――――. *Deschooling Society.* New York: Harper & Row, 1970, 1971.

――――. *Tools for Conviviality.* New York: Harper & Row, 1973.

――――. *Energy and Equity.* London: Calder & Boyars Ltd., 1974.

――――. *Toward a History of Needs.* New York: Pantheon, 1978.

――――. *Shadow Work.* London: Marion Boyars Publishers Ltd., 1981.

Illich, Ivan, and Verne, Etienne. *Imprisoned in the Global Classroom.* New York: Writers and Readers Publishing Cooperative Ltd., 1976, 1981.

Jencks, Christopher, et al. *Inequality: A Reassessment of the Effect of Family and Schooling in America.* New York: Basic Books, 1972.

Jerome, Judson. *Culture out of Anarchy.* New York: Herder & Herder, 1970.

Kaye, Michael. *The Teacher Was the Sea.* New York: Links Books, 1972.

Kohl, Herbert. *Reading: How To.* E. P. Dutton Co., 1973.

Kozol, Jonathan. *Death at an Early Age.* Boston: Houghton Mifflin, 1968.

――――. *Free Schools.* Boston: Houghton Mifflin, 1972.

――――. *The Night Is Dark and I Am Far from Home.* New York: Bantam Books, 1975.

――――. *Illiterate America.* New York: Anchor Books/Doubleday, 1986.

Laing, R. D. *The Politics of Experience.* New York: Pantheon, 1967.

――――. *The Divided Self.* New York: Pantheon, 1969.

Leary, Timothy. *The Psychedelic Experience.* New Hyde Park, N.Y.: University Books, 1964.

Liedloff, Jean. *The Continuum Concept.* New York: Warner Books, 1975; Reading, Mass.: Addison-Wesley, 1985.

McLuhan, Marshall, and Fiore, Quentin. *The Medium Is the Message.* New York: Random House, 1967.

Macrorie, Ken. *Uptaught.* Rochelle Park, N.J.: Hayden Book Co., 1970.

――――. *A Vulnerable Teacher.* Rochelle Park, N.J.: Hayden Book Co., 1974.

Marin, Peter, and Cohen, Allan Y. *Understanding Drug Use.* New York: Harper & Row, 1971.

Maslow, Abraham. *Toward a Psychology of Being.* Princeton: D. Van Nostrand Co., 1967.

May, Rollo. *Man's Search for Himself*. New York: W. W. Norton Co., 1953.

Neill, A. S. *Summerhill*. New York: Hart Publishing, 1960.

———. *Talking of Summerhill*. London: Victor Gollancz Ltd., 1967.

Paley, Vivian Gussin. *Wally's Stories*. Cambridge: Harvard University Press, 1981.

———. *Boys and Girls: Superheroes in the Doll Corner*. Chicago: University of Chicago Press, 1984.

Pearl, Arthur. *The Atrocity of Education*. St. Louis: New Critics Press, 1972.

Postman, Neil, and Weingartner, Charles. *Teaching as a Subversive Activity*. New York: Delacorte Press, 1969.

———. *The School Book*. New York: Delacorte Press, 1973.

Rasberry, Salli, and Greenway, Robert. *Rasberry Exercises: How to Start a School and Make a Book*. Berkeley: Freestone, 1970.

Reich, Wilhelm. *The Function of the Orgasm*. New York: Farrar, Straus & Giroux, 1986.

Reimer, Everett. *School Is Dead*. New York: Doubleday, 1971.

Schumacher, E. F. *Small Is Beautiful*. New York: Harper & Row, 1973.

Silberman, Charles. *Crisis in the Classroom*. New York: Random House, 1970.

Sizer, Theodore. *Horace's Compromise: The Dilemma of the American High School*. Boston: Houghton Mifflin, 1984, 1985.

Stallibrass, Alison. *The Self-Respecting Child*. London: Thames & Hudson, 1974; rpt., Reading, Mass.: Addison-Wesley, 1989.

Szasz, Thomas. *The Myth of Mental Illness*. New York: Hoeber-Harper, 1961.

Taylor, Edmond. *Richer by Asia*. Boston: Houghton Mifflin, 1964.

Terkel, Studs. *Working*. New York: Pantheon, 1974.

Terry, Charles, ed. *Knowledge Without Goodness Is Dangerous: Moral Education in Boarding Schools*. Exeter, N.H.: Phillips Exeter Academy Press, 1981.

van den Berg, J. H. *The Changing Nature of Man*. New York: W. W. Norton, 1961.

Wasserman, Miriam. *Demystifying School*. New York: Praeger, 1974.

Whitehead, Alfred North. *The Aims of Education*. New York: Macmillan, 1959.

INDEX

Acland, Sir Richard, 172–75, 189–90
Apple Hill Chamber Music Center, 167
Arlen, Michael, 182–83

Berg, Elliot, 212
Berg, Leila, 38, 242
Berkeley, University of California at: courses taught at, 49, 177; student strike at, 45–46
Bernstein, Basil, 213
Bissex, Glenda, 239–41
Black community, economics of, 51–52, 226–28
Blacks: improving schools of, 117–18; radical, 65–66
Boggs, Grace and James, 226–28
Boston University students, 60–65
Bowles, Samuel, 5, 6n
Bruner, Jerome, 44, 215
Bystrom, Åke, 236

Cancer, 274–76
Capitalist society, 36
Center for Intercultural Documentation (CIDOC): Everett Reimer's seminar at, 70; and school reform movement, 6; students at, 56–59; visiting, 90–91. See also Deschooling; Illich, Ivan; Reimer, Everett
Change: effective, 226, 233–34; on human level, 149–50; process of, 110–

11, 142–43. See also Revolution, effective
Children: anger of, 76–77, 158–62; art by, 270; fantasy play of, 273; Holt's love of, 223–24; needs of, 219–20, 233; observing, 55, 88; oversocialization of, 272; people deciding to have, 234; sleep of, 194; talk of, 270; violence of, 229
Chomsky, Noam, 105–8
Christianity, 113–14
Cleaver, Eldridge, 82
College: advice to young people about, 41–42, 264; Holt's experience of, 1, 13, 251–52
Collins, Marva, 256
Colorado Rocky Mountain School: friend from, 118; getting job at, 14–15; life at, 21–22
Commonwealth School, 15
Communes, 119–20
Continuum Concept, The (Liedloff), 224–26
Croall, Jonathan, 242–47
Crocker, Katharine, 15–22

Daitch, Jon, 221–23
Dant, Pamela, 85–87, 90–92, 95–96, 125
Death: control of, 147–48; Holt's feelings about, 113, 114, 276; talking about, 154

INDEX

DeMott, Benjamin, 96–97
Denmark, 155–56. *See also* Hughes,
 Peggy; Ny Lilleskole
Dennison, George: on Holt's career, 4;
 on Holt as teacher, 157, 188; memo-
 rial essay by, 276; public life of, 53,
 157; review of *How Children Fail*, 43;
 as romantic critic, 4. See also *The
 Lives of Children*
Dennison, Mabel, 10, 218–20, 223–24
Deschooling, 6–8, 56, 110. *See also*
 Center for Intercultural Documenta-
 tion; Illich, Ivan
Deschooling Society (Illich), 7
Dewey, John, 3
Dillon, Jim, 102–4
Duane, Michael, 38
Dutton, E. P., publishing company, 54n,
 138. *See also* Scharlatt, Hal; White-
 head, Bill
Dworkin, Ronald, 93–94

Energy: levels of personal, 150–51,
 229–30; small-scale forms of, 191–93
Escape from Childhood (Holt): planning
 of, 120–21, 139–40; public response
 to, 169, 181; sales of, 189; title of,
 140–41
Exeter Academy, 179–80, 247–49

Fader, Daniel, 97, 209–12
Ferry, W. H. (Ping), 47, 186, 200, 241–
 42
Forer, Lois, 70–71
Foster, Marcus, 117–18, 125–27
Freedom and Beyond (Holt): choosing
 title of, 123, 140; manuscript of,
 99; as political book, 221; sales of,
 141
Freedom in classrooms, 177–78, 179.
 See also Free schools
Free schools: Holt and, 4–5; raising
 children in, 154–55; teachers in, 97–
 98
Freudian analysis, 41

Friedenberg, Edgar, 127–30, 168–69
Friedman, Jerry, 46, 163
Fromm, Erich, 33, 127

Geiger, Henry, 68n, 200
Gintis, Herbert, 5, 6n
GNYS AT WRK (Bissex), 239–41
Goodman, Paul: bitterness of, 91; on
 oversocialization of children, 272;
 and "roles," 61; and Western civilization, 67–70; and work worth doing,
 265; and young people, 66–67
Greene, Felix, 31–32
Growing Up Absurd (Goodman), 66, 265
Growing Without Schooling: discussion of
 politics in, 221; founding of, 8, 199–
 200; growth of, 230; pressure of editing, 200, 216

Happiness, 150
Harvard Graduate School of Education. *See* "Student-Directed Learning" course
Hentoff, Nat, 141–43
Herndon, James: as comic writer, 90;
 and compulsory schooling, 92; on
 education as separate from life, 202–
 3; on *How Children Fail*, 3; and publishing, 53–54; as romantic critic, 3.
 See also *How to Survive in Your Native
 Land; The Way It Spozed to Be.*
Hicks, Gary, 34–38, 45–46, 51–52, 65–
 66
Hille, Tony, 187–89
Holt, John: on cancer, 274–76; college
 experience of, 1, 13, 251–52; and
 communal life, 119–20; Dennison
 on, 4, 157, 188, 276; on his father,
 113, 164–66; feelings about death,
 113, 114, 276; future books of, 255–
 58; future plans of, 26–29; influence
 of, 118; on his mother, 164–66; as
 tactician, 110; as teacher, 2, 157, 188;
 as writer, 185

Home education: Judson Jerome and, 80, 119; as practical deschooling, 8–9

How Children Fail (Holt): choosing title of, 123, 140; Dennison review of, 43; description of, 1; editor's influence on, 124; effect on reform movement, 1; Herndon on, 3; McGovern response to, 130; in manuscript, 22–23, 25–26; public response to, 3; reasons for popularity of, 190

How Children Learn (Holt): choosing title of, 140; reasons for popularity of, 190; reviews of, 35, 55

How to Survive in Your Native Land (Herndon): galleys of, 90; review of, 96; as sad book, 96–97, 203, 266–67

Hughes, Peggy, 76–78, 133–35, 154–56, 162–68

Hull, Bill, 2n

Illich, Ivan: and control of death, 147–48; and Holt's cello playing, 151; influence on Holt, 6; on institutions, 60–61; interest in measurement, 151; and language, 213–18; and limiting technology, 148; as prophet, 110; refusal to lecture, 109; social criticism of, 93. *See also* Center for Intercultural Documentation; Deschooling; Reimer, Everett

Instead of Education (Holt): central point of, 266; fears about, 186; finding others through, 199; idea for, 139; in manuscript, 190

Janeway, Elizabeth, 158–62, 175–76

Jencks, Christopher, 140

Jennings, Frank, 25–29, 254–55

Jerome, Judson: and communes, 119–20; and home education, 80, 119; meeting with, 136–38; organizing conference, 201–2; public life of, 121; and revolution, 99–101; and technology, 80–81

John Holt's Book and Music Store, 200

Jørgensen, Mosse, 137

Kohl, Herbert, 4, 97, 127

Kozol, Jonathan: Holt's differences with, 195, 221; public life of, 53; and reading machines, 237–39; as romantic critic, 4

Kros, Terry, 133n

Laing, R. D., 133–35, 151

Language, 213–18. *See also* Talking

Law: corruption of, 112; demystifying, 93–94

Lawrence, Merloyd, 255–58

Learning All the Time (Holt), 256n

Learning disabilities, 187–88, 259

Leary, Timothy, 85

Lecturing, deciding to stop, 106, 108–9

Lescher, Robert, 54n, 138–39

Lesley, Agnes, 41

Lesley Ellis School, 15

Lessing, Doris, 151

Liedloff, Jean, 224–26

Life, people's feelings about, 81–82, 152–54

Lives of Children, The (Dennison): Holt's review of, 43, 52–53; moved by rereading of, 218–19

Lord of the Flies, 41

McDermott, John, 206–8

McGovern, George: Holt's interest in candidacy of, 130; presidential defeat of, 130–31; rally for, 128–29; response to *How Children Fail*, 131

MacKenzie, Bob, 38, 242

McLuhan, Marshall, 156

Macrorie, Ken, 176–81

Man's Search for Himself (May), 33–34

Manas, 68

Marin, Peter, 46–48, 81–82

Maslow, Abraham, 76

May, Rollo, 33–34

INDEX

Mercer University, 170–71, 178
Metcalf, Elliot (Mike) and Hope, 22–24
Milwaukee Fourteen, 94
Mingl, Kathy, 259–63
Mitchell, Jo, 118–19
Moravian University, 206–8
Mother Earth News, The, 95n, 101
Ms., 104, 169
Music, 91, 151–52, 189–90
Music education, 144
Muste, A. J., 85, 135, 211

Naked Children, The (Fader), 97, 209
Navy, 17. *See also* Submarine
Neill, A. S.: on *Freedom and Beyond,* 113; health of, 113; influence on Holt, 3–4, 246; Holt's last visit with, 38, 242–43; meeting Holt, 242, 246; views on death, 113, 114, 243. *See also* Croall, Jonathan
Never Too Late (Holt), 202, 220
New Alchemists, 222, 223
New Schools Exchange, The, 5n
Nixon, Richard: fear of, 85, 129, 167; Laing on, 135; losing credibility, 141–42
Ny Lilleskole, 76, 154–55. *See also* Hughes, Peggy

Ozer, Jerome, 25

Paley, Vivian, 269–73
Pearl, Arthur, 115–16
Pearlstein, Steven, 267–69
Perceptual handicaps. *See* Learning disabilities
Personal Teaching (Dillon), 102–4
Picciotto, Joanna, 249–55
Pitcher, Jane, 14, 21
Pitkin, Joan, 97–98
Pitman, Sir Isaac, publishing company, 25, 138
Politics as education, 106–8
Postman, Neil, 156–58
Priest, Margot, 133n, 185

Publishers, 123–25. *See also* Dutton, E. P.; Pitman, Sir Isaac
Publishing, 183–85

Rafferty, Max, 89–90
Rasmussen, Lore, 25
Reading: children's learning of, 98, 125–26, 240; effect of "Sesame Street" on children's, 182–83; machines to teach, 237–39
Reich, Wilhelm, 114, 135
Reimer, Everett, 70–76. *See also* Center for Intercultural Documentation; Illich, Ivan
Revolution, effective, 99–101, 221–23, 226. *See also* Change
Rivard, Betty, 123–25
Roques, Catherine, 144–46
Rousseau, Jean-Jacques, 3
Rowan, Tim, 132–33

Scharlatt, Hal, 124, 138–41, 183. *See also* Dutton, E. P.
School Book, The (Postman), 156
Schooling: judging people by amount of, 79; making noncompulsory, 196–98; resistance to, 56–59, 60, 63–64
School Is Dead (Reimer), 70
School reform: difficulty of, 64–65; effective, 158; possibility of, 95, 102–4
School reformers: criticisms of Holt, 9; Holt's dislike of label, 31; response to failure of movement, 6
School reform movement, failure of: "Back-to-basics" as response to, 6; Bowles and Gintis on, 5–6; deschooling as response to, 6; Holt's response to, 6–8, 9–11; reformers' response to, 6
Schools: alternatives to, 201–2; critical thinking in, 157–58; lost sense of mission of, 230–31; as moral communities, 246–49; pool of talent in, 117; possibility of change in, 259–62; visiting British, 172–73

INDEX

Self-Respecting Child, The (Stallibrass), 193–94
"Sesame Street," 182–83
Shady Hill School, 15, 25–26
Sheffer, Susannah, 263–67
Siegel, Dr. Bernard, 274
Silberman, Charles, 211
Sizer, Theodore, 267
Society, educational quality of, 93, 95, 97
Solo, Len, 83–84
Solomon, Izler, 91
Stallibrass, Alison, 193–94
Steinem, Gloria, 104–5
Stephens, J. M., 55
"Student-Directed Learning" course, 39, 43, 48–50, 83–84
Submarine: as learning community, 13–14; no guilt about, 60; reunion of, 120; skipper of, 121; after war, 16–17
Sullivan, Dennis, 75n, 149, 150, 151
Summerhill, 243–46. *See also* Neill, A. S.
Summerhill Society, 31
Szasz, Thomas, 151

Talbott, Nelson (Bud), 191–93
Talbott, Strobe, 93, 191
Talking: children's, 270; Holt's feelings about, 136–38. *See also* Language
Talking of Summerhill (Neill), 38, 39–42
Teacher Drop-Out Center, 65, 83
Teachers: autonomy of, 261, 262; as "Dumb Class," 204–6; feelings about children, 31–32, 260, 263; feelings about society, 154–55; in free schools, 97–98; harmfulness of, 210–12; as observers of children, 55; as radicals, 122–23, 174–75; reluctance to change, 231–32; training of, 62–65, 83–84, 207–8; why people become, 260–61
Teaching: Holt's, 2; humane, 102–3
Teaching as a Subversive Activity (Postman), 156
Teach Your Own (Holt), 235

Technology, 80–81, 148
Terry, Charles, 247–49
Todd, Terry, 170–71
Tolstoy, Leo, 3

Underachieving School, The (Holt), 46, 123
United States, possibility of leaving, 127–29, 155–56, 167–68, 214
United World Federalists, 14, 20, 191. *See also* World Government movement
Urban School, The, 34
U.S.S. *Barbero. See* Submarine
Utopia, 236

Vietnam War, 57, 144–45
von Hentig, Hartmut, 122–23, 228–35
Vulnerable Teacher, A (Macrorie), 176–81

Walker, Gerald, 196–98
Way It Spozed to Be, The (Herndon): 44, 49, 53
What Do I Do Monday? (Holt): choosing title of, 140; Holt's thoughts on, 48, 78; jacket design of, 124; *New York Times* review of, 91
White, Kevin, 79–80
Whitehead, Alfred North, 73
Whitehead, Bill, 183–85
Women's Liberation movement, 105, 175–76
Wootan, Dr. George, 276
Work: helping young people find, 233; students' feelings about, 265, 266; who defines, 115
World Government movement, 1, 14, 19. *See also* United World Federalists
Writing, 139, 185, 267–69

Zarowitz, Ron, 88
Zuckerman, David, 48–50